A Critical Introduction to Scientific Realism

"COYOTE IS ALWAYS OUT THERE
WAITING, AND
COYOTE IS ALWAYS HUNGRY."
—NAVAJO PROVERB—

BLOOMSBURY CRITICAL INTRODUCTIONS TO CONTEMPORARY EPISTEMOLOGY

Series Editor:

Stephen Hetherington, Professor of Philosophy, The University of New South Wales, Australia

Editorial Board:

Claudio de Almeida, Pontifical Catholic University of Rio Grande do Sul, Brazil; Richard Fumerton, The University of Iowa, USA; John Greco, Saint Louis University, USA; Jonathan Kvanvig, Baylor University, USA; Ram Neta, University of North Carolina, Chapel Hill, USA; Duncan Pritchard, The University of Edinburgh, UK

Bloomsbury Critical Introductions to Contemporary Epistemology introduces and advances the central topics within one of the most dynamic areas of contemporary philosophy.

Each critical introduction provides a comprehensive survey to an important epistemic subject, covering the historical, methodological and practical contexts and exploring the major approaches, theories and debates. By clearly illustrating the changes to the ways human knowledge is being studied, each volume places an emphasis on the historical background and makes important connections between contemporary issues and the wider history of modern philosophy.

Designed for use on contemporary epistemology courses, the introductions are defined by a clarity of argument and equipped with easy-to-follow chapter summaries, annotated guides to reading, and glossaries to facilitate and encourage further study. This series is ideal for upper-level undergraduates and postgraduates wishing to stay informed of the thinkers, issues and arguments shaping twenty-first century epistemology.

Titles in the series include:

A Critical Introduction to the Epistemology of Memory, Thomas D. Senor

A Critical Introduction to the Epistemology of Perception, Ali Hasan

A Critical Introduction to Knowledge-How, J. Adam Carter and Ted Poston

A Critical Introduction to Formal Epistemology, Darren Bradley

A Critical Introduction to Skepticism, Allan Hazlett

A Critical Introduction to Testimony, Axel Gelfert

A Critical Introduction to Scientific Realism

PAUL DICKEN

Bloomsbury Academic
An imprint of Bloomsbury Publishing Plc

B L O O M S B U R Y
LONDON · OXFORD · NEW YORK · NEW DELHI · SYDNEY

Bloomsbury Academic

An imprint of Bloomsbury Publishing Plc

50 Bedford Square
London
WC1B 3DP
UK

1385 Broadway
New York
NY 10018
USA

www.bloomsbury.com

BLOOMSBURY and the Diana logo are trademarks of Bloomsbury Publishing Plc

First published 2016

British Library Cataloguing-in-Publication Data

A catalogue record for this book is available from the British Library.

ISBN: HB: 978-1-4725-7591-3
PB: 978-1-4725-7590-6
ePDF: 978-1-4725-7588-3
ePub: 978-1-4725-7589-0

Library of Congress Cataloging-in-Publication Data

A catalog record for this book is available from the Library of Congress.

Series: Bloomsbury Critical Introductions to Contemporary Epistemology

Cover design by Louise Dugdale
Cover image © Philip Habib/Gallerystock

Typeset by Fakenham Prepress Solutions, Fakenham, Norfolk NR21 8NN
Printed and bound in India

Contents

Acknowledgements

This book began life in the sunny eastern suburbs of Sydney and was completed under three feet of snow in a remote corner of upstate New York. There are various theories relating the effects of the weather on one's philosophical disposition – that rain and mist encourages scepticism, and that the more speculative metaphysical fauna grow best in warmer climates – and I have endeavoured to write the various sections of this book under their most agreeable conditions. In the end however, I fear that the New York winter prevailed.

I would like to thank Stephen Hetherington for suggesting this project to me, and Michaelis Michael for listening to me complain about it. I didn't always agree with everything Michaelis had to say about philosophy, but I defer to him completely on the far more important topics of test match statistics and where to get the best coffee in Sydney. Some of the issues in this book are the result of lengthy – and ongoing – conversations with other philosophers of science. I'd like to thank Juha Saatsi who has done a lot to make me think about base rates, and Stathis Psillos, whose influence on my work as a whole has been considerable. I would also like to thank audiences at the University of the New South Wales and Sydney University for all of their valuable feedback, and an anonymous referee for wading through some truly horrific typos and errors.

In the southern hemisphere, I would like to thank Maddy and Ian Gulliver for their extraordinary hospitality. I would also like to thank Debra Aarons, Mengistu Amberber, Belinda Jones, Matthew Mison and Peter Slezak for keeping me relatively sane on a weekly basis. I would also like to extend a special acknowledgement to James Squire and Dan Murphy for all of their sterling work. In the northern hemisphere, I would like to thank Mary-Ellen Campbell for providing such a great place to work, and David Carlson and Tim Smith for their warm welcome to the area. Thanks also to Suzanne Stein and Andrew Mitchell, Stephanie Richmond and Tommy Tavenner and Rebecca Goetz for making the East Coast memorable. I am also very grateful to the Brothers Meloi for their commendable philosophical defence of American brewing.

Finally, my love and thanks to Katrina Gulliver, to whom this book is dedicated.

Paul Dicken
Somerset
27 October 2015

Introduction

Scientific realism is the view that our scientific theories are approximately true. This might not seem like a very exciting philosophical thesis. It might even seem like nothing more than just good common sense. After all, our scientific theories are enormously successful, not just in the accuracy of the predictions they make, but also in the reliability of the various technological advances they support. Every time we step onto an aeroplane, or turn on the television, or go to the doctor, we are implicitly endorsing the approximate truth of a myriad different scientific theories concerning mechanics, electromagnetism, the physiology of the human body and so on and so forth. If these scientific theories were not largely correct in their descriptions of the world, it would be simply miraculous that our aeroplanes remain in the air, our favourite shows appear on the screen or that we haven't all managed to poison ourselves by now. And this indeed is the central intuition underlying contemporary arguments in favour of scientific realism – science *works*, therefore it is (at least approximately) true.

Since this is philosophy, however, there is no reason to expect common sense to prevail. One persistent challenge facing any scientific realist is of course the threat of radical scepticism. Our scientific theories may well appear to give us reliable knowledge about the world around us, but we cannot rule out the logical possibility that we are being deceived. Maybe this is all a dream or, putting the worry in its more modern formulation, some elaborate computer program. Maybe we are all just brains in a vat. Or to take a less exotic example, perhaps we are merely victims of a persistent fluke. It might be the case that our scientific theories are completely and utterly false, but that so far we have only ever tested them in such a limited range of circumstances that these systematic errors have been avoided. For the radical sceptic, the possibilities are endless.

These are all good questions, but they are not part of our present concern. The scientific realism debate takes as its point of departure the assumption that it is possible for us to have at least *some* knowledge about the external world. The point, however, is not that the radical sceptical challenge can be safely dismissed, or that such fundamental questions of epistemology are somehow wrong-headed. It is merely that when it comes to concerns about evil demons and the abstract possibility of universal error, considerations regarding the reliability of our scientific theories are not going to have very much to add to such a debate. They might provide us with slightly more interesting examples of course; but if all of this is really a dream, the fact that I can successfully self-medicate while watching old Jean-Claude van Damme movies at 30,000 feet is no more or less compelling than G. E. Moore waving both of his hands in the air.

Nevertheless, even once we leave the radical sceptic to one side, there still remain significant challenges for scientific realism. Our contemporary scientific theories may well be highly impressive with respect to their predictive accuracy – but they have also been repeatedly shown to be wrong throughout the history of science. Aristotle believed that the outer planets were affixed to great crystalline spheres revolving slowly around the Earth. Roughly 2,000 years later, they were liberated by Newton and placed orbiting the Sun, held in place by a mysterious gravitational attraction like some kind of cosmic centrifuge. Neither account, however, is currently held to be true. According to Einstein, the planets are merely constrained by the deformation of space-time itself, and would wander off into the blackness of space if it wasn't for the vast astronomical trough at the centre of our solar system.

The problem, however, is that both Aristotelian and Newtonian accounts were considered to be highly successful at one time or another. Newtonian Mechanics was considered to be so successful in fact that contemporary physicists complained that there was nothing left for them to do other than to polish and preserve the great man's accomplishments. It follows then that any scientific realist writing in the early modern period would have been just as convinced of the approximate truth of his scientific theories as we are of ours today, and would offer *exactly the same* kind of arguments in their support. We know now that they were wrong – but how can we be sure that our own scientific theories will not suffer a similar fate in the future?

The contemporary scientific realism debate is primarily framed around these two competing considerations. On the one hand, the success of our scientific theories gives us reasons to suppose that they are approximately true; whereas on the other hand, the history of our scientific theories gives us reason to suppose that they will eventually turn out to be false. These two arguments are known in the literature as the No-Miracles Argument and the Pessimistic Meta-Induction respectively, and a great deal of ink has been spilt discussing the merits of both lines of thought. What is most surprising, however, is not just that these debates have proved inconclusive – this is philosophy after all – but that a large number of philosophers have actually concluded that the whole issue is simply misguided, and that it is a mistake to suppose that one can offer any kind of meaningful philosophical evaluation of our scientific practice at all.

Of course, the tactic of dismissing a philosophical debate as nothing more than conceptual confusion is not unique to the issue of scientific realism. What is unusual, however, is the frequency with which such a complaint is voiced, and the sheer variety of diagnoses that have been offered in response. It has been objected for example that the scientific realism debate is nothing more than a confusion over the use of language, a mistaken application of the concept of truth, the foolhardy attempt to stand outside of our own epistemological limitations, bad probabilistic reasoning, an outdated notion of rationality … and all of this regarding the relatively simple observation that if our scientific theories weren't more or less on the right track, our aeroplanes wouldn't stay up in the sky.

It is this widespread suspicion concerning the very possibility of the scientific realism debate that provides the main focus of this book. Surprisingly enough, this suspicion turns out to be an immediate consequence of the way in which the debate is differentiated from the larger issues of epistemology and radical scepticism with which we began. If we suppose that it is indeed possible for us to have reliable knowledge about the external world, the central question of the scientific realism debate becomes not *whether* our scientific theories can accurately represent reality, but rather *how* they manage to accomplish this feat. Our scientific theories are, after all, highly curious beasts – they are abstract, often impenetrably mathematical and riddled with exotic and unobservable entities that lie far beyond the scope of our everyday experience. We might feel confident in trusting the deliverance of our senses, but it can seem like a very different prospect when confronted with differential equations and Hamiltonian operators.

This at least was the way in which the scientific realism debate was originally posed by Immanuel Kant, who therefore attempted to show that the most fundamental scientific principles of the day could be derived from the inner workings of our minds. The project was pursued by the logical empiricists in the beginning of the twentieth century, who attempted to show how the most fundamental scientific principles of their day followed from a series of linguistic definitions. By the mid-twentieth century, however, both strategies had been abandoned in favour of a more straightforwardly epistemological approach. Yet throughout this methodological evolution, the same underlying conviction remained. The challenge was not to show that our scientific theories are predictively successful, but rather to explain how this predictive success is achieved.

There is, however, a basic tension in this approach. Roughly speaking, the problem is that the relationship between our scientific theories and the external world *is itself* one of the many aspects of the empirical world which it is the business of science to investigate. Human beings are, after all, just another animal running around in the great wide world, and our scientific theories just another kind of tool that we use to help us reproduce and survive. If our scientific theories do accurately represent the world, therefore, this will have something to do with human psychology, our evolutionary background and the causal properties of whatever it is out there in the world that we talk about when constructing our theories. It follows then that any attempt to explain how our scientific theories manage to provide reliable knowledge about the world must at some point appeal to those very same scientific theories in framing its response.

The point then is that our scientific investigations are not just one source of knowledge about the world – they are our *best* source of knowledge about the world, which makes them especially difficult to evaluate in an objective and philosophically neutral manner. The scientific realism debate therefore occupies an awkward middle ground between radical scepticism and common-sense epistemology. On the one hand, we can choose to subject everything that we think we know to hyperbolic doubt, in which case the question of scientific realism reduces to nothing more than an illustration of a larger epistemological debate. While on the other hand, we can attempt to ask a series of more modest epistemological questions about the reliability of our scientific theories from a position of cautious optimism, in which case we risk having already presupposed what we were attempting to show. One of the many reasons that the scientific realism debate is of interest to the general epistemologist therefore is that it shows us something important about the limitations that constrain any such investigation.

Chapter 1 begins with the historical background to the scientific realism debate, and with the specific challenges posed by the increased mathematization of the natural sciences in the early modern period. This was seen as raising a problem concerning how our scientific theories were able to *represent* the external world, given that their central terms and concepts were so far divorced from our everyday experience. An early answer to this problem was offered by Kant, who argued that our fundamental scientific principles could be derived from the necessary conditions of our experience. Subsequent developments in geometry and physics put pressure on the precise details of Kant's picture, and it was argued by the logical empiricists that the role assigned to the structure of our cognition should instead be attributed to the structure of our language.

The linguistic reformulation of the Kantian framework meant that in the early half of the twentieth century, the scientific realism debate was predominantly understood as a question about the meaning of our scientific language. This is the topic of Chapter 2, which recounts the various attempts made to express our scientific theories within an entirely observational vocabulary. Such a result promised an extremely neat solution to the scientific realism debate, since if it could be shown that our scientific theories do not really talk about unobservable entities like electrons, quarks and neutrinos, there can be no corresponding philosophical question as to how such terms manage to refer. There were, however, a number of significant technical difficulties facing such a project, and under the influence of Quine in the 1950s the scientific realism debate abandoned these linguistic considerations in favour of a more explicitly epistemological orientation.

Chapters 3 and 4 are concerned with the traditional arguments framing the contemporary scientific realism debate. Chapter 3 focuses upon the so-called No-Miracles Argument, which maintains that we should believe that our scientific theories are approximately true since this provides the *best explanation* for their predictive success. Opposition to the argument concerns whether or not the approximate truth of our scientific theories really is the best explanation for their predictive success, and the grounds for supposing that our best explanations are likely to be true. More importantly, however, it is also objected that the No-Miracles Argument is circular, since the principle of inference to the best explanation upon which it depends is itself part of our scientific methodology. It seems then that the scientific realist must effectively presuppose that our scientific theories are approximately true in order to argue that our scientific theories are approximately true. Chapter 4 focuses upon the Pessimistic Meta-Induction, the principal consideration offered against scientific realism. This is the argument from history, and it maintains that since so many scientific theories have been shown to be false in the past, we have good reason to suppose that even our most successful contemporary theories will be found to be false in the future. Two different readings of this argument are distinguished, and some of the difficulties involved in interpreting the history of science are discussed. As in the case of the No-Miracles Argument, it is concluded that the Pessimistic Meta-Induction also does not offer a compelling line of reasoning.

Having drawn such a negative assessment of the two central arguments framing the scientific realism debate, Chapter 5 attempts to provide a general diagnosis of these difficulties. The claim is that both sides of the scientific realism debate are guilty of a particular species of statistical fallacy known as the Base Rate Fallacy. In simple terms, we cannot assess the likelihood of a scientific theory being approximately true on the basis of its predictive success unless we already know the underlying base rate probability of any arbitrary scientific theory being approximately true – yet it is precisely this fact which both the No-Miracles Argument and the Pessimistic Meta-Induction are supposed to establish. Recent responses to this problem have sought to refocus the scientific realism debate as a series of highly specific arguments targeting the approximate truth of individual scientific theories, rather than a sweeping assessment of the reliability of scientific practice in general. This is still very much a live issue in the current literature, although there remains the worry that if the scientific realism debate is focused too narrowly, it becomes unable to offer any kind of philosophical analysis of our scientific practice at all.

The final two chapters consider a slightly different approach to the scientific realism debate, which is to investigate *how much* of our scientific theories we need to believe in order to accommodate their predictive success, considerations that can be pursued independently of any issues relating to the No-Miracles Argument, the Pessimistic Meta-Induction or the Base Rate Fallacy. Chapter 6 examines the claims of the structural realist, who maintains that our scientific theories are only approximately true with respect to their mathematical structure. This is a position motivated primarily by the problem of scientific representation, and is therefore in many ways the most natural successor to Kant's original project. The difficulty with such an approach is to articulate an account of structure that is both broad enough to cover a wide range of scientific theories, but not so broad as to render the position trivial. Chapter 7 examines the claims of the constructive empiricist, who argues that the aim of science is to produce theories that are merely empirically adequate rather than approximately true. A theory is empirically adequate provided it is accurate with respect to the observable phenomena, and in this respect constructive empiricism can be thought of as an updated form of the sort of instrumentalist strategies that attempted to express our scientific theories within a purely observational vocabulary. The difficulty facing the position is to provide a principled distinction between the observable and the unobservable, and in recent work it has been articulated within a novel epistemological framework that seeks to finesse such questions altogether. Pursuing the various twists and turns of constructive empiricism therefore leads to yet another diagnosis as to why the scientific realism debate is nothing more than a philosophical pseudo-question.

While the present book is intended as an introduction to the topic of scientific realism, and its relationship to broader issues in epistemology, it cannot at times avoid offering a rather strong assessment of some of the topics covered. Some of the central issues in the contemporary literature – especially those concerning the No-Miracles Argument and the Pessimistic Meta-Induction – seem to me to be simply mistaken, and due in large part to a failure to adequately grasp the historical background of the scientific realism debate. If a large part of this book seems therefore to be devoted to nothing more than clearing the ground, so be it. There remain a number of interesting and promising topics in the scientific realism debate and it is therefore valuable to know where the important problems are to be found, and where the dead-ends are to be avoided. A crucial element of any philosophical debate lies not only in answering difficult questions, but also in discovering which are the right questions to ask in the first place. It is with this modest task that this book is concerned.

1

The historical background to the scientific realism debate

There are a number of different places from which to begin an historical introduction to the problems of epistemology, and to the philosophy of science in particular, depending upon the different themes and issues that one wishes to emphasize. An introduction to the methodology of the natural sciences for example – or indeed, to the very possibility of rational inquiry in general – could easily begin with Plato, or perhaps even earlier with the Pre-Socratics. The question of scientific realism, however, is primarily concerned with the *results* of our scientific investigations, that is to say, with the relationship between the theories that we construct and the world they seek to describe, and with our grounds for supposing the former to provide a reliable guide to the latter. These questions underwent an important transformation in the early modern period in response to both the increased mathematization of the natural sciences, and to the correspondingly unfamiliar picture they began to paint of the world around us. In broad outline, these developments led to what we might call a *problem of coordination*, for even if we put to one side whatever general worries we may have regarding scepticism and our knowledge of the external world, modern mathematical physics presents us with the further challenge of understanding how the abstract, symbolic representations offered to us by our scientific theories manage to tell us anything at all about the concrete physical world with which they are supposedly concerned.

The paradigmatic example of this kind of revolution in the natural sciences is found in the work of Isaac Newton, and its consequent development throughout the eighteenth century by other luminary figures such as Leonhard Euler and Pierre-Simon Laplace. For on the one hand, Newtonian Mechanics provided a theoretical framework of unprecedented predictive and explanatory power, a universal theory of motion that integrated both terrestrial and celestial phenomena. On the other hand, however, it offered a description of the physical world couched in a mathematical vocabulary that few could understand and which completely divorced the fundamental notions of space and time from our intuitive, everyday understanding. In the Newtonian worldview for example, the Earth no longer occupies a privileged position within an ordered hierarchy of revolving heavens, but rather constitutes just one frame of reference amongst many. More specifically, while Newtonian Mechanics does indeed preserve a notion of absolute space against which all physical events take place, there is no way of determining whether or not this is coextensive with our own terrestrial frame of reference. It follows then that we can no longer assume that a physical object is moving just because it *appears* to be moving, since we cannot assume that our frame of reference is any more privileged than that of the physical object – for all that we can tell, it may be us who are moving with respect to absolute space, rather than the other way around.

Without a doubt, the most influential response to this specific philosophical challenge was offered by Immanuel Kant, who attempted to show not only that Newtonian Mechanics can be reconciled with our everyday experience of the world, but that we can in fact know *a priori* that its fundamental principles are true. We will begin therefore in this chapter with a sketch of Kant's philosophical project (§1.1) and some of the difficulties it faced in response to subsequent developments in geometry and physics (§1.2). I should note immediately, however, that Kant's work is both sophisticated and challenging, and that the picture I present is something of a simplification. This is because our primary concern is not with the precise details of Kant's philosophy, so much as it is with the way in which Kant was *interpreted* by subsequent philosophers of science. As I will attempt to show, the contours of the contemporary scientific realism debate were developed as part of a specific response to what was seen as a specific set of difficulties with Kant's overall project – I will therefore have relatively little to say as to whether or not this really is the best way to read Kant, or as to whether or not there is a better way in which these difficulties could have been resolved. I will then discuss some of the general conclusions drawn from these episodes, and the ways in which they have continued to shape the scientific realism debate (§1.3). This chapter concludes with a summary of the key points discussed (§1.4), and some suggestions for further reading (§1.5).

1.1. The scandal of philosophy

The basic problem motivating Kant's philosophy concerns our knowledge of the external world. We have thoughts and ideas in our heads which are somehow supposed to represent real objects and processes out in the world, but it is far from clear why we should take the former to be a reliable guide to the latter. There is, after all, no *logical guarantee* that the ideas in our heads should accurately depict anything at all about the external world. One way to think about this problem is to note that the ideas in our heads differ from the objects they are supposed to represent in a number of important ways. For example, physical objects have both a shape and a size, and are located at a particular point in space. The ideas in our heads by contrast – whatever other properties they may possess – clearly lack these kinds of spatial attributes. Or to take another example, the apple on my desk is bright green and has a slightly bitter taste, yet my *idea* of the apple on my desk has neither colour nor flavour. So there is a *prima facie* worry about how our mental ideas can represent the external world, since they certainly do not resemble one another in any significant way.

The issue then is not simply the traditional sceptical worry that everything we think we know about the world might in fact be wrong. It is a more specific worry about the way in which we come to have knowledge, since on the face of it the ideas we form in our heads do not seem to be particularly well suited for the task at hand. This is of course just another way of stating the problem of coordination with which we began, and it invites one of two equally unpalatable conclusions. On the one hand, we can argue with Hume that since our mental ideas do not resemble the objects they are supposed to represent, we cannot have any reliable knowledge after all, and must therefore embrace an all encompassing scepticism. Or on the other hand, we can argue with Berkeley that since we clearly do have some knowledge about the world, our mental ideas must therefore resemble the objects they represent after all, and conclude therefore that the external world is itself just another mental idea (albeit a much more sophisticated idea entertained within the mind of God).

Both of these arguments of course assume that representation must consist in some form of resemblance, an assumption that we might reasonably challenge, and which is certainly not universally accepted by contemporary philosophers. This, however, is not enough to resolve the basic problem. If the ideas in our heads accurately represent objects in the world, then there must be some kind of representational relationship holding between the two; and if we are to be justified in trusting the ideas in our head, then we need to show that this relationship is reliable. Unfortunately, however, this is something that we can never do. In order to show that this representational relationship is itself reliable, we must first of all be able to *represent* that relationship in order to be able to say anything intelligent about it. But if that is the case, then any attempt we make to demonstrate the reliability of our representations will simply presuppose the reliability of other representations in turn – and the reliability of those representations will presuppose the reliability of yet more representations, and so on and so forth. The whole project is therefore doomed from the start, since there appears to be no way for us to stand outside of our representational practices in order to critically assess them.

According to Kant, the underlying cause of this difficulty lies in a particular conception of our epistemic lives. It is a picture of the world that posits a complete separation between subject and object – a mind-independent reality into which we find ourselves thrown, and which we must consequently attempt to investigate and understand. In such a picture, there must always remain a gap between the ideas in our heads and the objects they are supposed to represent, since the existence of one is quite independent of the existence of the other; and so long as this gap remains, the threat of scepticism is inevitable. The situation is for Kant simply scandalous, and the only solution lies in a radical revision of this otherwise intuitive picture. He writes in the beginning of his *Critique of Pure Reason*:

> Hitherto it has been assumed that all our knowledge must conform to objects. But all attempts to extend our knowledge to objects by establishing something in regard to them *a priori*, by means of concepts, have, on this assumption, ended in failure. We must therefore make trial whether we may not have more success in the tasks of metaphysics, if we suppose that objects must conform to our knowledge … We should then be proceeding precisely on the lines of Copernicus' primary hypothesis. (1781 [1929]: Preface, Bxvi)

Since the supposition that the objects of our knowledge are independent of our representations leads inevitably to scepticism, Kant's proposal is that they must actually *depend* upon our cognitive faculties in some way. This is a difficult idea to grasp, but the comparison with Copernicus is helpful. What Kant intends to show is that the apparent independent existence of the external world is an illusion. It is in fact merely an artefact of our own subjective point of view – it is part of the way that we perceive the world, and not a property of the world itself – and can be explained away in much the same way that Copernicus explained away the apparent motion of the Sun in terms of the actual orbit of the Earth.

1.1.1. *Experience and the* synthetic a priori

Another way to understand Kant's proposal here is as the claim that perception is not a purely passive activity. It is not simply a case of opening our eyes and letting the external world flood inside, since this would provide us with nothing more than an undifferentiated confusion of noise and colour. Rather, in order for us actually to *experience* the world around us, all of this sensory stimulation must be carefully packaged so as to be made intelligible. This then is the way in which the objects of our knowledge can be said to depend upon our cognitive faculties, for what we experience is not the external world in all its unmediated glory – what Kant calls the *noumena* or the *thing-in-itself* – but rather the external world as it appears through the filter of our senses and other intellectual operations. Since the objects of our knowledge are therefore partly constituted by our own cognitive faculties, the gap between our ideas and the objects they are supposed to represent can finally be bridged.

According to Kant, there are two principal ways in which our cognitive faculties shape the objects of our knowledge. In the first place, our sensory stimulations must be neatly ordered, so that we can tell when one experience ends and another begins. And secondly, once our sensory stimulations have been divided into distinct experiential episodes, these need to be labelled and conceptualized in such a way that we can tell when two different experiences are related to one another in various ways – for example, when two experiences are of the same object, or when one experience is invariably followed by another, and so on and so forth. These two functions are performed by two distinct components of our cognitive faculties, which Kant calls our *sensibility* and our *understanding* respectively, and it is only possible for us to experience the world when these two different faculties work together to turn our sensory stimulations into intelligible objects of knowledge.

It should be noted of course that none of this is sufficient to finally defeat the sceptic. Our cognitive faculties only shape the objects of our knowledge, they do not create them, and thus there will always remain room for mistakes and errors. However, by collapsing the traditional separation between our ideas and the objects they are supposed to represent, it is now at least *possible* for us to resolve the sceptical worries with which we began – unlike, say, in the case of Hume or Berkeley. Moreover, if our sensibility and understanding do indeed impose a structure upon the objects of our knowledge, then there will be certain very general things we can know with absolute certainty about any possible experience we might have, simply by investigating the inner workings of our own cognitive faculties. Delineating the extent of this knowledge is one of the central projects of Kant's *Critique of Pure Reason*, and in it he draws a number of extremely interesting conclusions about the necessary conditions of any possible experience. Most importantly for our present purposes, however, is Kant's contention that space and time are not objective features of the external world, but are in fact part of the framework we impose on the objects of our knowledge: they are the forms of sensibility, nothing more than the way in which we divide our sensory stimulations into discrete experiential episodes.

This is certainly a radical conclusion to draw, and Kant does indeed offer a number of arguments as to why we cannot conceive of space and time as features of the external world, but only as part of our contribution to the objects of our knowledge. By far the most important argument for Kant, however, is that this supposition allows him to answer another important epistemological problem. It is common for us to distinguish between those things that we know on the basis of experience, and those things that we can know independently of any experience – between our knowledge *a posteriori* and our knowledge *a priori* respectively. The most obvious examples of the latter form of knowledge are of course mathematics and geometry. We can know that 7 + 5 = 12, or that the interior angles of a triangle add up to 180 degrees, without having to perform any experiments or in any other way going out and investigating the world around us. Moreover, in the case of mathematics and geometry at least, such knowledge appears to be far more certain than anything we can know on the basis of experience. Not only can we know that 7 + 5 = 12 without relying upon any form of experience, but there is conversely no possible experience that could ever show this claim to be false. In contrast to what we may come to know about the external world, the truths of mathematics and geometry are said to be *necessary* truths.

The status of mathematical and geometrical truths posed a serious challenge for the various epistemological theories with which Kant was familiar. Since such knowledge is held to be independent of our experience, it was generally supposed that it must be about the operations of our minds in some respect instead. Hume for example argued that our *a priori* knowledge simply described the ways in which we organize our *a posteriori* knowledge – they are principles of reasoning, or relations between ideas, rather than claims with a specific content (this view was later revived by Wittgenstein to explain the status of logical truths). The problem with this, however, is that our mathematical and geometrical knowledge seems to have a content that goes beyond mere principles of reasoning. In order to grasp these truths, we need to do more than simply understand the meaning of the terms involved. According to Kant, while it is indeed necessarily true that the interior angles of a triangle add up to 180 degrees, and while it is indeed true that we can know this without investigating any particular triangle, there is, however, nothing about the *concept* of a triangle considered in isolation that entails that its interior angles add up to 180 degrees. It requires some further thought to convince us of this fact, albeit further thought of a highly abstract nature. This is in contrast to something like the claim that all triangles have three sides, which appears to be true simply as a matter of definition.

Kant therefore introduced a new category to account for our knowledge of mathematics and geometry. They are *synthetic a priori*, which means that while they are independent of experience, they nevertheless go beyond the mere analysis of concepts. Specifically, in order to grasp the truth of mathematical and geometrical statements, we need to understand them against the background of some larger conceptual framework. In the case of geometry, for example, this will be predominately spatial. There is nothing about the concept of a triangle alone that determines the sum of its interior angles – but once we attempt to *picture* or *construct* a triangle in space, then we can see that the angles must add up to 180 degrees. So the truth of geometrical statements presupposes a notion of space against which we can explore the further consequences of our geometrical concepts. However, since the truth of a geometrical statement is also *a priori*, this notion of space cannot be something that we learn from experience. The only remaining possibility for Kant is to see this notion of space as something that we contribute to the objects of our knowledge, since that is the only way in which it can add content to our geometrical concepts while remaining *a priori* valid for any possible object of knowledge. Similarly in the case of mathematics, the required conceptual framework will involve the notion of succession, which Kant understands in terms of time.

Kant concludes therefore that space and time are not objective features of the external world, but rather forms of our sensibility. This illustrates the way in which the objects of our knowledge are partly constituted by our own cognitive faculties, since while all of our experiences are necessarily spatial-temporal, there is no such thing as space and time in the external world. It also explains how our mathematical and geometrical knowledge can go beyond the mere analysis of our concepts, yet remain *a priori* valid. This then is the general outline of Kant's solution to the problem of coordination, one which he was to extend to an extremely influential account of Newtonian Mechanics and which was to set the stage for much of the contemporary scientific realism debate.

1.1.2. *The metaphysical foundations of natural science*

While the general outline of Kant's approach to the problem of Newtonian Mechanics is present in the *Critique of Pure Reason*, the details of his solution are not fully developed until his *Metaphysical Foundations of Natural Science*, published five years later in 1786. In this work, Kant attempts to accomplish two closely related goals. The first is to put the natural sciences on a secure epistemological footing by showing that the basic principles of Newtonian Mechanics can themselves be known *a priori* in much the same way as the basic principles of mathematics and geometry. The second goal is then to help make the Newtonian picture more intelligible by showing how some of its more problematic consequences – for example, the fact that we can in principle never detect the difference between absolute and relative motion – are simply part of the structure of any possible experience, as structured by the contribution of our cognitive faculties.

More specifically, since scientific inquiry must always begin with *some* empirical content if it is to be differentiated from the pure study of mathematics and geometry, we will of course have to begin with more than just the pure forms of our sensibility and understanding. The natural sciences are concerned with the behaviour of the physical world around us, rather than the abstract truths of mathematics and geometry, and so any derivation of Newtonian Mechanics must similarly begin with the most general concept that allows us to define its domain of application. According to Kant, this is the idea of something being 'moveable in space' (1786 (2002): §4:480), reasoning that the natural sciences are fundamentally concerned with changes in the physical world around us. Accordingly then, the basic project is to show how the principles of Newtonian Mechanics follow from the structure of our cognitive faculties *as applied to* the fundamental empirical concept of that which is moveable in space.

The precise details of this derivation are naturally enough somewhat complex, but it is possible to give a rough sketch of Kant's procedure. In the *Critique of Pure Reason*, Kant established that space was merely a form of our sensibility. Rather than an objective feature of the external world, space is part of the structure that our own cognitive faculties contribute to the objects of our knowledge. This does not mean, however, that we cannot form an idea about specific regions of space, or in particular, of the empirical space in which the laws of physics are supposed to operate. What it does mean though is that in order to take these specific regions of space as an object of knowledge, we must understand them in turn as located against the background of a larger spatial framework. This is just an instance of Kant's general epistemology: if we can only have experience of an object by supplying it with a spatial structure, then we can only have experience of empirical space by supplying it with a (further) spatial structure. The consequence of this, however, is that any space can always be regarded as contained within a larger space; or working in the opposite direction, that any space is infinitely divisible. In the context of the *Metaphysical Foundations of Natural Science*, this immediately gives us our first important result. For if any space can always be regarded as contained within a larger space, then the motion of any physical object in space (whatever is moveable in space) can itself always be regarded as moving with respect to a larger space (1786 [2002]: §4:481). What appears to be absolute motion may therefore be only relative motion, since our own point of view may in fact be moving with respect to a background spatial framework. Kant's contention that space is merely a form of sensibility therefore not only underpins his response to the problem of coordination and helps to explain the *synthetic a priori* status of geometrical knowledge, but can even show how one of the most unintuitive consequences of Newtonian Mechanics actually follows from some of the most general conditions for any possible experience.

We have already noted that in order to make sense of our sensory stimulations, they need to be both neatly ordered into distinct experiential episodes, and then conceptualized in such a way that we can compare, contrast and draw various links between them. The former function is performed by our faculty of sensibility, which, as we have seen, provides the spatial-temporal framework for our experiences. The second function is performed by our faculty of understanding, which in turn provides the general structure of any possible *judgement* that we might make about our spatial-temporal experiences. This part of Kant's account is one of the most difficult and controversial aspects of his entire philosophy, but in simple terms, Kant believes himself to have identified exactly twelve different ways in which we might judge two things to be similar or different, each of which corresponds to a specific way in which we can conceptualize the relationship between our spatial-temporal experience. So, for example, what Kant calls the categorical form of judgement is when we assert that one thing is another (x is F), whereas the hypothetical form of judgement is when we assert that one thing is conditional on another (if p then q). In the context of our spatial-temporal experience, these two forms of judgement lead to the conceptual categories of *substance* and *causality* respectively. The idea then is that since any attempt to understand our sensory stimulations will necessarily involve packaging our spatial-temporal experiential episodes in one or more of these general forms of judgement, the various conceptual categories to which they correspond will be *synthetic a priori* conditions for any possible experience in much the same way as the sensible forms of space and time.

All of this of course has further important consequences for Kant's epistemology, but for our present purposes it is sufficient simply to note the role it plays in our understanding of Newtonian Mechanics. We have seen how Kant's understanding of space as a form of our sensibility is applied to the fundamental empirical concept of the moveable in space to yield the relativity of motion. In a similar fashion, the forms of our understanding are also to be applied to this fundamental empirical concept to yield more specific principles of Newtonian Mechanics. The category of substance, for example, when applied to the concept of that which is moveable in space, gives us the principle that 'in all changes of corporeal nature, the total quantity of matter remains the same' (1786 [2002]: §4:541) – which is just another way of stating

Newton's First Law of Motion. The category of causality, when restricted to the concept of that which is moveable in space, entails that 'every body persists in its state of rest or motion, in the same direction, and with the same speed, if it is not compelled by an external cause to leave this state' (ibid.: §4:543) – which is of course Newton's Second Law of Motion. Slightly less convincing is the derivation of Newton's Third Law of Motion, which Kant argues follows from translating our abstract judgements of coexistence into the conceptual category of *reciprocity*, and hence to the empirical principle that 'in all communication of motion, action and reaction are always equal to one another' (ibid.: §4:544).

While some of the fine details may well be less than compelling, the general idea is at least clear. Kant argues – not implausibly – that in order for us to have any experience at all, we must in fact supply some of the sensible and conceptual structure of that experience. In broad terms, this has the consequence of helping to close the otherwise unbridgeable gap between our ideas and the objects they are supposed to represent, and thus providing the possibility of responding to the sceptic. More specifically, however, since the objects of our knowledge are now in part constituted by our own cognitive faculties, we are in fact in a position to know *with certainty* those things that we can deduce from the general structure of our cognitive contributions. The paradigmatic example here is of course our knowledge of mathematics and geometry, which are in fact made true by the structure of our forms of sensibility. Crucially, however, Kant also maintains that we can know the basic principles of Newtonian Mechanics with certainty, since these also follow from the general form of our cognitive contribution – in this case, our most basic conceptual categories, as applied to the fundamental empirical concept of that which is moveable in space. The upshot then is that not only can we be sure that our unintuitive and highly mathematized scientific theories nevertheless manage to accurately represent the external world, but we can know this with absolute certainty since the basic principles of Newtonian Mechanics actually codify our own cognitive contribution to any possible empirical experience.

1.2. From critique to conventionalism

Kant's solution to the problem of coordination, and its specific application to the puzzles raised by the increasing mathematization of the natural sciences, is both radical and ingenious. From its earliest inception, however, Kant's philosophical project attracted a number of criticisms. For our present purposes, the most important of these concerned the status of the external world. As we have seen, the way in which Kant attempts to bridge the gap between our ideas and the objects they are supposed to represent is by arguing that we never have knowledge of the external world in all its unmediated glory – the objects of our knowledge are not the things-in-themselves, but rather things *as they appear* to creatures with cognitive faculties like our own. But this seems to raise another sceptical challenge, for if we never have knowledge of things-in-themselves, how then do we know that there are any such things in the first place?

More specifically, we can put the worry as follows. If the point of Kant's philosophical project is to bridge the gap between our ideas and the objects they are supposed to represent, then it follows that there must be *something* – the things-in-themselves – that lies beyond our cognitive faculties, and which is in some way responsible for the phenomena we do eventually experience. Without this supposition, Kant's position would amount to a radical form of solipsism, where the only objects of knowledge are the contents of our own minds. However, if things-in-themselves lie beyond our cognitive faculties, then by Kant's own standards we can have absolutely no knowledge about them – including, for example, the fact that they exist and are responsible for the phenomena we experience. We appear then to be in the awkward situation of knowing something about those things about which we can have no knowledge. As Friedrich Heinrich Jacobi put it in an early and influential criticism:

> Even if it can be *conceded* under Kant's view, that a transcendental somewhat [i.e. things-in-themselves] *might* correspond to these merely subject beings [i.e. the phenomena we experience] … where this cause is, and what kind of connection it has with its effect, remains hidden in the deepest obscurity. (1787 [1994]: 336)

For Kant's solution to work, we must suppose that the things-in-themselves are somehow mediated through our cognitive faculties in order to produce the objects of our knowledge. But if our only possible objects of knowledge are those things that have been mediated through our cognitive faculties, then by definition we can know nothing of the things-in-themselves standing behind this process. All that we seem to have done therefore is just to shift the problem of coordination – for just as we cannot stand outside our own representational relationship in order to form an idea of its reliability, neither can we stand outside the conditions of our experience to make sure that they really do relate to an unconceptualized reality.

Such an objection may not be entirely fair to Kant. Implicit in the argument is the assumption that the only way in which the things-in-themselves could be related to the phenomena that we experience is through some kind of *causal* connection, and that since causality has been shown to be a form of our understanding, this will be a relationship that cannot apply to the situation in question. But there may well be other ways in which we can understand the relationship between things-in-themselves and the phenomena we experience that does not presuppose the contribution of our cognitive faculties. Nevertheless, the potentially paradoxical nature of the things-in-themselves proved to be a lasting source of contention, and much of the subsequent history of philosophy can be seen as a series of attempts to alleviate this difficulty. The general response was to eliminate the problematic notion of the things-in-themselves altogether and to attempt to articulate the broad outlines of Kant's philosophy without reference to an unmediated and pre-conceptualized external world.

In the case of the German Idealists, for example – thinkers such as Fichte, Hegel and Schelling, working in the immediate aftermath of Kant – this led to the endorsement of exactly the kind of solipsism mentioned above. Our interests, however, lie with another group of thinkers, loosely categorised as logical empiricists, and who also came to articulate what they saw as a sanitized version of Kant's philosophy. Unlike the German Idealists, however, who were primarily concerned with resolving what they saw as the internal tensions in Kant's system, the logical empiricists were more worried about extending Kant's philosophy to accommodate recent developments in mathematics and physics. Moreover, they also attempted to recast some of the central elements of Kant's philosophy within the powerful new tools of formal logic and semantics, a move that was to have significant consequences for the way in which we understand the contemporary scientific realism debate.

1.2.1. Non-Euclidean geometry

As we have already seen, Kant argued that space exists only as a form of our sensibility. It is not an independent substance or an objective feature of the external world, but rather one of the ways in which our own cognitive faculties order our sensory stimulations into intelligible experience. This in turn helps Kant to explain a curious feature of our geometrical knowledge: that it can be both *a priori* in that it does not depend upon experience, yet also *synthetic* in that it goes beyond mere conceptual analysis. Kant's solution, of course, is that insofar as space provides one of the conditions for us to have experience, and that since the principles of geometry are a description of this space, there is no way in which we could have experience to which the truths of geometry did not apply. One important consequence of this view therefore is that the principles of geometry cannot admit of any exception, since then they could hardly describe the conditions of any possible knowledge. At the beginning of the nineteenth century however, this was shown to be precisely the case.

What Kant understood as geometry is nowadays referred to as *Euclidean* geometry. This is the geometry with which we are all familiar, and in the two-dimensional case can be thought of as the geometry of a flat plane – that is, a space with no intrinsic curvature. This system was originally codified in Euclid's *Elements* (c. 300 BC), and was remarkable for its early axiomatic approach. What Euclid showed was that from a handful of definitions and postulates, it was possible to prove an enormous number of often extremely complex geometrical propositions on the basis of much simpler principles.

For all of its unrivalled success, however, there did remain one or two problematic issues with Euclid's system. For the most part, the definitions and postulates of Euclidean geometry seemed to be so self-evident as to preclude any coherent disagreement or discussion. They state, for example, that a straight line can be constructed between any two points, that a straight line can be extended in either direction and that all right angles are equal. The so-called *parallel postulate*, however, presented a slightly different state of affairs. What this says in effect is that if you have one straight line and a separate point, there is only one way to draw a second straight line that goes through this point but does not intersect with the first straight line. This claim, of course, seems intuitively plausible, since unless the two lines are perfectly parallel, they will eventually converge. Nevertheless, this postulate is certainly more difficult to state than the others, and indeed, Euclid himself attempted to avoid appealing to it in his proofs whenever possible. This relative complexity proved to be a source of some consternation for mathematicians, and there were various attempts to show that it could in fact be derived from the rest of Euclid's system, thereby confirming its legitimacy. Unfortunately, however, none of these attempts were successful. In fact, quite the opposite result was achieved, and by the beginning of the nineteenth century it was eventually shown that it was in fact perfectly consistent to *deny* the parallel postulate altogether.

The resulting systems are collectively known as *non-Euclidean* geometries since they differ from the original presentation in Euclid. They come in two broad flavours, depending upon the respect in which they deny the parallel postulate. In an *elliptic* geometry, there are no parallel lines whatsoever. This is the geometry of a positively curved space, and in the two-dimensional case can be approximated as something like the surface of a sphere where any two straight lines will eventually converge if extended far enough. In a *hyperbolic* geometry, by contrast, there will always be an infinite number of parallel lines that can be constructed through a point. This is the geometry of a negatively curved space, which is unfortunately much more difficult to picture – in the two-dimensional case, however, it can be thought of as something like the surface of a saddle or trough where any two straight lines will move further and further apart as they approach infinity. Other interesting consequences follow from the rejection of the parallel postulate. In an elliptic geometry, for example, the interior angles of a triangle will add up to *more* than 180 degrees (again, imagine trying to draw a triangle on the surface of a sphere), whereas in an hyperbolic geometry, the interior angles of a triangle will add up to *less* than 180 degrees.

The discovery of alternative geometrical systems was naturally enough a cause for some alarm amongst Kantians. If Euclidean geometry is just one option out of many possible systems, then it can hardly be necessarily true in the sense in which Kant assumed. Or to put the point another way, if we can readily imagine a variety of different geometrical systems – with different numbers of parallel lines, and where the interior angles of triangles add up to different amounts – then it seems very difficult to maintain that exactly *one* of them provides the spatial conditions for any possible experience.

There were roughly two different strategies employed by Kantians to meet this challenge. The first was to dismiss the new geometries as of merely technical interest, arguing that the mere existence of these formal systems with no apparent application could show us nothing about the spatial conditions of our actual experience. This line of reasoning came under greater pressure with the development of the theory of relativity in the early twentieth century (discussed in the next section), which maintained that non-Euclidean geometry was not merely of technical interest, but in fact offered a literally true description of the physical space we actually inhabit. At this point the strategy was then to distinguish between a number of different types of space, and to argue that while the *empirical space* of contemporary physics may well be non-Euclidean, nevertheless the *intuitive space* of our immediate experience remained Euclidean as Kant maintained.

A second option was to attempt to abstract from the orthodox Kantian picture. The thought was that Kant's real achievement was to have determined that our experiences were dependent upon some kind of spatial-temporal ordering, and that while Kant himself had identified this with the Euclidean geometry of his day, these specifics are not an essential part of his project. Indeed, one might even applaud the development of non-Euclidean geometries and their subsequent application as a refinement of Kant's philosophy, since they all at least agree that *some* of the apparent structure of the external world is in fact due to the way in which our cognitive faculties partly constitute the objects of our knowledge.

Neither of these responses, however, are completely satisfactory. The idea of distinguishing between the space of our immediate experience and the space of empirical science stands in stark tension with Kant's project, which explicitly holds that it is our intuitive space that determines the empirical geometry of the natural sciences. Similarly, while the essence of Kant's project can always be preserved by ascending to ever greater degrees of abstraction, at a certain point this becomes meaningless. Kant argued for the spatial-temporal conditions of our knowledge – but he also devoted considerable effort to showing exactly what these conditions amounted to, and how they shape the fundamental principles of our natural sciences. Nevertheless, despite many claims to the contrary, the development of non-Euclidean geometries alone was not sufficient to undermine Kant's philosophy of science. It did, however, prepare the ground for a more significant challenge from the realm of physics.

1.2.2. *Reflections on relativity*

One popular way of understanding the challenge posed by the development of Einstein's special and general theories of relativity is that they not only acknowledge the existence of non-Euclidean geometries, but also maintain that such geometries were in fact true of empirical space. However, as we have seen, such claims could be integrated within the broader Kantian picture by (for example) distinguishing between the empirical space of physics and the intuitive space of our immediate experience. A better way of understanding the challenge therefore – or at least one influential way of understanding the challenge, one with lasting consequences for the scientific realism debate – is to see the development of the special and general theories of relativity as not just attacking the details of Kant's philosophy of science, but in fact undermining its very possibility.

This line of thought is most strongly associated with Hans Reichenbach, although initially he saw himself as offering merely a modification of Kant's position. According to Reichenbach, what the special and general theories of relativity show us is that some of the principles that Kant regarded as being *synthetic a priori* can in fact come into conflict with experience. Such principles cannot therefore function in the way that Kant intended, since there is no way we could have experiences that conflict with what are supposed to be the conditions for any possible experience. The solution to this problem, however, is to draw a very careful distinction within Kant's account. As Reichenbach (1920 [1965]: 48–9) sees it, there are in fact two different ways to understand the notion of the *a priori* in Kant's work: those statements which are necessarily true (or true for all time); and those statements responsible for the constitution of the objects of our knowledge. What the developments in the special and general theories of relativity show, Reichenbach maintains, is that these two notions can come apart. There are statements responsible for the constitution of the objects of our knowledge and which can be thought of as the conditions for our experience – but these statements are not eternal truths and are in fact open to revision like any other claim.

We can illustrate this in the case of the special theory of relativity. Despite its radical and unintuitive consequences, the special theory of relativity is actually a rather conservative proposal. In essence, it is merely an attempt to reconcile two independently well-established principles: one concerning the invariance of physical laws between different observers or frames of reference; and one concerning the speed of light in a vacuum. Both principles were extremely successful in their respective domains, but when taken together appeared to entail some awkward consequences. In most of our everyday experience, the velocity of an object will depend in part upon our motion with respect to it. For example, if we run towards a speeding vehicle, it will approach us at a much greater velocity than if we run in the opposite direction. However, the speed of propagation of an electromagnetic wave is not like the velocity of a car. It is rather a law of nature, determined solely by the energy and frequency of the electromagnetic wave in question. But if the velocity of light is a law of nature, then by our first principle it must remain constant for all observers in all frames of reference. It follows then that we could have two different observers, one moving towards a source of light and one moving away from it, who nevertheless agree in how quickly the beam of light approaches them. The result seems paradoxical, since we are tempted to say that the beam of light will approach the observer moving towards the source of light at a much greater velocity than it will approach the observer moving away from it. Yet according to our basic principles (and indeed, countless experimental evidence), this is simply not the case. The velocity of light is a constant for all observers.

Since velocity is a function of distance and time, the only way for the two observers to agree upon the velocity of the beam of light is therefore to *disagree* as to the distance travelled by the beam and the time it took to do so. However, since all inertial frames are equivalent and none are privileged when it comes to making these assessments, there will be no fact of the matter as to which of these judgements is correct: hence the relativity of time and space. This proved to be a source of some consternation to the scientific community, and various attempts were made to understand this phenomenon, including the idea that light must propagate through some all-pervasive medium or *ether* that has the effect of systematically distorting our measuring instruments in such a way as to explain why our two observers will reach the different results that they do. What Einstein proposed is a considerable simplification of these attempts. Rather than postulating the existence of the ether and the mysterious and systematic distortion of our measuring instruments, we should instead take the phenomena at face value and conclude that distances of space and durations of time really do vary systematically for different inertial frames. In more technical terms, the two Newtonian invariances of absolute space and absolute time are replaced by the single invariance of the velocity of light.

One of the crucial ideas underlying all of this concerns the notion of *simultaneity*. It is one of the unintuitive consequences of our two basic principles that different observers in different frames of reference will come to different conclusions about when exactly different events take place. This can seem absurd if we also suppose that there is some objective fact of the matter as to when different events occur, quite independently of our ability to know when this might be. According to Einstein, however, in order to provide a precise definition for what it means for two events to occur simultaneously, we must first of all specify a procedure for *determining* when two events occur simultaneously, such as travelling between the two locations and comparing any suitably calibrated clocks found there. Since any such procedure must itself consist of some kind of physical process, it would therefore be subject in turn to the laws of nature and limited by its own velocity. It follows then that if two events were so far apart that they could never be compared, we simply cannot make any sense of them occurring simultaneously or otherwise.

The relevance of all of this for the *synthetic a priori* can now be stated quite simply. In order to provide a definition of the simultaneity of events, we must first of all offer an empirical hypothesis concerning the velocity of whatever process we use to determine the simultaneity of events. Given this assumption, we can see that any claim about the nature of time will therefore entail an empirical hypothesis concerning the velocity of this process. So, for example, the claim that time is absolute – the idea that any two events anywhere in the universe can intelligibly be thought of as happening at the same time – entails the existence of a physical process with an infinite velocity, since otherwise we would be unable to make an unrestricted comparison of events occurring anywhere in space. But the idea that time is absolute is *synthetic a priori* for Kant, whereas the claim that there exists a physical process with an infinite velocity is an *empirical* hypothesis. Moreover, it is one that we also know to be straightforwardly false.

The conceptual developments of the special and general theory of relativity therefore do not simply show the applicability of non Euclidean geometry. What they show is that in order to make sense of advances in our scientific understanding, we must suppose that many of the principles Kant took to be conditions for any possible experience can be revised in the face of empirical evidence. The fundamental notion of the *synthetic a priori* is therefore seriously undermined, and with it, the essence of Kant's philosophical system. The result, however, is purely negative – the problem of coordination is revived, and so too the mysterious nature of mathematics and geometry. The challenge therefore was to find a way of maintaining as much as possible of Kant's epistemology, and the idea that the objects of our knowledge are in part constituted by the knowing subject, yet while acknowledging the contingent and historical flexibility of this process.

1.2.3. Analyticity and the semantic turn

According to Reichenbach, the basic outlines of Kant's philosophy were correct. We do not have unmediated access to things-in-themselves, and thus in order to experience the world around us we must somehow provide the structure for the objects of our knowledge. Kant was wrong, however, to suppose that this structure could be provided by the general forms of our cognitive faculties, since recent developments in mathematics and physics had shown that whatever contribution we make to our experience is in fact contingent, temporary and revisable in the face of further empirical evidence. The underlying idea is therefore one of us freely choosing to lay down various stipulations and conventions about the way in which we are to organize our experience (what Reichenbach calls *coordinate definitions*), rather than having these constraints imposed upon us by the nature of our cognitive faculties.

However, while this modification of Kant's account may be better able to accommodate recent developments in mathematics and physics, Reichenbach still finds himself struggling with a difficulty. He acknowledges the 'strange fact' that in the process of applying these coordinate definitions

> it is the defined side [i.e. the objects of our knowledge] that determines the individual things of the undefined side [i.e. things-in-themselves], and that, vice versa, it is the undefined side that prescribes the order of the defined side. *The existence of reality is expressed in this mutuality of coordination.* (1920 [1965]: 42; original emphasis)

For Reichenbach, the objects of our knowledge are constituted through the application of various coordinate definitions, and in order for us to be able to apply these coordinate definitions there must of course be some undefined *something* to which these definitions are applied. The problem, however, is that these undefined somethings will themselves impose a constraint upon the coordinate definitions we apply – remember that we now have a choice as to which system of coordinate definitions to apply, and that some of these systems (e.g. those associated with the theory of relativity) will just be better at accommodating our experiences than others. But how can this undefined side impose any kind of constraint when it is – by definition – undefined?' The problem, of course, is precisely the same problem Jacobi encountered with Kant's original formulation. For Jacobi, we seem to be faced with the uncomfortable position of knowing that there must be something about which we can have no knowledge; for Reichenbach, we seem to be left with undefined objects that can nevertheless help to define the structure of our experience.

The crucial question, of course, concerns the nature of these coordinate definitions, and the picture that would eventually emerge is one where the objects of our knowledge are partly constituted by the language we use to represent them, rather than the cognitive faculties in which those representations take place. What this amounts to in effect is the drawing of a second important distinction within the framework of Kant's original account – between the *act of representing* an object and the *resulting representation* of that object. But once we make that distinction, Reichenbach's problem is resolved. To say that some systems of coordinate definition are better than others is to acknowledge that there are some external constraints on the way in which we represent the undefined things-in-themselves. But since we have now introduced the idea of a language standing as an intermediary between the things-in-themselves and our cognitive faculties, we do not need to understand this constraint in terms of the undefined objects simultaneously structuring the very activity that is supposed to give them structure. Rather, we apply our linguistic framework to the undefined things-in-themselves in whatever way we choose without fear of external constraint, and it will be the *resulting representation* – rather than the act of representation itself – that is subsequently assessed in the face of empirical evidence.

The distinction between the act of representation and the content of that representation is of course by now standard fare in contemporary philosophy. It does not seem, however, to have been fully appreciated by Kant, as is perhaps best illustrated with respect to his account of mathematical and geometrical truth. We have already seen that Kant argued that while these are clearly *a priori*, they nevertheless appear to go beyond the mere conceptual analysis of the terms involved. One of the weaknesses in this argument is that Kant tries to establish this conclusion on psychological grounds – we are simply asked to note that it is far from *obvious* that the internal angles of a triangle add up to 180 degrees without further background knowledge. The problem with this, of course, is that it is difficult to distinguish between those consequences that we fail to grasp because the concepts do not in fact entail one another, and those consequences that we fail to grasp simply because we're not trying hard enough.

The reason for this dependence upon a psychological criterion is that Kant does not seem to distinguish between those statements which are true in virtue of the concepts involved, and those statements that we *know* to be true via a process of conceptual analysis. That these two categories can come apart is easily illustrated (see Coffa 1991: 19–20). It may seem obvious that we need to analyse the concept of *bachelor* in order to realize that all bachelors are unmarried men. But it should also be obvious that if this analysis goes through, then the content of this statement is equivalent to the claim that all unmarried men are unmarried men, which clearly *does not* require any conceptual analysis in order for us to grasp its truth. We can know that all unmarried men are unmarried men, even if we do not understand any of the concepts involved.

The point then is that while analysis may well provide a good guide to those statements that are true in virtue of the concepts involved, it is not the analysis itself that makes those statements true. In modern terminology, we would say that such statements are true in virtue of the *meaning* of the concepts involved, rather than whether or not we have actually undertaken the analysis of those concepts. It follows therefore that an analytic truth need not be immediately obvious as Kant supposed – which is to say that just because our mathematical and geometrical knowledge *appears* to go beyond the mere conceptual analysis of the terms involved, it does not follow that it really does. It might just be that such truths are difficult to spot. As Frege put it, in an influential account of mathematical knowledge developed in opposition to that of Kant:

> The truth is that they [i.e. the conclusions of our mathematical delibera-tions] are contained in the definitions, but as plants are contained in their seeds, not as beams contained in a house. (1884 [1980]: §88)

The distinction between the act of representation and the content of that representation – or more broadly, the focus upon *semantics* – was therefore to serve two important roles in the subsequent development of Kant's philosophy of science. It was to provide a linguistic alternative to the forms of our cognitive faculties, sufficient to structure the objects of our knowledge, but flexible enough to be revised in the face of scientific development; and it was to undermine the role of the *synthetic a priori*, by explaining away its role in terms of the distinction between analytic truth and our ability to readily grasp those truths.

1.3. A scientific philosophy of science

At the root of the scientific realism debate lies a problem of coordination. Even if we are willing to reject the general sceptical challenge that attends to any of our attempts to gain knowledge of the external world, we may nevertheless still entertain the worry as to how it is that our scientific theories manage to be successful in this respect. This particular problem arose in the early modern period in response to the increased mathematization of our scientific theories and was further motivated by the increasingly unintuitive consequences they entailed. We have also seen how this worry illuminated a more general problem about *representation* that was diagnosed with particular clarity by Kant.

The specific details of Kant's solution to this problem of coordination faced a number of challenges in the light of subsequent developments in mathematics and physics, and were significantly transformed in the context of a more sophisticated understanding of the role of semantics in our philo-sophical analyses. In particular, Kant's central argument for the existence of the *synthetic a priori* was seen to depend upon an overly restricted understanding of analytic truth – which was in turn seen to depend upon a conflation between the act of conceptual analysis and the resulting content of that analysis. This sudden appreciation of the role of semantics was then seen to provide the framework for the necessary modifications to Kant's account. The way in which the subject structures the objects of his knowledge was now to be provided by the revisable forms of our language, rather than the timeless constraints of our cognitive faculties. Moreover, by carefully distin-guishing between the act of representation and the *semantic content* of those representations, we can account for the way in which the objects of our knowledge are partly determined by external constraints, but without thereby having to attribute structure to the pre-conceptualized things-in-themselves.

It should be immediately noted, however, that not all these developments proved to be ultimately successful. For example, while it is certainly true that Kant's argument for the *synthetic a priori* status of mathematics and geometry fails, subsequent attempts to accommodate them in terms of a broader understanding of analytic truth ran into insurmountable technical difficulties in the 1930s and were largely abandoned. Similarly, the resulting emphasis upon semantics – and in particular, the expectation that a detailed investigation into the language of our scientific theories would be sufficient to resolve many of the outstanding philosophical problems associated with scientific practice – was also to run aground in the second half of the twentieth century, although again, not without shaping the resulting debate in a number of important ways (discussed in detail in the next chapter). Nevertheless, one feature that has remained persistent throughout the contemporary scientific realism debate has been a particular *methodological orientation* inherited directly from Kant, and which is crucial for understanding some of the central meta-philosophical themes discussed in this book.

1.3.1. *The transcendental method*

The central idea behind Kant's philosophical project is his so-called Copernican Revolution. Traditional philosophical debate had concerned itself with the question of whether or not we have any knowledge of the external world, a question that had proved quite intractable. Kant's solution was therefore to turn this problem on its head – we were to begin with the assumption that we do have knowledge of the external world, and then seek to explain how this could be possible. The precise details of Kant's answer to this question were of course challenged by subsequent developments in mathematics and physics, and some of the fundamental components of his philosophy rejected in favour of advancements in logic and formal semantics; nevertheless, his underlying methodology was to remain a crucial component for any philosophy of science, and for the scientific realism debate in particular.

We will see this fact illustrated throughout the rest of this book. The starting point for all sides to the scientific realism debate is the acknowledgement that our scientific theories are predictively successful. The question then is not whether or not our scientific theories can give us knowledge about the external world, but how this fact can be best explained. According to the scientific realist, any such explanation will have to maintain that the rest of our scientific theories – the unobservable entities and theoretical structures postulated in order to make these predictions – are approximately true, while his opponents maintain that this predictive success can be explained by more parsimonious assumptions, or perhaps doesn't really require any philosophically deep explanation at all. In any case, no one in the scientific realism debate seriously questions the fact that our scientific theories do provide us with knowledge (to a greater or lesser degree), and it is this methodological constraint that helps to differentiate the scientific realism debate from the larger epistemological debate of which it is a part.

This transcendental methodology, however, does more than simply delimit the scope of the scientific realism debate. It also has interesting consequences for the type of argument offered in the debate. If it is already accepted by all sides that certain claims of our scientific theories are justified, then one way in which the scientific realist can proceed is to show how some of the disputed claims of our scientific theories are in fact *relevantly similar* to those claims which we already accept. We will see this strategy of justification-by-association repeatedly employed by the scientific realist in defence of their position (see Chapter 3). We will also see this kind of reasoning used against those alternatives to scientific realism that maintain that we need only believe some of the claims of our scientific theories, such as structural realism (see Chapter 6) and constructive empiricism (see Chapter 7).

But while the contemporary scientific realism debate remains committed to Kant's transcendental methodology, there remains nevertheless one crucial difference. Kant was concerned with the preconditions for our knowledge in general, and once he had provided his answer in terms of the forms of our sensibility and understanding, he then attempted to show how the science of his day could itself be deduced from this basis. In Reichenbach's terminology, he attempted to provide an analysis of our faculty of reason, rather than the scientific theories that result from it, and it is this that accounts for the eventual rejection of the *synthetic a priori*. As Reichenbach puts it:

> If he [i.e. Kant] searched for the conditions of knowledge, he should have analysed *knowledge*; but what he analysed was *reason* ... There cannot be a logical analysis of reason, because reason is not a system of fixed propositions but a faculty that becomes fruitful in application to concrete problems. Thus his method always leads him back to the criterion of self-evidence ... Essentially, the system of his a priori principles represents merely a canonization of 'common sense', of that naive affirmation of reason which he himself occasionally rejects with sober incisiveness. (1920 [1965]: 72–3; original emphasis)

It was because Kant was committed to a timeless set of principles ultimately responsible for all scientific theorizing that his position had such difficulties accommodating subsequent developments in our scientific knowledge – if there is one set of principles, and our scientific theories are to follow deductively from these principles, then once we have successfully analysed one scientific theory there simply isn't any possibility for that theory to change. By contrast, the contemporary scientific realism debate takes our current and most up-to-date scientific theories as their point of departure; we are to show not the preconditions for any *possible* experience, but merely the preconditions for our *actual* scientific knowledge.

Yet this shift – from the transcendental analysis of the methods of science to the transcendental analysis of their results – raises difficulties of its own. The fact that our scientific theories evolve and develop means that no analysis of our scientific knowledge can ever be considered complete, but will only ever be provisional on our currently accepted scientific worldview. This is a consequence that most philosophers of science will happily concede, since they would also maintain that our epistemological investigations are continuous with our best scientific practices, and that there is no higher perspective from which we can approach these questions. We are to undertake what has been championed as a thoroughly *scientific* investigation of our scientific practices. But one must proceed cautiously here. For while all parties to the scientific realism debate will agree that our scientific theories are predictively successful, there nevertheless remain important questions as to how much of our scientific theories we should therefore believe – and if the ultimate standards for answering these epistemological questions depend upon the very scientific theories about which they are asked, we risk arguing ourselves into a circle. This is an extremely broad and highly abstract way of presenting the issue, but it is one that underlies much of the contemporary literature. In particular, it is responsible for the perennial conviction that the scientific realism debate is not in fact philosophically well formed, but is rather a pseudo-debate arising out of a misunderstanding of the central issues involved.

1.4. Chapter summary

- The scientific realism debate arose as a very specific epistemological concern over the status of our scientific theories. The problem was not the general sceptical worry as to whether or not we could have knowledge of an external world, but whether our scientific theories in particular could be considered a reliable means to this end.
- The issue was ultimately a *problem of coordination* between the abstract mathematical language of our scientific theories, and the concrete physical world they attempted to describe. This in turn can be seen as a particular instance of a more general worry about *representation* that was only just beginning to be understood in the early modern period.
- An early and influential answer to this problem was offered by Kant, who attempted to close the gap between our ideas and the objects they are supposed to represent by arguing that the objects of our knowledge are in fact partly constituted by our own cognitive faculties. He then argued that some branches of our knowledge – geometry, mathematics and the fundamental principles of Newtonian Mechanics – are simply descriptions of the way in which we structure the objects of our knowledge, and so can be known with certainty merely through the introspection of our own cognitive faculties.
- Unfortunately, subsequent developments in geometry and physics put pressure on the precise details of Kant's picture. It was argued that while the subject is partly responsible for constructing the objects of his knowledge, these constraints are contingent, flexible and can be revised in the face of new empirical evidence.
- Similarly, Kant's account of the *synthetic a priori* was eventually seen to rest upon a conflation between the act of analysing our concepts and the resulting content of that analysis. It was consequently argued that much of the role Kant assigned to the fundamental forms of our cognitive faculties could in fact be accomplished by the structure of our language.
- The contemporary scientific realism debate therefore began as an attempt to answer a set of distinctively Kantian questions, through the novel perspective of a careful analysis of the language of our scientific theories. As we shall see in the next chapter, the emphasis upon language was to be short-lived. Crucially, however, the underlying Kantian methodology was to persist, although with less and less of the larger philosophical framework within which such an approach makes sense.

1.5. Further reading

For an accessible introduction to Kant and his so-called Copernican Revolution, see Gardner, S. (1999) *Kant and the Critique of Pure Reason* (London: Routledge). Also recommended is Guyer, P. (2006) *Kant* (London: Routledge), which provides a more general overview of Kant's philosophy. Detailed discussion of Kant's account of Newtonian Mechanics can be found in Friedman, M. (1992) *Kant and the Exact Sciences* (Cambridge, MA: Harvard University Press), and in the more recent Friedman, M. (2013) *Kant's Construction of Nature* (Cambridge: Cambridge University Press), although it should be noted that both books are pitched at a much more advanced level. A particularly helpful overview of some of the epistemological background to Kant's project that emphasizes some of the issues of representation discussed in this chapter can be found in Musgrave, A. (1993) *Common Sense, Science and Scepticism* (Cambridge: Cambridge University Press).

For a philosophically informed introduction to non-Euclidean geometries and the theory of relativity, and to their consequences for the philosophy of science, see Dainton, B. (2001) *Time and Space* (Durham: Acumen). More details concerning mathematics and the history of the *synthetic a priori* can be found in Potter, M. (2000) *Reason's Nearest Kin* (Oxford: Oxford University Press), although again the material can become quite advanced. Probably the most important overview of this period of philosophy, tracing the emergence of the contemporary philosophy of science from its Kantian origins, is Coffa, J. A. (1993) *The Semantic Tradition from Kant to Carnap* (Cambridge: Cambridge University Press).

2

The legacy of
logical empiricism

In the previous chapter, we have seen how the scientific realism debate arose in response to a specific epistemological worry about the status of our scientific theories – not with the possibility of knowledge in general, but rather the extent to which our increasingly abstract and mathematized scientific theories could nevertheless accurately represent the physical world. This problem was articulated with particular clarity by Kant, who has continued to influence the contemporary debate with respect to its general methodological assumptions, although his own solution to the problem was transformed in response to developments in mathematics and physics and came to be articulated in terms of the much more flexible device of a linguistic convention. In order to ground the reliability of our scientific theorizing, it was no longer deemed necessary to inspect the fundamental structures of our cognitive faculties, but rather simply to lay down precise definitions for the terms we wanted to use.

This conclusion naturally raises further questions as to the nature of these definitions, and in particular, how our theoretical terms are related to the more familiar everyday terms that are introduced in order to help systematize and explain. Such an investigation naturally raises the prospect that maybe the meaning of our theoretical discourse is not given in terms of mysterious unobservable entities to which they struggle to refer, but can in fact be cashed out in terms of the observational evidence by which they are tested and confirmed. This line of thought in turn offers an extremely neat resolution of the scientific realism debate, since the predictive success of a scientific theory can hardly raise difficult questions about the accurate representation of unobservable phenomena if that theory does not even *mention* such phenomena in the first place.

In the first half of the twentieth century, therefore, the scientific realism debate was primarily understood as a debate concerning the language of our scientific theories. The principal issue was one of *semantic realism* – whether the language of our scientific theories was to be taken at face value, and as therefore committing us to the existence of electrons, quarks and neutrinos, or if our theoretical discourse could be somehow revised or reinterpreted in such a way as to eliminate any reference to anything lying beyond the limits of our senses.

In this chapter we will investigate two strategies for removing any reference to unobservable phenomena from our scientific theories: the programme of logical reductionism (§2.1), whereby we attempt to provide explicit definitions of the theoretical terms of our scientific theories in terms of our observational vocabulary; and the programme of instrumentalist reaxiomatization (§2.2), whereby we attempt to eliminate our theoretical vocabulary *en masse* in favour of an alternative reformulation of our scientific theory couched within a purely observational vocabulary. As we shall see, however, both programmes are ultimately unsuccessful in capturing the full content of the theoretical discourse that they attempt to remove. For on the one hand, logical reductionism is unable to accommodate the essentially open-ended nature of our scientific investigations, while on the other hand, eliminative instrumentalism is unable to accommodate the full inferential role performed by our scientific theories. We will also consider the view of Rudolf Carnap (§2.3), who argued that a proper investigation into the semantic structure of our scientific theories demonstrates that the entire scientific realism debate is in fact a *philosophical pseudo-problem* that we should attempt to overcome. This approach also has its difficulties, but the idea that the whole question of scientific realism is somehow confused, or otherwise not properly formulated, is a recurring theme throughout the history of the debate, and many of these misgivings have their roots in Carnap's work. The chapter concludes with a summary of the key points discussed (§2.4) and some suggestions for further reading (§2.5).

2.1. The explicit definition of theoretical terms

The programme of explicit definition is essentially the attempt to replace certain terms of our scientific theories with (possibly rather complex combinations of) other already existing terms. Intuitively speaking, the idea is that while some of the terms of our scientific theories are well understood and grounded in our everyday experience, others are introduced in the process of our scientific investigations and need to be somehow connected with our everyday experiences in order for us to make sense of them. Following convention, we shall refer to these as the *observational terms* and the *theoretical terms* of our scientific language respectively. The purpose of an explicit definition is therefore to replace our theoretical terms with a precise definition couched entirely within our observational vocabulary.

As a purely logical exercise, there is no difficulty in drawing such a distinction. We can simply stipulate for every term in our scientific language whether or not it is to count as an observational term or as a theoretical term. The problem is that the programme of explicit definition is supposed to have some kind of philosophical relevance for the scientific realism debate, whereby we gradually increase our understanding of our scientific theories by replacing new and unfamiliar terms with those that we already grasp. Arguably then, we need to provide some kind of justification for the way in which we are to draw the boundary between our observational and theoretical vocabularies.

One tempting proposal that immediately suggests itself is to specify our observational vocabulary as being those terms that refer to entities that we can directly observe, and our theoretical vocabulary as those terms that do not. The idea then would be that since we have more reliable knowledge about the former, we can ground our semantic distinction between the observational and the theoretical upon this underlying epistemological distinction between the observable and the unobservable. Unfortunately, there are a number of difficulties with such a strategy. Perhaps the most significant issue is whether or not we really do have more reliable knowledge about those things that we can directly observe. We might argue, for example, that we have extremely reliable knowledge about the unobservable world through the use of electron microscopes and other sophisticated scientific instruments (some of these issues are discussed in more detail in Chapter 5). Moreover, even if such problems can be resolved, it is not clear that our epistemological and semantic distinctions will line up in the right sort of way. For even if we can clearly distinguish between those things that we can directly observe, and those that require instrumental mediation, it does not follow that our scientific language can be similarly divided between those terms that only refer to the former, and those that only refer to the latter. Indeed, provided we are willing to make use of a simple semantic device like negation, it seems that we can in fact easily talk about unobservable entities using what are in fact clearly observational terms (van Fraassen 1980: 54–5). For example, electrons are entities that we *cannot* directly observe; a quantum superposition is one where particles *do not* have simultaneously determinate positions and momentums; absolute space *is not* empirically detectable. These are all descriptions of unobservable entities using what we would assume to be our observational vocabulary.

Most of those engaged in the programme of explicit definition, however, were not concerned with this kind of foundationalist epistemology. The distinction between observational and theoretical terms was not intended to mark some fundamental epistemological distinction, but rather to reflect the contingent fact that some of the terms of our scientific theories are considered to be better understood than others. Carnap (1936: 454–5), for example, was happy to identify the observational vocabulary as those terms that just happen to enjoy a relatively high degree of intersubjective agreement within the scientific community. Such an approach may seem to leave many of the most pressing questions unanswered, yet it is also very much in line with the broadly Kantian methodology we identified in the previous chapter – to analyse the necessary conditions of an already existing practice, rather than attempting to justify that practice against sceptical challenges.

2.1.1. From explicit definition to partial definition

Let us leave to one side then issues concerning the justification of the distinction between our observational and theoretical vocabularies. In what follows we will assume that we can draw such a distinction, and that while it may not correspond to anything of profound epistemological significance, it nevertheless reflects a genuine semantic distinction that is of at least *some* interest for the scientific realism debate. Nevertheless, even with these provisos in hand, the programme of explicit definition still encounters serious problems.

The difficulties in attempting to provide explicit definitions of our theoretical terms are well documented in Carnap's (1936, 1937) investigation into testability and confirmation. Consider, for example, a simple dispositional predicate such as having a temperature of 30°C. There are, of course a number of observable states of affairs that we would naturally associate with an object satisfying this theoretical predicate, but for simplicity let us focus on the proposal that if we place a thermometer next to such an object, the bar of mercury will rise to the point marked '30'. This then suggests a pretty straightforward format for our attempted explicit definition: to say that something has a temperature of 30°C *is just to say* that if we place a thermometer next to the object, the mercury rises to 30. In symbols:

$$\forall x \ [Tx \leftrightarrow (O_1x > O_2x)]$$

where T is the theoretical property of having a temperature of 30°C, O_1 is the observational property of having a thermometer in the vicinity and O_2 is the observational state of affairs of the thermometer reading '30'. The proposal as it stands however is far too strong. We are saying that something has a temperature of 30°C provided it satisfies the conditional claim that if we measure it with a thermometer, then the mercury points to '30'. The problem is with the conditional, which by the standard truth-tables comes out as true whenever the antecedent is false. It would follow then that anything which is *not* currently being measured with a thermometer counts as having a temperature of 30°C by default, which is clearly absurd.

Carnap (1936: 440–3) concludes, therefore, that the most that we can hope for will be a *partial definition* of our theoretical terms. In essence, this consists in stating some of the observable consequences of our theoretical terms, but without stipulating that these consequences exhaust the meaning of those terms. So, for example, a *reduction sentence* of the form:

$$\forall x \, [O_1 x \supset (O_2 x \supset Tx)]$$

tells us that *if* we place a thermometer next to an object, and *if* the mercury rises to the '30', *then* the object of our investigation can be attributed a temperature of 30°C. A reduction sentence for T will not erroneously include vacuous cases within its extension, since it does not strictly speaking provide a definition for T, but rather a set of conditions under which T can be said to hold. The downside of course is that partial definitions are not exhaustive – if we don't actually perform the requisite experimental test, the reduction sentence will imply absolutely nothing whatsoever regarding the attribution of T one way or the other.

The upshot of all of this is that if we wish to establish explicit definitions for our theoretical terms, we need to *legislate* for those cases where the initial conditions do not hold. There are two obvious ways in which this can be done (Carnap, 1936: 448). The first is to stipulate that our experimental conditions actually exhaust the theoretical predicate in question, that is:

$$Tx \equiv (O_1 x \, \& \, O_2 x)$$

This will establish that using a thermometer ($O_1 x$) and having it point to '30' ($O_2 x$) is the *only* condition under which something has a temperature of 30°C (Tx) and that therefore any other experimental technique that appears to measure an object's temperature is in fact measuring some other property. The second is to stipulate that an object only *lacks* a temperature of 30°C whenever our thermometer explicitly gives us a negative result:

$$Tx \equiv (\neg O_1 x \, v \, O_2 x)$$

although it is admittedly a little harder to give an intuitive sense to this second proposal.

As a simple matter of logical formalism, there is nothing illegitimate in either amendment, and so in a purely technical sense the programme of explicit definition can go through. But there is no encouragement for the logical empiricist here, and no solution to the problem of explicit definition. We were attempting to show that one can make sense of *actual scientific practice* without talking about particular theoretical entities, and while our amended explicit definitions may allow us to dispense with these theoretical terms, such definitions no longer reflect the actual scientific practice with which we began. As Carnap puts it:

> Although it is possible to lay down either [of the above stipulations], neither procedure is in accordance with the intention of the scientist concerning the use of the predicate ... the scientist wishes neither to determine all the cases ... positively, nor all of them negatively; he wishes to leave these questions open until the results of further investigations suggest the statement of a new reduction pair; thereby some of the cases so far undetermined become determined positively and some negatively. (1936: 449)

The problem is that the terms of our theoretical vocabulary are essentially dynamic – they are 'open-ended' in such a way as to outstrip any particular legislation as to the future usage of that term, a usage that will be endlessly refined as we develop more and more disparate measurement techniques for the property in question. For the logical reductionist, however, any such amendment will require a new reduction sentence, along with a new stipulation for the future usage of the term. It will in effect constitute an entirely new theoretical term, with no obvious connection to the previous one with which we began. It is an unfortunate consequence of the logical reductionist programme therefore that our theoretical terms can no longer be said to grow and develop, but are rather replaced wholesale every time something new comes along.

2.1.2. Introducing the Ramsey Sentence

In what has become a justly influential paper, Frank Ramsey (1929) draws much the same conclusion as Carnap does with respect to the programme of reducing one fragment of our scientific language to another, and then proceeds – characteristically – to also suggest a solution. In order to better understand the meaning of our theoretical terms, it is of course natural to try to sketch the various semantic relationships that we know to hold between them and our more familiar observational vocabulary. However, since these semantic relationships are always open to revision in the face of our ongoing scientific investigations, such a procedure can never eliminate the theoretical terms in question. When we discover a new technique for measuring temperature for example, we want to be able to compare this with our already existing techniques for measuring the same property, which is something we cannot do if we have already *defined* the theoretical term in question with those already existing techniques. So it would appear then that theoretical terms are an indispensable component of our scientific theories. What Ramsey noted, however, was that from a purely logical point of view, it doesn't seem to matter *which* theoretical terms these are. In order to make sense of scientific practice, we certainly need to talk about more than just the observational content of our scientific theories. But we don't need to talk about specific theoretical entities like electrons, quarks and neutrinos for this to be the case. All that we really need is for there to be *enough things* such that the observational consequences of our scientific theories hang together in the right sort of way.

The basic idea then is that while the structure of our scientific theories requires some kind of theoretical placeholder in order to help systematize and explain our observational experience, this is not the same thing as our scientific theories committing us to the existence of specific unobservable entities. There is, however, some technicality involved, so we will proceed slowly. Let us begin with a simple example. Suppose our scientific theory consists of nothing more than the claim that whenever a philosopher argues with Frank Ramsey, they learn a lot about the status of our scientific theories. Symbolically we might express this as follows:

$$\forall x \, [(Px \, \& \, Axf) \supset Lx]$$

where P is the property of being a philosopher, A is the two-place relational property of having an argument, L is the property of learning a lot and where we have introduced the proper name f for Frank Ramsey. The idea then is that if this really is all that we know about Frank Ramsey – nothing about his character or appearance, but merely his argumentative influence upon other philosophers – then we can preserve *all* of the inferential structure of this theory without having to name him at all. We can simply replace the name with a suitably quantified variable:

$$\exists y \forall x \, [(Px \, \& \, Axy) \supset Lx]$$

The original theory told us that any philosopher will learn a lot if he argues with Frank Ramsey; our second theory simply tells us that *there is someone* such that any philosopher who argues with him will learn a lot about the status of our scientific theories. We call the resulting expression the *Ramsey Sentence* of the original theory.

Of course, when it comes to our scientific theories we are usually more interested in the theoretical predicates that can be attributed to different entities, rather than with the proper names of these entities. For example, in our attempt to provide a partial definition of having a temperature of 30°C, we were considering theories of the form:

$$\forall x \, [O_1 x \supset (O_2 x \supset Tx)]$$

which does not include any proper names at all. In order to construct the Ramsey Sentence for this theory, therefore, we need to replace the theoretical predicate T with an existentially quantified variable. This is not a well-defined operation for standard first-order predicate calculus, and in fact requires us to work within a more powerful logical system that does allow such quantification. We call this system *second-order* predicate calculus to indicate the fact that it allows us to quantify over *both* object-variables and predicate-variables and write the resulting Ramsey Sentence in the form:

$$\exists X \forall x \, [O_1 x \supset (O_2 x \supset Xx)]$$

where the lower case variables stand for objects in the usual way, and the upper case variables stand for predicates. Since it is natural to think of a predicate in terms of its extension, that is, the set of objects which satisfy that predicate, the resulting Ramsey Sentence can be read as saying that *there is some set* of objects X such that, if something has a thermometer placed near it ($O_1 x$) and if the mercury rises to the '30' ($O_2 x$) then that object is a member of that set (Xx). Nevertheless, it should be obvious that the Ramsey Sentence has all and only the observational consequences of the original theory, and that from the perspective of our scientific practice – if perhaps not our philosophical analysis – it is entirely equivalent.

There are a number of further interesting issues relating to the use of second-order logic, but fortunately they need not concern us here (we return to some of these issues in Chapter 6). The important point to note is that by replacing our theoretical terms with the appropriate number of existentially quantified variables, we can both illuminate the meaning of our theoretical discourse in terms of its relationship to our observational vocabulary, and do so in such a way that respects the open-ended nature of our scientific investigations. This is because a Ramsey Sentence does not attempt to provide an explicit definition of our theoretical terms so much as make a claim about the structure of our scientific theories. It tells us about how our observational experiences hang together and the number of theoretical posits required in order for it to do so in the right sort of way (although not of course the exact nature of those theoretical posits). This gives us a way of better understanding the meaning of our theoretical vocabulary in terms of the role it plays in systematizing our observational experiences, but without thereby committing ourselves to any kind of rigid definition. It follows then that as our scientific investigations progress, we can take this as simply providing more information about the structure of our theories, rather than undermining or in any other way revising any existing definitions. If we discover new techniques for determining whether or not something has a temperature of 30°C for example, this information can be added within the scope of our original variables, producing a more complex Ramsey Sentence of the form:

$$\exists X \forall x \{[O_1x \supset (O_2x \supset Xx)] \vee [O_3x \supset (O_4x \supset Xx)] \vee \ldots \}$$

In such a situation, it is clear that we are *extending* our original Ramsey Sentence, rather than replacing it with another.

The second thing to note, however, is that in so doing, the Ramsey Sentence of a theory also helps to make explicit the way in which our theoretical vocabulary has an excess content over any putative reduction to our observational vocabulary. Replacing theoretical predicates with existentially quantified variables does not eliminate reference to unobservable entities and processes from our scientific theories altogether – indeed, it makes explicit exactly the minimum sort of ontological commitments that are really associated with the usage of our theoretical vocabulary. In order to understand the meaning of our theoretical terms, we require a semantic framework that explicitly posits the existence of *something* beyond the observable entities and processes with which we are familiar. The Ramsey Sentence can therefore be seen as marking something like the limits of logical reductionism, and it shows us how much we can hope to achieve simply by analysing the meaning of our scientific vocabulary.

2.2. Theories as instruments

It would appear then that the theoretical terms of our scientific theories can only be reduced to our observational vocabulary if we are willing to violate the essentially open-ended aspect of our scientific investigations. However, the fact that we cannot systematically replace each individual theoretical term with some complex of observational statements does not necessarily commit us to taking these terms at face value, nor to believing in the existence of whatever it is that satisfies the existential structure of our scientific theories, since it may be possible to eliminate our theoretical vocabulary *en masse* without loss of predictive power. This is the position of the eliminative instrumentalist, who maintains that the theoretical terms of our scientific theories do not refer to unobservable entities, and nor do they describe complex elements of the observable world. They do not even function as undefined existential place-holders. For the eliminative instrumentalist, the theoretical terms of our scientific theories are quite literally *meaningless* – they are nothing more than symbolic devices introduced into the language of our scientific theories in order to help us organize our observational experiences, and have no more semantic content than any other of the grammatical devices we might use, such as brackets, commas and full-stops.

An early articulation of this view was put forward in the later nineteenth century by the famous philosopher, physicist and psychologist Ernst Mach. In Mach's view, the purpose of our scientific theories is to provide an *economy of thought*. They give us a way of summarizing our past experiences in a way that facilitates their easy use in future situations, in much the same way as our natural language gives us a way of keeping track of objects without having to physically carry them around. As our scientific investigations become more highly developed, greater and greater numbers of past experiences can be captured by fewer and fewer expressions, giving us an ever increasing cognitive economy. According to Mach:

> Thus, instead of noting individual cases of light-refraction, we can mentally reconstruct all present and future cases, if we know that the incident ray, the refracted ray, and the perpendicular lie in the same plane and that $\sin\alpha/\sin\beta = n$ ... In nature there is no *law* of refraction, only different cases of refraction. The law of refraction is a concise compendious rule, devised by us for the mental reconstruction of a fact, and only for its reconstruction in part, that is, on its geometrical side. (1893 [1960]: 582)

For the eliminative instrumentalist then, our scientific theories are not in the business of offering explanations. When we talk about laws of nature for example, we are not talking about the metaphysically substantive entities, or about the fundamental structure of reality – we are merely talking about our most useful and wide-ranging generalizations.

The crucial issue for the eliminative instrumentalist, of course, is whether or not the theoretical vocabulary of our scientific theories *is* dispensable as maintained. But suppose for the sake of argument that we agree that the purpose of a scientific theory is simply to systematize our observational experiences, and to provide a tool for summarizing and clarifying the various inferences that we are allowed to draw between one observational experience and another. All of this would suggest a fairly obvious sense in which our theoretical discourse can be eliminated: for if the role of our theoretical discourse is exhausted by its heuristic value, then one merely needs to find an *alternative* systematization of our observational experiences that preserves the same inferential structure, but does not include any theoretical terminology. Undoubtedly, such an alternative will be less elegant than its theoretical predecessor. But if it can be shown – at least in principle – that this heuristic role can be fulfilled by a non-theoretical equivalent, then it can be shown that our theoretical discourse can indeed be eliminated; and given the eliminative instrumentalist's conception of what it is that our theoretical discourse *does*, this task is actually rather straightforward.

In an extremely influential article, Carl Hempel (1958: 75–6) helps to make this idea precise. Consider an arbitrary scientific theory, the terms of which have been divided into an observational vocabulary $\{O_1, O_2, O_3, \ldots O_n\}$ and a theoretical vocabulary $\{T_1, T_2, T_3, \ldots T_m\}$. Given our assumption that the purpose of a scientific theory is merely to systematize our observational experiences, it follows that the purpose of our theoretical discourse will be merely to facilitate the derivation of observational consequences from observational antecedents. Simplifying somewhat, we can therefore represent the general structure of our scientific inferences as being of the form:

$$(O_1 \,\&\, T_1) \rightarrow O_2$$

where O_1 will be some initial experimental set-up or observational state-of-affairs, O_2 will be the predicted observational result and T_1 will be whatever (combination of) theoretical assumptions are used in the prediction. It should be perfectly clear that if such an inference holds, and we can logically derive O_2 on the basis of O_1 and T_1, then it will also be the case that:

$$T_1 \rightarrow (O_1 \supset O_2)$$

since otherwise such an inference will fail to hold. As far as the systematization of observational experience goes, then all reference to T_1 can be happily replaced in favour of this much more direct conditional claim. Consequently, we could just as well represent the general structure of our scientific reasoning as being of the form:

$$[O_1 \,\&\, (O_1 \supset O_2)] \rightarrow O_2$$

which will clearly facilitate all (and only) those inferences licensed by the original formulation. None of this of course is to say that our theoretical terms are to be *defined* in terms of conditional claims couched within an observational vocabulary – rather that, once we make clear the inferential role that our theoretical discourse plays, it becomes rather straightforward to find another syntactic device, stripped of all theoretical vocabulary, that can play the same inferential role.

2.2.1. Craig's Theorem

If we are willing to assume that our scientific theories are simply tools for the systematization of our observational experience, then it is a relatively straightforward procedure for us to eliminate our theoretical discourse. The problem, however, is that such a procedure leaves us with an untidy mess of seemingly disconnected statements, rather than something with which we could reasonably expect to conduct our scientific investigations. In order to be taken seriously, therefore, the eliminative instrumentalist needs to show how all of these statements can be tied together to constitute a *genuine replacement* for our original scientific theory. The way in which this can be done was first demonstrated by William Craig (1953), and although Craig himself did not endorse the position, his work has become of central importance to eliminative instrumentalism.

Craig's original result is rather technical and does not necessarily have any immediate consequences for eliminative instrumentalism. What he actually proved was the following:

> Every theory that admits of a recursively enumerable axiomatization can be recursively axiomatized.

This requires some unpacking. In simple terms, what this means is that if we have a theory for which we can systematically produce a complete list of its axioms (i.e. one that admits of a recursively enumerable axiomatization), then there will be *another* way of producing a complete list of axioms for that theory, one that also admits of a decision procedure (i.e. that can be recursively axiomatized). More importantly, Craig proved as a corollary to this result that if we have a theory for which we can systematically produce a complete list of its axioms, then there will be another way of producing a complete list of axioms for that theory *entirely within a specified sub-vocabulary of our scientific language* that also admits of a decision procedure. The problem facing the eliminative instrumentalist was to show that his seemingly disconnected observational paraphrases could be brought together to constitute a genuine scientific theory; what Craig proved was that provided our original scientific theory satisfies some minimal technical desiderata, then there will be an alternative way of expressing the content of that theory, couched entirely within our observational vocabulary, that actually satisfies even more demanding technical desiderata than the original.

The above account is obviously rather compressed, and it will be helpful for assessing the eliminative instrumentalist position to follow the proof in a little bit more detail. We begin with our original scientific theory Φ and the stipulation that it must admit of a recursively enumerable set of axioms. A set is recursively enumerable provided its elements can be listed off by an effective procedure; and an effective procedure is one that can be carried out systematically by some machine or by someone with absolutely no understanding of what they are doing, and without need of further instruction or interpretation. We further stipulate that the language of Φ can be divided between its observational vocabulary V_O and its theoretical vocabulary V_T. Since Φ admits of a recursively enumerable set of axioms, it will also admit of a recursively enumerable set of *theorems*: our effective procedure here need be nothing more taxing than writing down all of the axioms (in some lexicographical order), then writing down all of the formulae that can be obtained by applying one rule of inference to an axiom, then writing down all of the formulae that can be obtained by applying two rules of inference to an axiom, and so on and so forth. Finally, since Φ admits of a recursively enumerable set of theorems, it will also admit of a recursively enumerable set of theorems *couched entirely within the observational vocabulary V_O*. The procedure here is even more straightforward than before: we simply take our recursively enumerable set of theorems and go through them one by one, removing anything that includes an element of our theoretical vocabulary V_T. What we are left with will be an exhaustive list of all of the observational consequences of Φ, in some well-defined lexicographical order. Call this list $S = \{S_1, S_2, S_3, \dots \}$.

Essentially, all that we have done so far is to give a more precise description of the eliminative instrumentalist position. We still have nothing more than a list of the observational consequences of our original scientific theory Φ, even if we have shown that there is a systematic method of producing that list. But from here we can prove Craig's main result, that every theory that admits of a recursively enumerable set of axioms can be recursively axiomatized in a sub-vocabulary of that theory. A theory is said to be recursively axiomatizable if it has a set of axioms that is decidable; and a set is said to be decidable if there exists an effective procedure for determining whether or not any arbitrary formula in the language of the theory belongs to that set. The result is not trivial, since it is not the case that all recursively enumerable sets are decidable. For example, in order to produce a recursively enumerable set of natural numbers, we need only have a machine that will methodically produce each natural number in turn, and which we can leave running away forever in the corner of the room. But for such a set to be decidable, that machine must also be able to tell us in advance, for any particular number that we choose to feed it, whether or not it is going to appear in the final list. But that is clearly a much more sophisticated type of computation and not one that it is necessary to be able to perform in order to carry out the original task of simply producing a list of all the natural numbers. Essentially, it requires the machine to be able to make some kind of self-reflective judgement about its own future behaviour, which is several steps beyond the rather simplistic operation of continually adding one to its previous output. In the crudest possible terms, the potential slack between being recursively enumerable and being decidable consists of the fact that while the former is an entirely positive concept of future-directed behaviour (the machine will keep on doing such-and-such), the latter also involves a negative concept of future-directed behaviour (in addition, the machine will not do this-and-that).

Not all recursively enumerable sets are decidable; but given the foregoing construction of our set of observational consequences S, it is always possible to construct at least one such set for Φ entirely within the observational vocabulary V_O. Let S be the effectively produced sequence $\{S_1, S_2, S_3, \dots \}$ as before. We now construct a new effectively produced sequence S* of the form $\{S_1, (S_2 \& S_2), (S_3 \& (S_3 \& S_3)), \dots \}$. That is to say, the first member of S* consists of the first member of S, the second member of S* consists of *two* instances of the second member of S, the third member of S* consists of *three* instances of the third member of S, and so on and so forth. More generally, for each positive integer i, S* contains the formula $S_i \& (S_i \& (S_i \& \dots))$ with i conjuncts of the form S_i. What we have done then is to build into each member of S* a location marker. For any arbitrary formula in the language of the theory, it is therefore extremely straightforward to determine whether or not it is a member of S*. We noted above that one way to think about how recursive enumeration and effective decidability could come apart was that, in order to determine that an arbitrary formula was *definitely not* a member of a recursively enumerable set, we had to know something about the future-directed behaviour of our machine. What Craig provides is a conclusive method for circumventing this problem. Since every member of S* is constructed in such a way that one can tell – purely on the basis of its syntactic structure – its ordered location within any recursive enumeration of S*, one can always tell exactly how long we need to leave the machine running in order to tell for certain if that formula is going to appear on the final list.

If our original scientific theory Φ admits of a recursively enumerable set of axioms, it will admit of a recursive axiomatization couched entirely within its observational vocabulary V_O – we simply take the recursive axiomatization S* as constituting the axioms of our new theory. Let us call such a theory Craig(Φ) to indicate the result of applying all of the above operations to our original scientific theory Φ. Given the method of its construction, it should be obvious that Craig(Φ) preserves all of the observational consequences of Φ, that it is entirely stripped of any theoretical terms and that it satisfies a number of formal requirements for counting as a genuine alternative to our original theory Φ.

2.2.2. Axiomatization, simplicity and scope

The eliminative instrumentalist initially appealed to Craig's Theorem in response to the worry that his proposed reconstruction of our scientific theories would be an unwieldy mess – and while we have seen that Craig(Φ) will satisfy some fairly robust technical properties, there still remains a sense that this is all just a trick. As Hempel (1958: 76–8) points out, while Craig(Φ) is indeed both axiomatizable and decidable, it will nevertheless still consist of an infinite number of axioms; and while we may now possess an effective procedure for enumerating and checking these axioms, we have not made any progress regarding the usability of the resulting reconstruction. Indeed Craig himself, reflecting upon the possible philosophical significance of his formal result, dismissed the eliminative instrumentalist appropriation of Craig(Φ) as '[failing] to simplify or to provide genuine insight' (1956: 49). Another way to put the point is to argue that what Craig really showed was not that the eliminative instrumentalist reconstruction can be made technically respectable, but that some of our formal criteria of what counts as a genuine theory are so easily satisfiable as to not really impose any significant constraints at all.

This, however, is perhaps not entirely fair to the eliminative instrumentalist. Without a doubt, Craig(Φ) is considerably less user-friendly than our original scientific theory Φ. This is something that the eliminative instrumentalist happily concedes. His claim, after all, is that our theoretical terms help to systematize and simplify our observational experiences, and so it goes without saying that a scientific theory that employs such labour-saving devices will be more elegant and easier to use than one which does not. The question then is whether or not we can find a *precise* sense in which Craig(Φ) is worse than our original scientific theory Φ, one that doesn't appeal to such vague aesthetic standards of *being messy* or *being inelegant*. What Craig's Theorem shows is that one plausible way of fleshing out this intuition in terms of axiomatization and decidability does not impose any significant constraints after all. Craig(Φ) may therefore fail either to 'simplify' or to provide any 'genuine insight' into our scientific theories; but until his critics can come up with more precise desiderata as to what this actually means, it is not clear that this is an objection that need concern the eliminative instrumentalist.

A more interesting worry concerns not so much the nature of Craig(Φ) but the way in which it was constructed. In order for his reconstruction to go through, the eliminative instrumentalist must first of all be in possession of a successful scientific theory, one that is formulated in terms of both its observational and theoretical sub-vocabularies. But if that is the case, then it looks as if eliminative instrumentalism can only get going once the scientific realist has done all of the hard work. As Ernest Nagel puts it:

In order to specify the axioms for [Craig(Φ)] we would have to know, *in advance* of any deductions made from them, *all* the true statements of [Craig(Φ)] – in other words, Craig's method shows us how to construct [Craig(Φ)] only *after* every possible inquiry into the subject matter of [Craig(Φ)] has been completed. (1961: 137)

The idea is that, since the eliminative instrumentalist is only interested in replacing those theoretical terms that have been shown to facilitate genuine observational inferences, he must wait until he knows which scientific theories provide the best guides to the subject matter in question (i.e. he must wait until after every possible inquiry into the subject matter has been completed). In which case, since our theoretical terms play an ineliminable role in those initial investigations, any attempt to eliminate them after the investigation is complete is simply disingenuous. Or to put it another way, it is one thing to show that the inferential role of our theoretical vocabulary can be replaced with a purely observational reformulation, but if one could never uncover these inferential relations without the employment of theoretical terms in our scientific investigations, then such terms cannot really be eliminated in any philosophically interesting sense.

Again, however, this complaint may not be completely fair to the eliminative instrumentalist. We need to distinguish between two different claims that might be made here. The first is that our theoretical vocabulary can be completely eliminated from all aspects of our scientific practice. This is an extremely strong claim to make, and one against which Nagel's complaint may well have some force, since it may well be the case that our theoretical vocabulary plays an indispensable *methodological* role in the construction of our scientific theories. A second and weaker claim, however, would be merely that our theoretical vocabulary does not impose any ontological commitments. We may well need to *use* our theoretical terms as an intellectual crutch for understanding and systematizing our observational experiences, but the fact that these terms can subsequently be eliminated shows that we don't *need* to believe in the entities to which they supposedly refer. The fact that we need to begin with a successful scientific theory already articulated in both observational and theoretical terms is a fact about us and our limited intellectual capabilities; but that in itself does not necessarily show us anything about our theories, or the unobservable structure of the external world.

Underlying both of the previous objections is a more fundamental dissatisfaction with eliminative instrumentalism. It is natural to distinguish between two different functions that our scientific theories might perform: the systematization and prediction of observational experience, and the explanation of those observational experiences. Most philosophers of science attempt to strike a balance between these two functions, with the eliminative instrumentalist representing the extreme case of privileging the former at the expense of the latter. Ultimately then, those objections that challenge the nature of Craig(Φ) or the method of its construction are ultimately objections to the fact that it fails to provide us with any kind of understanding of the world around us. This is the line taken by Hilary Putnam, who argues:

> Why theoretical terms? ... *Because* without such terms we could not speak of radio stars, viruses, and elementary particles, for example – and we *wish* to speak of them, to learn more about them and to explain their behaviour and properties better. (1965: 257)

Many of the objections to Craig(Φ) therefore are only compelling if one already endorses scientific realism – and many of the defences of Craig(Φ) are only compelling if one already endorses eliminative instrumentalism. As we shall see, this sort of dialectical impasse is widespread in the contemporary scientific realism debate. Just as in the case of explicit definition, however, there are some more forceful considerations concerning the *scope* of Craig(Φ) which do not depend upon one's prior philosophical commitments.

2.2.3. *Probability and prediction*

When we considered the case of explicit definition, we saw that while it was possible to completely reduce our theoretical terms, we could only do so at the expense of their future refinement. A similar worry has been raised concerning the open-ended nature of our scientific investigations regarding the programme of eliminative instrumentalism. Let us suppose for the sake of argument that Craig(Φ) provides a genuine reformulation of our original scientific theory Φ, one that captures all of the observational consequences of Φ without appeal to any theoretical terms. Our scientific theories, however, do not exist in a vacuum, and one of the ways in which we attempt to further our understanding of the world is by *combining* our successful scientific theories. This is obviously a complex and sophisticated procedure, but at an abstract level we can think of it as the idea that if we have a successful scientific theory Φ_1 about some domain of inquiry, and another successful scientific theory Φ_2 about another domain of inquiry, it is natural to consider the conjunction (Φ_1 & Φ_2) as a way of investigating what happens when these domains interact. This, however, seems to be a feature of our scientific practice that the eliminative instrumentalist cannot accommodate. As John Earman (1978) argues, it might well be the case that (Φ_1 & Φ_2) entails novel observational consequences that we could not predict from considering Φ_1 and Φ_2 in isolation, due to the way in which their theoretical terms interact. However, given its method of construction, the eliminative instrumentalist conjunction [Craig(Φ_1) & Craig(Φ_2)] will not entail anything not already contained in its individual conjuncts.

The argument then is not so much that Craig(Φ) provides an unsatisfactory reformulation of our original scientific theory Φ, but rather that once such a reformulation is constructed, we are no longer able to accommodate some widespread features of scientific practice. The argument, however, is a little quick. While it certainly is true that the conjunction [Craig(Φ_1) & Craig(Φ_2)] will not entail any observational consequences not already entailed by Craig(Φ_1) or Craig(Φ_2), this is not the only way in which the eliminative instrumentalist needs to think about combining his scientific theories. If the conjunction (Φ_1 & Φ_2) entails novel observational consequences, then so too will the reformulation Craig(Φ_1 & Φ_2). In other words, rather than attempting to combine two scientific theories that he has already reconstructed, the eliminative instrumentalist can combine the two original theories, and then apply Craig's method to the resulting whole. The real issue therefore is not whether or not the eliminative instrumentalist can accommodate the practice of combining our successful scientific theories, but rather how he is supposed to *justify* this practice. Earman's objection therefore comes down to the issue of whether or not eliminative instrumentalism is parasitic upon a non-instrumentalist understanding of scientific practice, which we have already discussed in the previous section.

A more serious objection concerning our scientific methodology, however, notes that we don't just use our scientific theories to deduce observational consequences. We often use our scientific theories to make inductive inferences as well, and this is something that the eliminative instrumentalist cannot capture. Consider the following example due to Hempel (1958: 78–80). We have a simple scientific theory that expresses the following relationships between some observational and theoretical properties:

$$\forall x \, (T_1 x \supset O_1 x)$$
$$\forall x \, (T_1 x \supset O_2 x)$$
$$\forall x \, (T_1 x \supset O_3 x)$$
$$\forall x \, (T_1 x \supset T_2 x)$$
$$\forall x \, (T_2 x \supset O_4 x)$$

As we can clearly see, there is no deductive relationship that holds between the observational properties O_1, O_2, O_3 and the observational property O_4. In fact, if we attempted to apply Craig's Theorem to this simple scientific theory, we would not be left with any observational theorems at all out of which we could construct an eliminative instrumentalist alternative. However, argues Hempel, such a scientific theory does support an *inductive* inference between these observational properties. Suppose we discovered some object that satisfied the first three properties, that is $(O_1a \,\&\, O_2a \,\&\, O_3a)$. This fact does not entail that this object also satisfies T_1 since there may well be other reasons for this to be the case. But it does make it quite *likely* that this object satisfies this theoretical property, that is, T_1a – and if that is the case, then it does follow that this object has the fourth observational property too, that is, O_4a. The argument can be made more plausible by increasing the number of instances, but the basic point is clear enough, which is that even if we assume that Craig(Φ) can capture all of the observational consequences of our original scientific theory Φ in a satisfactory manner, we sometimes use our scientific theories to draw *non-deductive* consequences and this is something that is completely lost on the eliminative instrumentalist reformulation.

As it stands, Hempel's argument is pretty compelling. Given its method of construction, and given the underlying conception of what a scientific theory is supposed to do, there just is no way for the eliminative instrumentalist to capture any kind of inductive, statistical or probabilistic reasoning. In contrast then to the programme of explicit definition, which was able to completely capture the role of a theoretical term at any one time, but unable to accommodate how that term would change and develop, the eliminative instrumentalist can capture the future development of our scientific theories by repeated application of Craig's Theorem, but seems unable to capture the full role performed by these theories at any one time. In order to maintain eliminative instrumentalism, one would have to defend further (highly controversial) philosophical views about the role of induction, or the nature of probability. But that lies very much outside the scope of this discussion.

2.3. Pseudo-questions in the philosophy of science

We have seen then that neither logical reductionism nor eliminative instrumentalism can offer a completely satisfactory account of the structure of our scientific theories. On the one hand, any attempt to provide an explicit definition of our theoretical terms will fail to respect the essentially open-ended nature of our scientific investigations, while on the other hand, any technique for systematically eliminating our theoretical vocabulary will fail to capture the full range of (non-deductive) inferences for which it is used. The general moral seems to be that we are therefore committed to taking the language of our scientific theories at face value, and that any further concerns we may have regarding the conditions of their predictive success will have to be pursued by other means. Before turning to the contemporary debate, however, I want to consider one last semantic investigation into the status of our scientific theories. This is the considered view of Carnap, who argues that a closer analysis of the language of our scientific theories actually shows the entire scientific realism debate to be nothing more than a philosophical pseudo-problem.

According to Carnap, the content of a scientific theory is most clearly expressed in terms of its Ramsey Sentence – that is to say, as an existentially quantified claim regarding the structure of our observational experiences – along with a set of definitions or meaning-postulates for the terms of that theory. The meaning of our observational vocabulary is generally taken to be unproblematic by Carnap, and will simply require an empirical investigation into the speaking habits of the linguistic community in question (Carnap 1955; see also Carnap 1974: 257–64). The crucial issue concerns our theoretical vocabulary. We have already seen that simply constructing the Ramsey Sentence of a scientific theory will not in itself illuminate the meaning of our theoretical vocabulary, since all it really does is to make explicit the theoretical commitments imposed upon us by the inferential structure of our observational experiences. Nevertheless, we can still use it to help us define the meaning of our theoretical terms. More specifically, Carnap proposes that the meaning-postulates for our theoretical vocabulary can be given by the conditional statement that *if* the Ramsey Sentence of a theory is true, *then* the original theory is true. In symbols:

$$\text{Ramsey}(\Phi) \supset \Phi$$

where Φ is our original scientific theory, and Ramsey(Φ) is the result of replacing all of the theoretical predicates of that theory with the appropriate number of existentially quantified variables. This conditional is known as the *Carnap Sentence* of the theory, and in effect it expresses the idea that the meaning of our theoretical vocabulary as a whole can be given in terms of the role it plays in structuring our observational experiences (Carnap 1958; see also Carnap 1974: 265–74). In a sense, then, Carnap's proposal can be thought of as a kind of synthesis of the two strategies already discussed in this chapter — an explicit definition in the style of the logical reductionist, but of our theoretical vocabulary considered as a whole in the style of the eliminative instrumentalist.

Defining the meaning of our theoretical vocabulary in such an abstract manner may not seem like much of an achievement. It amounts to the claim that when we say that something has a particular temperature for example, what we really mean is that there is *some property* such that the mercury in our thermometer will point to a particular number, and our electromagnetic spectrometer will register a particular frequency, and so on and so forth – which clearly does not take us very far in resolving any questions we might have about how best to explain the predictive success of our scientific theories. Nevertheless, it turns out, however, to be quite a controversial move. If the Carnap Sentence of a scientific theory does indeed stipulate the meaning of our theoretical vocabulary, then presumably it must be true by definition – it determines the conditions under which we can meaningfully employ this aspect of our scientific language, and can be thought of therefore as providing something like a coordinate definition for our theoretical vocabulary, or as specifying our own linguistic contribution to the way in which we structure the objects of our knowledge.

The problem, however, is that the Carnap Sentence of a scientific theory does not look much like an analytic truth. In fact, it looks as if there will be lots of situations where the Carnap Sentence will be just straightforwardly *false*. This is because the Ramsey Sentence of a scientific theory is much easier to satisfy than the original theory, since it does not require the existence of specific unobservable entities, but merely the existence of enough things (whatever they might be) such that our observational experiences hang together in the right sort of way. So for example, the kinetic theory of temperature posits the existence of atoms and molecules bouncing around with different levels of energy, and would be shown to be false if these particles didn't actually exist. By contrast, however, the Ramsey Sentence of this theory only requires there to be *something* such that our thermometers give the right readings, and this could still be the case even if the kinetic theory of temperature is mistaken about their identity.

It might look then as if Carnap's proposal is in fact just another form of eliminative instrumentalism, since to claim that the Carnap Sentence of a scientific theory is analytically true amounts to the claim that the truth-conditions of a scientific theory are the same as the truth-conditions of its Ramsey Sentence – which is just to say that the existence of specific unobservable entities is actually irrelevant to the truth of our scientific theories. For Carnap, however, the question as to whether or not the meaning-postulates for a scientific theory are true is not to be understood as a substantial issue regarding the existence of unobservable entities, but merely a pragmatic issue about how we choose to regiment our language. He writes:

> I believe that the question should not be discussed in the form: 'are theoretical entities real?' but rather in the form: 'shall we prefer a language of physics (and of science in general) that contains theoretical terms, or a language without such terms?' From this point of view the question becomes one of preference and practical decision. (Carnap 1974: 256)

In this view, then, scientific realism reduces to the claim that the Carnap Sentence is false, since merely satisfying the existential commitments of our Ramsey Sentence is not sufficient to establish the truth of our scientific theories. By contrast, eliminative instrumentalism reduces to the view that the Carnap Sentence is true, since ultimately our scientific theories are nothing more than a tool for systematizing our observational experiences. So for Carnap, then, the entire scientific realism debate is nothing more than a disagreement over how we should parse the Ramsey Sentence of our scientific theories. But this is not a substantial philosophical issue about the nature of the external world – it is a pragmatic issue about how we should *talk* about that world.

2.3.1. *Internal and external questions*

In order to better understand Carnap's approach here, we need to grasp his underlying conception of what it even means to discuss questions of existence. According to Carnap (1950), if a long-running philosophical debate appears to be particularly troublesome or intractable, it is probably because the central terms of that debate have not been properly defined. These twin problems of intractability and imprecision are especially rife in the area of metaphysics, and with questions of ontology in particular. If we are to make any progress then, questions of existence must be made *precise*; and in order to do that, we must first of all lay down some well-defined standards as to what counts as the confirmation, verification or falsification of an existential claim. In most cases of course, this will be relatively straightforward. The crucial move for Carnap, however, is to acknowledge the possibility of different standards of confirmation against which one and the same existential claim may be evaluated very differently with respect to one and the same body of evidence.

One significant consequence of this view is that it entails a principled distinction between two different types of existential claim. For each different standard of confirmation that can be employed, there will always be certain background assumptions in place that help us to define the framework in question. For example, if we are considering whether or not there exists a highest prime number, we will naturally appeal to the framework of arithmetic and its associated methods of proof, which in turn will presuppose that there really are such things as numbers for us to be asking these questions about. In such a situation, since the existence of numbers helps to constitute the framework that we are using – and therefore helps to define our standards for judging whether or not something exists – any attempt to question *their* existence will leave us running in a circle. We cannot work within an arithmetic framework without presupposing the existence of numbers. From that perspective, therefore, it is analytically true that numbers exist, although it remains an open question as to whether or not any of those numbers is the highest prime.

For Carnap then, the question as to whether or not there is a highest prime is a well-defined existential query. He calls this an *internal question* of existence, since it must be answered from within a particular framework. By contrast, the question of whether or not numbers really exist is not a well-defined existential query. He calls this an *external question* of existence, since it really comes down to whether or not we wish to use arithmetic as part of our overall linguistic framework. This is not to say, however, that we can bring numbers into existence simply by choosing to talk about them. The point is rather that once we make explicit exactly what it means to ask such an existential question, *there just will be nothing more for us to say* about their existence than whether or not we wish to use certain criteria of confirmation.

All of this, of course, has immediate consequences for the way in which Carnap understands the scientific realism debate. On the face of it, the disagreement between realists and instrumentalists is over the existence of unobservable entities. As we have seen, though, the motivation under-lying this disagreement lies in very different conceptions as to the aim and purpose of scientific inquiry. For the scientific realist, an important function of our scientific theories is to provide explanations for the observational predictions they produce, and the existence of unobservable entities helps us to furnish such explanations. For the instrumentalist, by contrast, the purpose of our scientific theories is merely to provide concise systemati-zation of these observational predictions, and the existence of additional, unobservable entities (as opposed to the existence of additional, symbolic devices) is ultimately superfluous to this requirement. Yet for this conflict to constitute a substantial, metaphysical disagreement, we must first of all have some linguistic framework in place with well-defined criteria for assessing the existence of the entities in question. We can easily provide such frame-works to ask about the existence of *specific* unobservable entities – we use subatomic physics to ask about electrons, molecular biology to ask about cells, and so on and so forth – but it is not clear what framework allows us to assess the existence of *unobservable entities in general*. Here we seem to face the same sorts of issues relating to the existence of numbers; the existence of unobservable entities appears to be the sort of claim that constitutes a linguistic framework, rather than something that can be settled from within a linguistic framework. But once we realize that the most we can squeeze out of the issue is whether or not we want to *talk about* unobservable entities, then we can just say that it depends upon how much you want to increase your stock of explanations at the expense of streamlining your predictive tools. Insofar as the realist and the instrumentalist represent extreme positions along this axis, they can therefore both be acknowledged as being correct regarding the 'existence' of theoretical entities, with respect to their own particular scientific goals.

What it is important to realize, therefore, is how the entire issue over Ramsey Sentences, and Carnap's proposed logical reconstruction of a scientific theory, depends upon the secondary issue of how to understand an ontological dispute. When the realist objects that the Ramsey Sentence of a theory is much easier to satisfy than the original theory (since it could be made true by set-theory rather than atoms of gas), he is presupposing a substantive conception of ontology where quantification over sets is metaphysically distinct from quantification over atoms, or quantification over nothing at all. But this, of course, is precisely what Carnap denies: in his picture, where questions of existence are understood to be language-relative, one's ontological commitments are nothing more than one's choice of how to speak – it simply makes no sense in Carnap's account for the Ramsey Sentence of a theory to be 'easier' to satisfy than the original theory, only for it to be a more or less expedient way of talking with respect to some purpose or another.

2.3.2. The analytic and the synthetic revisited

We began this chapter with the idea that Kant's basic approach to the problem of coordination should be articulated in terms of something like a linguistic convention. This in turn prompted the idea that maybe some of the objects of our knowledge could be accounted for through a process of semantic analysis, either through explicit definition or instrumentalist reaxiomatization. Such an approach reaches its logical fulfilment in the work of Carnap, who argues that once we appreciate the structure of our scientific theories, these troubling questions of existence actually collapse into nothing more than a pragmatic decision over how we want to talk about the external world. But in presenting the issue so clearly, Carnap also exposed the vulnerabilities of the entire approach. Carnap's views on ontology – or perhaps better, his views on the *explication* of ontological questions – commits him to a principled distinction between analytic and synthetic statements. If there was no such distinction, then there would be no principled distinction between those existential claims that are dependent upon a framework and those that are constitutive of a framework; and if there are no existential claims that constitute a framework, then there would not be any *alternative* linguistic frameworks, and ontology could not be understood in the deflationary sense that Carnap intends. But unfortunately, this is exactly what W. V. O. Quine (1951a) showed.

Immediately, however, the standard story begins to fragment, as the precise respect in which Quine is taken to have refuted the analytic/synthetic distinction enjoys remarkably little consensus in the contemporary debate. Richard Creath (2007: 327) gives an informative survey of some of the options, from those who take the central argument of Quine's paper to be that the analytic/synthetic distinction is vague or circular, through those who take it to be that the distinction is insufficiently general or even empty, to those who understand the complaint to be that the distinction lacks explanatory value or behavioural significance. Creath's own view is that while Quine may establish that there is no unproblematic notion of analyticity for natural language, this can hardly be an objection to Carnap who uses the distinction in order to establish a philosophical framework.

We can perhaps try a little harder. With respect to the philosophy of science, the central lesson has generally been taken to be *epistemological*, a reading that Quine himself recognized in retrospect when he writes in his autobiography:

> I now perceive that the philosophically important question about analyticity and the linguistic doctrine of logical truth is *not* how to explicate them; it is rather the question of their relevance to epistemology. (Quine 1986: 207)

The idea can be put as follows (Hylton 2007: 68–74). Any distinction between the analytic and the synthetic entails a corresponding distinction with respect to justification: synthetic statements will be justified with respect to the standards of confirmation and evidence of the linguistic framework in question; while analytic statements will be justified insofar as we take the linguistic framework they constitute to be pragmatically beneficial. For Quine, however, confirmation is a holistic enterprise, since the confirmation of any statement will depend upon the confirmation of a whole range of other inter related statements, and thus 'any statement can be held true come what may, if we make drastic enough adjustments elsewhere in the system' (1951a: 40). The confirmation of any statement therefore will involve a pragmatic element, as we balance the weight of evidence against the overall utility of making adjustments elsewhere in our web of beliefs. For Quine, then, the justificatory distinction between the analytic and the synthetic is one of degree, not of kind; and without a principled epistemological difference between the two, the distinction collapses.

Another way to put Quine's misgivings is to note that if our existential questions can be divided into those that are analytic with respect to a linguistic framework, and those that are synthetic with respect to that framework, then we must also be able to draw a sharp distinction between the *variables* of our existential quantifiers. In Carnap's account, to ask whether or not a particular entity exists (e.g. the highest prime) is to ask whether or not there is such an entity within our domain of quantification; by contrast, to ask whether or not a particular type of entity exists (e.g. numbers) is to ask about the domain of quantification as a whole. For each linguistic framework, we therefore have to distinguish between those variables over which we can quantify (prime numbers, even numbers, any particular number) and those variables over which we cannot (numbers in general); on this account, quantification will always be restricted. However, Quine (1951b) complains, any such distinction will always be arbitrary, for while an arithmetical framework will not allow straightforward quantification over numbers, there will always be a broader linguistic framework in which we can – in a set-theoretic framework, for example, numbers will only constitute a subset of the total domain of quantification (these being defined as particular sets); within a more philosophical framework of abstract entities, we will be able to quantify over both numbers and sets (and many other things besides); and given a maximally general framework, we could presumably quantify over anything at all. In Quine's view, then, we can have no philosophically substantive reason for any kind of segregation of our variables – both general existential claims and particular existential claims are therefore to be taken on a par, and if that is the case, the sort of distinction between the analytic and the synthetic upon which Carnap depends is undermined.

The essence of Quine's criticism therefore is that Carnap's distinction between the analytic and the synthetic lacks adequate philosophical motivation. Quine therefore does not so much object to Carnap's deflationism as he does to the *extent* of Carnap's deflationism. If the distinction between the analytic and synthetic is to be abandoned because the confirmation of all existential claims is ultimately pragmatic, then what we have is a more thoroughgoing – maybe even more streamlined – articulation of Carnap's view. Similarly, to object to the notion of a linguistic framework on the grounds that there is no non-arbitrary way in which we can segregate our variables is not to object to a deflationary ontology, but merely to the degree of pluralism such deflationism allows. In Carnap's account, certain existential claims will constitute our linguistic framework and will therefore be unrevisable except through the adoption of an entirely new framework; in Quine's account, while certain existential claims will no doubt be harder to revise than another, there is only a difference in degree and not of kind.

Nevertheless, if the distinction between analytic and synthetic statements is as flexible as Quine maintains, then we no longer have the resources to provide a coordinate definition in the sense intended by Reichenbach and others. As Donald Davidson (1974) would put it in a later context, if different linguistic frameworks really do constitute the objects of our knowledge, there must be a sense in which *different* linguistic frameworks give *different* answers to the same ontological questions. But the very fact that we can so easily translate between them – treating one and the same existential statement as constitutive of our linguistic framework in one context, and as being answered within our linguistic framework in another – shows that these frameworks are not genuinely in competition. But if all of our different linguistic frameworks are ultimately the same, then we cannot really make sense of the idea of how different frameworks give different ontologies, which means that we cannot really make sense of how questions of existence can be reduced to questions of language after all. In the end, therefore, a linguistic framework is just *too* flexible for the job at hand.

2.4. Chapter summary

- The linguistic reformulation of the Kantian framework meant that in the early half of the twentieth century, the scientific realism debate was predominately understood as a question about the meaning of our scientific language – in particular, with how the novel, theoretical terms of our scientific theories were related to the better understood observational terms with which we begin our scientific theorizing.

- We introduce theoretical terms into our scientific theories in order to help systematize and explain our observational experiences. This therefore raises the prospect that the meaning of our theoretical terms can be somehow cashed out in terms of the various observational experiences by which they are tested and confirmed, and perhaps thereby shown to make no further existential demands on the conditions of their predictive success.

- However, we cannot reduce our theoretical vocabulary to our observational vocabulary through a process of explicit definition, since the meaning of our theoretical terms is essentially dynamic and constantly revisable in the face of future scientific developments. Similarly, we cannot eliminate our theoretical vocabulary altogether in favour of a reaxiomatization couched purely within our observational vocabulary without thereby curtailing the inferential power of our scientific theories.

- The most it seems that we can do is to illuminate the role played by our theoretical terms in the structure of our scientific theories taken as a whole. This is done by constructing the Ramsey Sentence of the theory, which while preserving the open-ended nature of our theoretical terms involved, and capturing the full range of scientific inferences that they perform, also makes explicit the fundamental existential commitments of the theory's predictive success.

▶

- Carnap essentially proposed that these abstract claims about theoretical structure could in fact play the role of Reichenbach's coordinate definitions. In conjunction with his deflationary views about metaphysics in general, this entailed the conclusion that the entire scientific realism debate was nothing more than a pragmatic disagreement about our choice of linguistic framework.
- It is generally agreed, however, that Quine showed this to be unfeasible. Carnap's understanding of a linguistic framework is too flexible to impose any rigid constraints on how we construct the objects of our knowledge, thus undermining this element of the Kantian approach. Subsequent discussion of the scientific realism debate was therefore to abandon altogether the idea that we structure our experiences, although it continued to maintain the essentially transcendental methodology that distinguishes these questions from the broader epistemological debate.

2.5. Further reading

Some of the best material on this period of the philosophy of science is written by the people involved. In addition to the work already cited, the essays collected together in Hempel, C. G. (1965) *Aspects of Scientific Explanation, and Other Essays in the Philosophy of Science* (New York: Free Press) are an extremely useful and accessible resource on many of the issues discussed in this chapter. Also recommended is Hanfling, O. (1981) *Logical Positivism* (New York: Columbia University Press) as an introductory overview. For more contemporary scholarship, see the essays in Friedman, M. (1999) *Logical Positivism Reconsidered* (Cambridge: Cambridge University Press). The project of somehow reducing or eliminating one part of our language to another has continued in various forms in both the philosophy of science and the philosophy of mathematics: Burgess, J. and Rosen, G. (2000) *A Subject With No Object: Strategies for Nominalistic Interpretation of Mathematics* (New York: Oxford University Press) is a difficult book, but an extremely detailed analysis of most of the contemporary approaches.

Similarly, the best introduction to Carnap's work is also by the man himself. See Carnap, R. (1974) *An Introduction to the Philosophy of Science* (New York: Basic Books) for an accessible overview of much of his philosophy. Appreciation of Carnap's thought and its scholarly analysis has accelerated over the past few decades. The articles in Friedman, M. and Creath, R. (eds) (2007) *The Cambridge Companion to Carnap* (Cambridge: Cambridge University Press) bring together work by some of the leading Carnap experts, yet are still very accessible. See also Demopoulos, W. (2013) *Logicism and its Philosophical Legacy* (Cambridge: Cambridge University Press), who discusses some of the more contemporary applications of Carnap's thought in the philosophy of science.

3

The No-Miracles Argument

So far I have argued in this book that the scientific realism debate is best understood as what we might call a problem of coordination. It is not the general sceptical worry as to whether or not we are able to have any kind of knowledge of the external world, for it takes as its starting point that our scientific theories are at least predictively successful to a greater or lesser extent. The issue is rather to investigate the necessary preconditions for that predictive success, and whether these preconditions impose any substantial limitations upon our scientific knowledge – for example, if we really need to commit ourselves to the existence of various unobservable entities and processes in order to accommodate that predictive success, or if more modest assumptions will suffice. It is this specific methodological orientation that distinguishes the scientific realism debate from broader epistemological debates of knowledge and scepticism, and which traces its origin to Kant's early and influential account of Newtonian Mechanics. It also explains the semantic preoccupations of the logical empiricists, who saw the idea of a linguistic convention as a way of reconciling the essential details of Kant's approach with the modern developments in mathematics, physics and formal logic that threatened to undermine it.

With the widely acknowledged failure of logical empiricism, however, the scientific realism debate began to take on an important new direction. Since our theoretical vocabulary cannot be reduced to our observational vocabulary, or in any other way eliminated in favour of a purely observational paraphrase, it seems that we must take the language of our scientific theories at face value. Moreover, if all of our linguistic conventions are mutually inter-trans-latable as Quine and Davidson maintain, then there is no philosophically substantive sense in which they can be said to construct the objects of our knowledge, since there is no longer any philosophically substantive sense in which different linguistic conventions would provide different constructions. These two difficulties together in turn led to a kind of naive realism – the view that our scientific theories purport to give us a *literally true* description of the external world, and that in turn we have good reasons to believe that they are largely successful in this task.

This is the classic statement of scientific realism, and the initial arguments offered in its support were in effect a rhetorical appeal in favour of a common-sense understanding of scientific practice over the intractable semantic complexities of logical empiricism. Such reasoning, however, proceeded at an extremely high level of abstraction, and it was quickly seen necessary to articulate this conviction along more robust epistemological lines. In particular, the intention was to try and reformulate what was essentially an *a priori* appeal to the greater philosophical plausibility of scientific realism over its instrumentalist rivals to an *a posteriori* argument based upon our more widely accepted standards of scientific plausibility (§3.1). A key issue here concerns the general reliability of the principle of inference to the best explanation – that we have good reasons to believe that our best explanations are likely to be true – which has continued to offer a focus of disagreement for those engaged in the contemporary scientific realism debate (§3.2). The combination of an appeal to a common-sense understanding of scientific practice, articulated in terms of an inference to the best explanation, is generally known as the *No-Miracles Argument* for scientific realism, and is one of the principal considerations that define the contemporary debate.

Unfortunately, however, despite its central role in the debate, the No-Miracles Argument is widely dismissed as an unsuccessful piece of reasoning. The basic problem seems to be that the argument is only compelling for those who already endorse scientific realism, and that therefore the scientific realism debate can amount to nothing more than a simple trading of philosophical intuitions. There have been a number of attempts to diagnose why this problem arises (§3.3); the argument of this chapter is that such an eventuality is to be expected, given what we have seen concerning the history of the scientific realism debate. For on the one hand, the contemporary scientific realism debate rejects one element of the Kantian framework, insofar as it no longer accepts that the objects of our knowledge are partly constructed by our cognitive faculties or linguistic conventions, seeking instead to offer a scientific argument for taking our theories at face value. On the other hand, however, it still retains the general methodological approach associated with this framework, insofar as it seeks to analyse the necessary preconditions of an already existing scientific practice, rather than attempting to question the reliability of that practice. The result is an epistemological investigation into the preconditions of our scientific success, which simultaneously takes our scientific investigations to constrain our epistemological investigations – which is to work within a very tight intellectual circle indeed. The chapter concludes with a summary of the key points discussed (§3.4) and some suggestions for further reading (§3.5).

3.1. Cosmic coincidences

An early articulation of this new realist intuition was offered by J. J. C. Smart (1963), who presented what he called a *plausibility argument* for scientific realism. The basic idea is that even if we could somehow dispense with our theoretical vocabulary through some process of explicit definition or instrumentalist elimination, our resulting picture of science would leave a great many things unexplained. For the eliminative instrumentalist, for example, our scientific theories are to be understood as tools for the systematization of our observational experience – they are purely symbolic devices that state that whenever a particular observational state of affairs obtains, another particular observational state of affairs will follow. But there is nothing in the eliminative instrumentalist's picture that can tell us *why* these regularities hold. On this account, it is simply a 'cosmic coincidence' that our observational experiences are related in this way, and regardless of the technical merits of the position, this is just unacceptably mysterious. Smart writes:

> Is it not odd that the phenomena of the world should be such as to make a purely instrumental theory true? On the other hand, if we interpret a theory in the realist way, then we have no need for such a cosmic coincidence: it is not surprising that galvanometers and cloud chambers behave in the sort of way they do, for if there are really electrons, etc., this is just what we should expect. (1963: 39)

Suppose that we are attempting to explain why it is that different magnetic fields produce different patterns in a saturated cloud chamber. For the scientific realist, there is an extremely straightforward story that can be told. It tells us that radioactive materials emit subatomic particles which ionize the gas in the cloud chamber as they pass, leaving a visible trail in their wake; moreover, many of these subatomic particles are intrinsically charged, and will therefore be attracted or deflected in the presence of a magnetic field, resulting in a corresponding change in their path taken through the cloud chamber. Such an account clearly involves commitment to various unobservable entities and processes, but it is nevertheless an integrated and intelligible account of the phenomena we are trying to explain. By contrast, the story provided by the eliminative instrumentalist seems to depend more upon dumb luck than any kind of causal mechanism. On this account, the most that we can say is that it is a brute fact of nature that whenever certain materials – the ones that glow in the dark and make you ill – are placed near a cloud chamber, various tracks appear; moreover, it is also a brute fact of nature that placing magnets in the vicinity of such an experimental set-up makes some of these tracks turn into spirals. There is, however, no particular reason to suppose that these facts are related.

The idea then is that scientific realism is just intrinsically more plausible than any of its instrumentalist rivals. We should note, however, that this isn't merely the old dispute as to whether or not our scientific theories should both systematize *and* explain our observational experiences, and nor is Smart simply stating that our scientific theories can provide us with knowledge of the unobservable world – an accomplishment that the eliminative instrumentalist would in any case reject as irrelevant to our scientific practice. Rather, the claim is that scientific realism provides us with a better account of our *observational experiences* and why we should expect the world to turn out the way that our theories say that it will. This is a goal that both realists and instrumentalist share, and therefore promises to provide a positive argument for scientific realism.

Nevertheless, at the centre of Smart's argument lies the idea of one philosophical position just being intrinsically more plausible than another. One can certainly feel the force of his reasoning, but at the end of the day the strength of the argument relies upon our pre-theoretical intuitions about what makes one account better than another. It therefore follows that if another philosopher simply denied that they found scientific realism more plausible than its rivals, there would be very little that Smart could say to try and convince them otherwise. For example, a committed instrumentalist might well maintain that while scientific realism offers a more intellectually pleasing account of the relationship between our observational experiences, none of this assists us in the fundamental task of deductive systematization, and is therefore actually superfluous to the real issues relating to the scientific realism debate. Or to take a more contemporary example, an empiricist like Bas van Fraassen might well maintain that while the instrumentalist explanation for the tracks in the cloud chamber leaves a lot unexplained, the scientific realist is really in no better a situation – it is not a virtue of an explanation to merely replace one mystery with another, and while talk about electrons and charge may explain the tracks in the cloud chamber, we are simply left with another set of unanswered questions about why electrons have such-and-such properties and act in the way that they do (we will return to some of these issues below). The point then is not that Smart is wrong about the plausibility of scientific realism, but only that the notion of plausibility under discussion seems to be too subjective to help us make any progress in the debate.

3.1.1. A scientific explanation for scientific success

The more contemporary articulation of this general realist intuition is usually credited to Hilary Putnam (1975a) and Richard Boyd (1984). There are a number of ways in which to understand how this version of the argument differs from – and thus attempts to improve upon – the account given by Smart. In both cases, the idea is to show how scientific realism is somehow more plausible than its rivals and can therefore provide a better explanation for why our scientific theories manage to be predictively successful. In the case of Smart, however, this notion of plausibility was to be understood in terms of our *a priori* intuitions and was therefore powerless to convince those who simply did not share these assumptions. In the case of Putnam and Boyd, by contrast, we are presented with an *a posteriori* argument for scientific realism, one where the central notion of plausibility is to be grounded in our everyday inferential practices.

More specifically, the idea is that since there is no way to adjudicate between competing *a priori* standards of plausibility, we should instead appeal to those standards of plausibility already in use within our most successful empirical investigations. Both realists and instrumentalists of course agree that our scientific theories are predictively successful; it is, after all, willingness to endorse this epistemological starting point that defines the scientific realism debate. Presumably then, both realists and instrumentalists will agree that whatever standards and criteria we use to adjudicate between competing scientific theories are themselves generally reliable, since they have allowed us to select those which are predictively successful. The proposal then is that we can appeal to these same standards and criteria to adjudicate between competing philosophical theories about the status of our scientific theories. The contemporary articulation of the realist intuition is therefore an explicitly *scientific argument*, the thought being that by looking at our most successful scientific investigations, we can adopt standards of plausibility that all sides to the scientific realism debate can accept. As Putnam puts it:

> The positive argument for realism is that it is the only philosophy that does not make the success of science a miracle. That terms in mature scientific theories typically refer ... that the theories accepted in a mature science are typically approximately true, that the same terms can refer to the same even when they occur in different theories – these statements are viewed not as necessary truths but as part of the only scientific explanation of the success of science, and hence as part of any adequate description of science and its relations to its objects. (1975a: 73)

This has become the canonical articulation of our starting intuition and is known in the literature as the No-Miracles Argument for scientific realism.

In order to properly assess this reasoning, it will be helpful to outline the structure of the argument in more detail. We begin with the claim that since the approximate truth of our scientific theories is the best explanation for their predictive success, we should conclude that our scientific theories are indeed approximately true. The argument is therefore an instance of inference to the best explanation (IBE), where the idea of one explanation being better than another is to be understood in terms of those theoretical virtues by which we choose one scientific theory over another, such as simplicity, scope, coherence with the rest of our theoretical background, and so on and so forth. This gives us a more concrete sense in which one philosophical theory can be more plausible than another, but it raises the obvious question as to why we would suppose that IBE is a reliable method of inference. The idea, however, is that IBE is part of our scientific methodology, and thus once we accept that we should appeal to our scientific methodology in order to help us adjudicate between competing philosophical theories, we *ipso facto* have reason to suppose that IBE is in fact reliable. The real force behind the No-Miracles Argument is therefore a kind of epistemological slippery slope: that once we endorse a little bit of our scientific methodology in order to break our philosophical deadlock, we end up endorsing so much of that scientific methodology that we cannot help but accept scientific realism.

More specifically, we can think of the argument as proceeding in two steps. The first step begins with the claim that our scientific theories are predictively successful, something that all parties to the scientific realism debate will accept. We then note that our scientific theories do not exist in a vacuum, but are themselves the result of a number of important considerations, including for example the various constraints imposed upon our reasoning by those background theories that we already accept. To take a very simple example, if our background theories entail that a particular sort of entity cannot exist, then any contemporary scientific theory that posits the existence of such an entity will be rendered extremely unlikely, no matter what other theoretical virtues it may possess. We conclude therefore that since our contemporary scientific theories depend so heavily upon our already existing background theories, they wouldn't have turned out to be so predictively successful unless these background theories were themselves approximately true. Or alternatively, if our background theories were not themselves approximately true, then it is hard to see how the contemporary scientific theories that we select on their basis could turn out to be as predictively successful as they are.

This might seem like a somewhat roundabout way to proceed, but it is by taking this detour through our background theories that the scientific realist is able to establish the reliability of the *a posteriori* standards of plausibility upon which his argument depends. The second step of the argument then continues with the claim that our background theories are themselves the result of previous instances of IBE. After all, we come to accept one scientific theory over another because it provides the *best explanation* for the phenomena in question, where the idea of one explanation being better than another is again to be understood in terms of the familiar theoretical virtues of simplicity, scope, coherence with other scientific theories, and so on. This claim is also fairly uncontroversial, since both realists and instrumentalists will agree that this offers an accurate description of actual scientific practice. The point though is that since we have already established in the previous step that our background theories are approximately true, the fact that they were formulated on the basis of IBE now gives us a good reason to suppose that IBE is a reliable method of inference. The rest of the argument then proceeds swiftly. According to the scientific realist, the *best explanation* for the predictive success of our scientific theories is that they are approximately true; and since we have concluded that IBE is a generally reliable method of inference, we can therefore conclude that our contemporary scientific theories are indeed approximately true as the scientific realist maintains.

3.1.2. Vicious circles and virtuous circles

Although there is certainly something compelling about the way in which the No-Miracles Argument attempts to show how even a limited endorsement of our scientific methodology inevitably leads to full-blown scientific realism, there are also a number of reasons why we might feel suspicious of this particular line of reasoning. The argument attempts to show that scientific realism offers the most scientific explanation for the predictive success of our scientific theories, and while it might well have greater simplicity and scope than its instrumentalist alternatives, there is still a sense in which it offers a very poor explanation as judged by contemporary scientific standards. The problem is that a good scientific explanation is usually one that generates novel predictions. It does not simply tell us how things have been in the past, but also makes concrete claims about how things will turn out in the future. Indeed, we saw in the previous chapter that one of the principal arguments against eliminative instrumentalism was its inability to accommodate this feature of scientific practice. But the claim that our scientific theories are approximately true does not itself lead to any novel predictions over and above those already made by the scientific theories in question (see for example Frost-Arnold 2010). This is because scientific realism is not so much a scientific explanation of predictive success as an *evaluation* of that predictive success. Or to put the same point another way, it is one thing to explain the tracks in a cloud chamber by claiming that subatomic particles exist, but it adds very little to that explanation also to claim that *it is true* that subatomic particles exist. Consequently, it is far from clear why an appeal to our scientific methodology should have anything to say about the status of scientific realism after all.

So there is a worry then that maybe the No-Miracles Argument is not a convincing piece of reasoning after all, and in fact depends upon an illegitimate understanding of our scientific practices. This concern has been put forward with particular force by Arthur Fine (1984a), who notes that the scientific realist is offering us a philosophical argument concerning the nature and reliability of our scientific methods, while simultaneously *appealing* to those very scientific methods in order to justify his philosophical argument. This then immediately raises the suspicion that whatever conclusions we are able to draw concerning the approximate truth of our scientific theories will simply depend upon whatever interpretation of our scientific theories we choose to build into our initial premises.

We have already noted that the No-Miracles Argument is an instance of IBE, and that therefore in order to proceed, it must demonstrate that IBE is a reliable method of inference. Fine's concern, however, is that the way in which the No-Miracles Argument attempts to show that IBE is reliable *is itself* an instance of IBE. As the argument was reconstructed above, we began by acknowledging the fact that our contemporary scientific theories depend heavily for their formulation upon a great number of background theories, and then concluded that since our contemporary scientific theories are predictively successful, the background theories upon which they depend must themselves be approximately true. The scientific realist then goes on to argue that since these background theories are the result of previous instances of IBE, we have reason to suppose that this particular method of inference is indeed generally reliable. But the approximate truth of our background theories is not logically entailed by the predictive success of the theories that they produce, and nor is it the only explanation available. It might be the case that all of our background theories are systematically false, yet by a series of fortuitous happenstances nevertheless lead us to the formulation of predictively successful theories. Of course, the approximate truth of our background theories may well be the *best explanation* for the predictive success of our contemporary scientific theories, but this is not something that we can appeal to when the entire purpose of the argument is to establish the reliability of IBE. In summary then, unless we already assume the reliability of IBE, we cannot conclude that our background theories are approximately true; and if we cannot conclude that our background theories are approximately true, we have no reasons to suppose that the IBE is generally reliable.

In the previous section it was noted how the No-Miracles Argument proceeds by trying to show how once we endorse some limited reliability in our scientific methods, we cannot help but endorse the general reliability of those methods. The weakness in this particular instance of the strategy, however, is that its starting point is too controversial. All sides to the scientific realism debate will happily concede that our background theories play an important role in the formulation of our contemporary scientific theories, and that these background theories are themselves the product of earlier instances of IBE. But that is not the same as the much stronger claim that our background theories must therefore be *true*, and are thus the product of *reliable* instances of IBE. Indeed, it is precisely this stronger conclusion that the scientific realist is attempting to establish.

The No-Miracles Argument is therefore a straightforwardly circular piece of reasoning, only capable of producing whatever conclusions one initially builds into its premises. As an argument against the eliminative instrumentalist, or anyone else not already committed to scientific realism, it is therefore completely ineffectual. But not all circles are vicious; some are quite benign, and some can even positively support their application. It all depends upon the purpose to which they are put to use. Certainly, no committed instrumentalist will be converted to scientific realism on the basis of the foregoing reasoning. According to Stathis Psillos (1999: 81–90; see also his 2009: 49–52), however, the No-Miracles Argument may nevertheless make a positive epistemological contribution to those already favourably predisposed towards scientific realism, and is therefore not completely empty. The idea is that such an argument can help to demonstrate the *internal coherence* of the position and thus provide further justification for those who already accept the broad outline of scientific realism.

Psillos recommends therefore that we think of the No-Miracles Argument as providing additional resources for the scientific realist who, having concluded that a scientific theory is probably true on the basis of its predictive success and other theoretical virtues, may nevertheless still entertain the meta-theoretical worry as to why we should trust our scientific methodology in this respect. The answer offered by the No-Miracles Argument is that *in general* our scientific reasoning is reliable, and while this inference will itself be an instance of IBE and therefore part of the very scientific methodology under dispute, it does at least speak to the overall consistency of the scientific realist's position. This is in fact a non-trivial result, since it could easily be the case that one's commitment to our first-order scientific practices actually sat in tension with our second-order philosophical assessment of those practices. Consider, for example, the self-refuting attempt to argue that enumerative induction is an unreliable method of inference, based upon an inductive extrapolation of all the ways in which it had gone wrong in the past (Lipton 2000).

This way of understanding the No-Miracles Argument is therefore still an instance of the broadly Kantian methodology that underlies the entire scientific realism debate, although with a less controversial set of initial premises. We use an inference to the best explanation to justify inference to the best explanation – but they are at least *different* inferences to the best explanation. The general success of our contemporary scientific theories invites us to conclude that our background scientific theories are generally reliable, while the reliability of our background scientific theories in turn invites us to conclude that our contemporary scientific theories are generally successful. This then completes the justificatory circle, and any meta-theoretical doubts we might have entertained are shown to be inconsistent with our starting philosophical intuition.

3.2. Inference to the best explanation

According to the scientific realist, it is a matter of some surprise that our scientific theories are predictively successful, something that calls out for an explanation in terms of their approximate truth. There are, however, other potential explanations available. According to Bas van Fraassen:

> The success of science is not a miracle. It is not even surprising to the scientific (Darwinist) mind. For any scientific theory is born into a life of fierce competition, a jungle red in tooth and claw. Only the successful theories survive – the ones which *in fact* have latched on to actual regularities in nature. (1980: 40)

In contrast to the scientific realist then, van Fraassen proposes a *selectionist* explanation for the predictive success of our scientific theories, an account that can be thought about along broadly evolutionary lines. Suppose that we begin with a large number of competing scientific theories, all of which make different predictions about the world. As time goes on, some of these predictions will be vindicated and others will be shown to be wrong. Whenever this happens, we eliminate the unsuccessful theories from our pool. As we continue our scientific investigations and encounter new and varied phenomena, we will both add new theories to our pool and eliminate old theories that no longer make the grade. It follows then that at any particular moment of time, all of the scientific theories left under consideration will be predictively successful – for if a theory was not predictively successful, it would no longer be one of the theories left under consideration.

According to van Fraassen then, the approximate truth of our scientific theories is not the best explanation for their predictive success, which is sufficient to undermine any attempted articulation of the No-Miracles Argument even on the more modest reading suggested by Psillos. There are, however, a number of difficulties with van Fraassen's account. First, while van Fraassen may be able to explain why it is that our scientific theories are in general predictively successful, he is not in a position to explain why it is that any *individual* scientific theory is predictively successful. Consider the following analogy. We might be able to explain why everybody in the room has red hair by noting that it is a meeting of the Red Hair Society, and that they have a very strict door policy. This, however, will not explain why it is that *James* has red hair, a fact that presumably has something to do with his genetic make-up rather than the presence of the bouncer on the door. Another way to put the point is to note that in a good evolutionary explanation, we try to identify those specific features of an organism that contributed to its survival; in van Fraassen's account, however, that level of analysis is conspicuously lacking. By contrast, the scientific realist can explain the predictive success of an individual scientific theory by appealing to its approximate truth (Lipton 2004: 193–4).

It seems then that van Fraassen's explanation does not possess the same scope as the scientific realist's explanation. But there is another respect in which we might think that a selectionist explanation for predictive success is lacking. For while it may be the case that van Fraassen can explain why our scientific theories have been predictively successful so far, he does not appear to be able to explain why many of them *continue* to be predictively successful in the future. For many scientific realists, this is the real surprise that calls out for explanation, and something that can of course be explained on the assumption that our theories are indeed approximately true. By contrast, van Fraassen's account is entirely retrospective, and there is nothing about his suggested selection mechanism that can tell us which of our currently successful theories are going to make it in the long run.

On the other hand, though, if a scientific theory remains predictively successful for a long period of time, then there will be a reasonable (inductive) expectation that it will continue to be predictively successful in the future – and if pushed on the question as to *why* our current scientific theories will continue to be predictively successful, it is presumably open to someone like van Fraassen to claim that this is just a brute fact of nature. The scientific realist will of course respond that this is a very poor explanation, and that we would therefore be better off on the supposition that our scientific theories are approximately true. At this point, however, we find ourselves back in a familiar situation. For the scientific realist, postulating the existence of unobservable entities and processes provides a more satisfying explanation of our theoretical success. But for someone like van Fraassen, we have simply replaced one set of concerns over predictive success with an equally problematic set of concerns about the nature of these unobservable entities; and if we are allowed to take unobservable entities as a brute fact of nature, why not just take the predictive success of our scientific theories as a brute fact of nature instead?

3.2.1. The best of a bad lot

The approximate truth of our scientific theories is therefore not the only explanation for their predictive success, and the extent to which it might be considered the *best* explanation is going to depend upon more fundamental considerations about what we are trying to explain when we come to assess our scientific theories. A more serious challenge to the way in which IBE underpins the No-Miracles Argument, however, is to argue that such a method of inference is just straightforwardly unreliable – that even if we grant that the approximate truth of our scientific theories is the best explanation for their predictive success, there is no reason to suppose that our best explanations are thereby likely to be true. This objection is again to be found in the work of van Fraassen (1989), although it should be noted that while the following argument can be taken on its own terms, the precise consequence that van Fraassen draws from these considerations is rather subtle (this will be discussed in more detail in Chapter 7).

In order to understand van Fraassen's objection, it is helpful to think of IBE as a two-stage process: the ranking of competing explanations in order to determine which one is the best; and then the inference to the effect that our best explanation must therefore be true. For van Fraassen (1989: 142–9), the basic problem with this is that there is no guarantee that we will have considered *enough* competing explanations during the first stage of the process. Since we are only ever capable of considering a tiny fraction of all of the possible competing explanations for any particular phenomenon, there is always going to be the risk that there exists a better explanation that we just haven't thought of yet. So in fact, we are never really engaging in an inference to the best explanation, but rather an inference to the best explanation *of those that we have actually considered*. No matter how reliable our ranking of explanations then, the worry is that our inference may well be 'the best of a bad lot' (ibid.: 142).

A satisfactory response to van Fraassen's objection therefore requires finding some way of guaranteeing that the range of explanations that we consider will be such as to include the best possible explanation. There are two ways in which this might be accomplished. The first is by exhaustion, that is, to make sure that we are in fact ranking every possible explanation for the phenomenon in question. As Peter Lipton (1993: 93–5) notes, this need not necessitate the unfeasible task of considering an infinite number of distinct hypotheses. Rather, all we really need to do is to make sure that we have exhausted the logical space of competitors by including the *negation* of all the possible explanations under consideration. So for a very simple example, if we are attempting to rank competing explanations E_1 and E_2, we can exhaust the logical space of possibilities by also considering $\neg (E_1 \vee E_2)$ as one of our competing explanations. Of course, one might well object that this last possibility is not much of an explanation: for the argument by exhaustion to work, we would have to be happy with an explanation that stated that all of the alternatives we had considered were not likely to be true, rather than chalking this up as the *failure* to come up with a compelling explanation for the phenomenon in question.

A better strategy would therefore be to show that while our range of competing explanations is not exhaustive, we nevertheless do have reasons to suppose that it is an epistemically privileged selection, one likely to contain the best possible explanation after all. As we noted above, van Fraassen is willing to grant that we are at least capable of reliably ranking the competing explanations under consideration – he merely challenges the assumption that this set of potential explanations is likely to include the truth. This is an important concession on van Fraassen's part. It would be easy enough to challenge the reliability of IBE on familiar sceptical grounds, such as the uncertainty of inductive inference in general, or other radical possibilities undermining our knowledge of the external world. As we have repeatedly noted, however, these sorts of extreme arguments are out of place in the content of the scientific realism debate, committed as it is to a broadly Kantian methodology. The issue is not whether or not we can have knowledge of the external world, but whether or not *these particular scientific theories* can furnish us with *this particular knowledge* about the external world. This is why van Fraassen is willing to grant the reliability of the first stage of IBE, since his intention is not to show that we have no scientific knowledge whatsoever, but merely that this reliability does not stretch as far as the scientific realist maintains.

But if this is the case, then the scientific realist can avail himself of the same sort of slippery slope considerations that we encountered above. As Lipton (1993: 95–101) argues, the ranking of potential explanations does not take place in a theoretical vacuum, and the various background theories that we already accept will play an important role in how we make these assessments. But if we are willing to grant that our ranking of potential explanations is a reliable process, and we concede that such a ranking depends heavily upon our accepted background theories, then we must also accept that our background theories must enjoy some privilege or success in order to play such a role. Lipton argues therefore that if we grant that we can reliably rank competing explanations, we must also grant the approximate truth of our background theories. The argument then proceeds along familiar lines, as we note that these background theories were themselves the product of earlier instances of IBE – and since we have reasons to believe that they are approximately true, we must also have reasons to believe that the instances of IBE by which they were produced were also generally reliable. We therefore conclude that in general our set of potential explanations does tend to enjoy the necessary degree of privilege and include the best possible explanation. Once we grant the reliability of one stage of the process, it is no longer coherent to cast doubt upon the second stage of the process.

The argument of course is simply a generalization of the No-Miracles Argument with which we began; and for all of its ingenuity, the same problems emerge. In order to grant the reliability of our ranking of potential explanations, we may well need to suppose that the background theories against which such comparisons are made are themselves epistemically privileged so as to not lead these comparisons astray. But we need not thereby suppose that these background theories are *true* since there are other explanations for their success. Indeed, any further argument here would itself be another instance of IBE – that the truth of our background theories is a better explanation for our reliable ranking of explanations than a persistently lucky coincidence – which just takes us back to where we began.

3.2.2. IBE and Bayesianism

Let us suppose then for the sake of argument that the approximate truth of our scientific theories really is the best explanation for their predictive success, and moreover, that the best explanations we actually formulate are also likely to be the best possible explanations. But there may still be a more fundamental problem with IBE as a method of inference, and in particular with how it fits in with our other methods of reasoning. The issue ultimately concerns the relationship between our available evidence and the various competing hypotheses that such evidence supports. IBE, of course, tells us that we should favour whatever hypothesis best explains our evidence, but another important consideration is to work in the opposite direction and look at how our evidence affects the *likelihood* of those hypotheses. The worry then is that these two assessments actually conflict with one another, which would seriously challenge the plausibility of any kind of IBE.

The way in which we assess the relative likelihoods of our hypotheses is given to us in terms of Bayes' Theorem, which is really just the method of calculating the conditional probability of a hypotheses on the basis of a particular piece of evidence. More specifically, our subjective probability for a hypothesis H given a piece of evidence E (our 'posterior probability' for H given that E) should be a function of our prior subjective probability for H (independently of this new piece of evidence E), our prior subjective probability for E (independently of our hypothesis H) and our prior subjective probability for how likely E would be to occur if H were the case. More formally:

$$P(H/E) = \frac{P(E/H) \cdot P(H)}{P(E)}$$

Suppose that we are initially very doubtful of a new hypothesis H, but that it predicts an extremely unlikely phenomenon which we subsequently observe. Let us say that P(H) = 0.2 and P(E) = 0.3, but that the conditional probability P(E/H) = 0.9 since this particular piece of evidence is predicted by our hypothesis. Plugging these numbers into our formula, we find that our conditional probability P(H/E) = 0.6 – in other words, our confidence in our hypothesis has increased dramatically, which is what we should expect given the circumstances described.

Bayes' Theorem therefore gives a precise sense in which we can say that a piece of evidence confirms an hypothesis and provides an important constraint upon our rational deliberations. Indeed, it is easy to show that if someone did not update their subjective probabilities in accordance with this formula, then they would endorse all sorts of inconsistent sets of beliefs. It would be like believing that A, believing that if A then B, but not believing that B. The problem is that IBE seems specifically designed to add something over and above these probabilistic relationships. Faced with two competing hypotheses equally supported by the data, we should consider the one that provides the better explanation more likely to be true. Yet once we allow explanatory virtue to provide this kind of boost to our subjective probabilities, we will have clearly violated Bayes' Theorem (van Fraassen 1989: 160–70). It would be like believing that A, coming to believe that if A then B, but on the grounds that it carries little explanatory weight, refusing to believe that B. It seems then that since the whole point is to provide more content than a straightforwardly probabilistic assessment, IBE is essentially probabilistically incoherent.

This objection is not insurmountable, but it does require some careful thinking about the scope of both IBE and Bayesianism. As Lipton (2004: 106) notes, while Bayes' Theorem may impose a certain *structure* upon our beliefs, it says absolutely nothing about the *content* of those beliefs. Or to put the point another way, while it may tell us which combinations of beliefs are incoherent, it doesn't tell us which beliefs need to be revised. There is nothing logically inconsistent in believing that A, coming to the belief that if A then B, and refusing to believe that B *provided* that one is thereby willing to go back and give up the belief that A. Similarly, there is nothing probabilistically incoherent in adopting an extra-high subjective probability for H given E on explanatory grounds *provided* one is also willing to retrospectively recalibrate one's prior subjective probabilities. What Bayes' Theorem tells us therefore is not that explanatory considerations cannot influence our subjective probabilities, but only that these explanatory considerations must be applied consistently across the board.

Moreover, Lipton goes on to argue that our explanatory practices might in fact help us to implement our probabilistic reasoning. Generally speaking, while we might well agree that our distribution of subjective probabilities should satisfy Bayes' Theorem, it does not follow that we are any good at meeting this desideratum (2004: 109). Such calculations are often quite complex, and we need to follow various non-probabilistic heuristics in order to stop us from falling into error. Going with the hypothesis that best explains the available evidence need not then be understood as a rival method of inference that affords extra probabilistic value to those hypotheses that meet certain theoretical virtues, but rather as a *guide* for finding those hypotheses that are in fact best supported by the evidence. Similarly, while Bayes' Theorem tells us to revise our subjective probabilities in the face of a particular piece of evidence, it tells us very little about how to determine the initial probabilities upon which that calculation is based. In those cases where the hypothesis does not logically entail the evidence in question for example, we may well need to appeal to considerations such as how well the hypothesis would explain the evidence in order to determine the conditional probability of E given H (ibid.: 114–16). Finally, not only does Bayes' Theorem tell us nothing about the input values for the process of revising our subjective probabilities, it also tells us nothing about *when* such revisions should take place. When a new piece of evidence comes to light, we should update our beliefs – but what counts as a new piece of evidence? We may worry that since any aspect of the world will have *some* relevance for any hypothesis, the Bayesian account will leave us constantly tweaking our subjective probabilities in the light of anything that transpires. Yet this is clearly not what happens. One natural rejoinder then is to note that our selection of what counts as a relevant piece of evidence will have to appeal to some non-probabilistic considerations, such as when a piece of evidence has particular explanatory consequences (ibid.: 116–17).

Bayes' Theorem is an important constraint on our inferential practices, and is clearly a necessary condition for any rational behaviour. But it is far from sufficient, and one natural way to fill in the gaps is by appealing to various non-probabilistic factors, such as the extent to which a hypothesis explains the evidence in question. However, such a reconciliation also imposes important constraints upon IBE. Once we reconceive of the process as an heuristic, we can no longer simply say that a hypothesis is probably true *because* it is the best explanation. Rather, we have to say that being the best explanation is a *good guide* to some more fundamental property, in virtue of which an hypothesis is more likely to be true. The worry then is that this would make IBE something of a side-show to the main event, with little to add to whatever reasons we already have for making one inference over another – a conclusion very much in line with our original assessment of the No-Miracles Argument.

3.3. Arguing concerning scientific realism (Part I)

Although every philosophical debate will eventually come down to a clash of competing, fundamental intuitions about the matter in hand, the scientific realism debate appears to be particularly intractable. For unlike other philosophical disagreements, this clash of intuitions manifests itself right at the surface of the debate since the No-Miracles Argument simply presupposes an assessment of our scientific practices that no one other than a committed scientific realist would accept. We have already seen how Carnap believed that the dispute over the semantics of our scientific language was in fact a philosophical pseudo-debate over the pragmatics of different ways of talking. In a similar manner, many contemporary philosophers have argued that the impotence of the No-Miracles Argument is indicative of how questions over the explanation of scientific success are also somehow ill-formed.

An early example of this kind of diagnosis is due to Allison Wylie (1986), who argues that the problem lies in a certain blurring of the philosophical and meta-philosophical issues. In other words, the scientific realism debate is not just a disagreement over the approximate truth of our scientific theories, but also a disagreement over how we should evaluate different philosophical accounts concerning the approximate truth of our scientific theories. She writes:

> The debate persists because the most sophisticated positions in either side now incorporate self-justifying conceptions of the aim of philosophy and of the standards of adequacy appropriate for judging philosophical theories of science. (1986: 287)

More specifically, the scientific realist is committed to the idea that the philosophy of science should be conducted in scientific terms, as evidenced by the fact that the No-Miracles Argument is explicitly articulated as an instance of IBE, which is in turn defended as an accepted principle of our most successful scientific reasoning. By contrast, the opponent of scientific realism is committed to a degree of epistemic caution and the idea that we should seek to find the minimal commitments necessary for making sense of scientific practice. The conflict then arises because there is nothing about our scientific methodology that guarantees its philosophical economy – that just because the approximate truth of our scientific theories is the best explanation for their predictive success, it is not necessarily the least epistemically risky explanation for their predictive success. It follows then that since both sides of the debate have a different conception of *what sort* of explanation we should be seeking, it is inevitable that the debate should prove so intractable.

Ultimately, Wylie thinks that there are, however, pragmatic reasons for favouring scientific realism over its rivals. She argues that while the anti-realist can help to keep the scientific realist honest through his various criticisms and objections, he nevertheless struggles to provide a positive account of our scientific practice. In order to properly assess this claim, we will need to wait until we have discussed in detail the main alternatives to scientific realism and the extent to which they are able to provide an internally coherent picture of our scientific practice (see Chapter 6 for a discussion of structural realism, and Chapter 7 for a discussion of constructive empiricism). But in any case, there still remains the question as to *why* the scientific realism debate should manifest this problematic blending of philosophical and meta-philosophical issues, and whether it is possible to provide a deeper diagnosis of this fact.

3.3.1. *The natural ontological attitude*

One interesting and influential account of the apparent intractability of the scientific realism debate is due to Fine (1984a). We have already encountered Fine's criticism of the No-Miracles Argument as simply presupposing what it is attempting to establish; he goes on to suggest that this may be indicative of the scientific realism debate as a whole. Generally speaking, he believes that the problem lies in the attempt to add unnecessary philosophical substance to what is in fact a perfectly autonomous scientific enterprise. In the case of the No-Miracles Argument, we begin with the predictive success of our scientific theories and then attempt to provide an explanation for this success by showing that our scientific theories are somehow reliable in a way that goes beyond what is already explicit in our day-to-day scientific practice. The problem, of course, is that this explanation is only compelling if we already presuppose that our scientific theories are reliable in this additional, philosophically motivated sense, and so is unable to add anything to our original starting point. More generally, Fine argues that everyone in the scientific realism debate begins with a set of widely accepted scientific truths – what Fine calls the 'core position' – but then goes on to add their own philosophically substantive account concerning *the nature of truth*. The intractability arises therefore since each side of the debate is working with a different conception of what it really means to say that a scientific theory is successful, and so cannot help but talk past one another.

More specifically, Fine seems to suggest that all sides to the scientific realism debate will accept the results of our scientific investigations in the same way that they accept the results of our more familiar and everyday sources of knowledge about the world, such as the use of our unimpaired senses, or testimony from a trusted source. Of course, one could always maintain a more sceptical attitude and deny that any of our usual sources of knowledge are in fact reliable – but as we have already noted, these concerns fall outside the scope of our present concerns. Instead, the scientific realism debate consists of the various attempts to add something to this core position of widely accepted truths. Fine writes:

> Let us say then, that both realist and anti-realist accept the results of scientific investigations as 'true', on par with more homely truths ... And call this acceptance of scientific truths the 'core position'. What distinguishes realists from anti-realists, then, is what they add onto this core position. (1984a: 96)

For the scientific realist this will consist of the attempt to justify our scientific practice from an external perspective, and he will add to the core position a metaphysically robust account of truth in terms of the correspondence between our scientific theories and an external reality. For the anti-realist, by contrast, this will consist of the attempt to justify our scientific practice from an internal perspective, and he will add to the core position a more anthropocentric account of truth in terms of the conclusive verification of our scientific theories, or their warranted assertability, pragmatic utility, and so on (ibid.: 97–8).

Broadly speaking, this analysis fits well with the contrast between prediction and explanation that we have also seen to characterize the scientific realism debate. The scientific realist believes that we need to posit the existence of an external reality beyond the limits of our unaided senses, because ultimately he thinks that our scientific theories should explain why our observational experiences turn out the way they do. The eliminative instrumentalist, by contrast, is content to remain at the level of the inferences we actually make, because ultimately he believes that our scientific theories are merely tools for the systematization of our observational experiences. Moreover, Fine's analysis also provides a diagnosis of why the scientific realism debate should prove so intractable, and why exactly it is that the debate seems to blur philosophical issues concerning our scientific theories and meta-philosophical issues about how those theories should be investigated. In short, since our concept of truth will in part determine how we interpret our scientific practice, we should not be surprised when further appeal to the nature of that practice fails to take us any further in resolving our original dispute.

The only solution according to Fine is to abandon this rarefied philosophical dispute and rest content with the core position with which we began. He calls this the *Natural Ontological Attitude* (NOA), and writes that:

> The attitude that marks NOA is just this: try to take science on its own terms, and try not to read things into science. If one adopts this attitude, then the global interpretations, the 'isms' of scientific philosophies, appear as idle overlays to science: not necessary, not warranted, and in the end, probably not even intelligible. (1984b: 62)

Since NOA is essentially the *rejection* of the scientific realism debate – a sort of 'no-theory' theory of scientific practice – it is understandably a little bit difficult to describe it in more detail. The end result, however, can usefully be thought of as a kind of revamped version of what Carnap had to say regarding the scientific realism debate. Both Carnap and Fine agree that our scientific practice does not require philosophical legitimization in order to be successful; but whereas Carnap understood the debate as predominately linguistic, and therefore saw the continuing philosophical debate as an ultimately dispensable disagreement over the interpretation of our Ramsey Sentence that in no way impacts the nature of our scientific investigations, Fine understands the debate in more explanatory terms and locates it as an equally superfluous squabble over a concept of truth that explicitly goes beyond any role it might play in our scientific practice.

Before continuing this line of thought, however, it is important to note some serious problems in the details of Fine's analysis. As Alan Musgrave (1989) points out, there is no such thing as a core position of widely accepted scientific truths agreed upon by all sides to the scientific realism debate – unless the idea is that the NOA restricts itself to only believing those claims of our scientific theories that concern our observational experiences. For while a scientific realist may well take the existence of electrons to be a scientific truth, the eliminative instrumentalist, for example, will object that talk of electrons has no semantic content whatsoever. Similarly, despite the helpfulness of Fine's account, it is difficult to see how the contemporary scientific realism debate has anything to do with the concept of truth. The disagreement between scientific realists and eliminative instrumentalists for example concerns whether or not the claims of our scientific theories can be expressed within a particular fragment of our overall scientific language: it is a debate about what our scientific theories actually *say*, rather than the esoteric disagreement over their truth-conditions. Generally speaking, the contemporary scientific realism debate is a disagreement over how much of our scientific theories we need to believe in order to accommodate our scientific practice, a disagreement that is completely independent of any philosophical dispute over the fundamental nature of truth.

What has happened then is that Fine has misunderstood the peculiarly Kantian origins of the contemporary scientific realism debate. We begin with the fact that our scientific theories are predictively successful and then ask about the necessary preconditions for that success, whether that be in terms of our own contribution to the construction of the objects of our knowledge, or in the additional existential commitments demanded by the structure of our scientific reasoning. Broad philosophical questions about the nature of truth may well be characteristic of the debate over realism in other areas of philosophy, but they fail to capture the specific epistemological issues and defining methodological commitments that have evolved with the contemporary scientific realism debate. Nevertheless, while Fine is wrong to suppose that the scientific realism debate is about the nature of truth, his analysis does at least *motivate* an extremely interesting response to the apparent intractability of the debate, one that has been strongly influenced by these broader questions of the nature of truth.

3.3.2. Minimalism and deflationism in the philosophy of science

We have already noted that the exact details of Fine's position are difficult to interpret, but presumably it is the case that if NOA is intended to capture the common ground between realist and anti-realist theories of truth, it is best understood as a *minimalism* about truth (see Psillos 1999: 228–45). Roughly speaking, the proposal is that truth is not a metaphysically substantive property such as correspondence to an external reality, nor an epistemic property such as warranted assertability or conclusive verification. It is in fact nothing more than a meta-linguistic predicate, a semantic device that allows us to correlate the expressions of our object-language with their truth-conditions in a meta-language. To put the point another way, an inquiry into the nature of truth can seem like an impossibly deep philosophical task. To ask in virtue of what the expressions of our language are true appears to require that we adopt some kind of perspective outside of our own representation practices, in order to investigate the relationships that hold between the things that we say and the things that we say them about (recall a similar problem discussed in Chapter 1). It was one of the great achievements of Alfred Tarksi (1944), however, to show that at least some of these issues can be resolved provided that we have *another* language with enough expressive power such that we can simultaneously talk about our original expressions and the features of the world to which they supposedly refer.

Suppose, for example, that we were originally talking in German. In that case, we could use another language such as English in order to both express our original expressions and their truth-conditions. We might say for instance that:

'Schnee ist weiss' is true iff snow is white

where we are correlating an expression in German with a description of its truth-conditions. Similarly, if we were originally speaking English, we might use German as our meta-language. In actual fact, though, most natural languages are expressively powerful enough to serve as their own meta-language, which means we could just as easily say that:

'snow is white' is true iff snow is white

where again the quotation marks indicate that we are merely *mentioning* an expression in English. More generally, our concept of truth is given by its role in a variety of truth-schemata of the form:

'p' is true iff p

where 'p' is an expression in our object-language, and p is a description of its truth-conditions in our meta-language. In any case, the point is simply that if we want to say something about what makes the expressions of our language true, we do not need to step outside of our representational practices altogether, but merely utilize a language capable of talking about the expressions of the first language. This might not of course answer all of the questions we have about truth. It does not for instance give us a general theory of truth. For any object-language, there will be an infinite number of different meta-languages in which we can correlate expressions with their truth-conditions, and there is nothing in Tarski's account that can tell us what all of these schemata have in common. Nevertheless, it is the basic claim of minimalism that this is all there is to the concept of truth – Tarski's proposal should perhaps be thought of as a technique for clarifying what is really at stake when we ask questions about truth, in much the same way that Carnap proposed a way of clarifying what was really at stake when we ask questions about existence.

Let us leave to one side the question of whether or not minimalism provides a fully satisfactory theory of truth. What is important for our present concerns is the general strategy involved, namely the idea that we can answer some of our questions about truth not by seeking some underlying metaphysical relationship between our expressions and the external world, but merely by utilizing some suitably expressive language in which such questions can be clearly stated and resolved. Such a line of thought can appear particularly attractive in the case of the No-Miracles Argument, which as we have seen attempts to offer a deeper explanation for the predictive success of our scientific theories, yet struggles to move beyond the content of the scientific theories in question. But maybe that is because there is no deeper explanation available, just as the minimalist proposes that there is no more philosophically substantive concept of truth beyond the mere correlation of object-language and meta-language. Our scientific theories already provide us with our most explanatory framework for understanding the world around us, and any attempt to seek a more profound level of understanding must either run into confusion or end up repeating what was already explicit at the beginning of our investigation. This at least is the conclusion offered by Simon Blackburn (2002), who writes:

> We see here a very different way of responding to [the No-Miracles Argument], and a way that may account for its apparent attraction. Suppose my practice is successful: my space rockets land where and when they should. What is the best explanation of this success? I design my rockets on the assumption that the solar system is heliocentric, *and it is*. Why is our medicine successful? Because we predicted that the viruses would respond in such-and-such a way, *and they do*. In saying these things we are not at all 'stepping outside our own skins' and essaying the mythical transcendental comparison. We are simply repeating science's own expla-nation of events. There is no better one – unless there is a better scientific rival. Once we believe that the best explanation of geographical and optical data is that the world is round, we also believe that the best explanation of our success as we proceed upon this hypothesis is that the world is round. It is not that there was a *further* set of data about science (its success) that required something like an independent, sideways explanation. (2002: 130)

For the minimalist about truth, there is no philosophically substantive difference between the claim that snow is white and the claim that it is true that snow is white. Similarly for the minimalist about science, there is no philosophically substantive difference between explaining the predictive success of the kinetic theory of gases in terms of atoms and molecules and the claim that the *best explanation* for that predictive success is the fact that atoms and molecules really exist.

I think that Blackburn's analysis successfully captures the insight behind Fine's NOA, and moreover provides a good framework for understanding why the No-Miracles Argument can appear so plausible and yet at the same time manage to be so unconvincing. If we are going to take seriously the idea that our best scientific practice provides the criteria for adjudicating between different philosophical theories as the contemporary scientific realist maintains, then it should hardly be surprising that when we come to make a philosophical assessment of our scientific theories we have very little left to say. In a way, minimalism in the philosophy of science could be thought of as a way of reconciling Carnap's observation that the entire issue comes down to our choice of language, with Quine's insistence that all of these languages are essentially one and the same.

In Blackburn's view – and presumably in Fine's view as well – this should be seen as a positive result, since it has shown (again) that the scientific realism debate is a philosophical pseudo-problem. Once we recognize that all explanations must take place from within some framework, and since there is no better explanatory framework than our best scientific theories, we should welcome this default victory of scientific realism as a triumph of common sense over excessive philosophical speculation. There are, however, a number of reasons to be suspicious of this result. We have already seen how most of the issues concerning truth simply misconstrue the structure of the contemporary scientific realism debate. In most cases, the issue is not whether our scientific theories provide our best explanatory framework, but rather how much of the framework we really need to believe. A default argument for scientific realism could just as easily become a default argument for eliminative instrumentalism were we able to provide a satisfactory reaxiomatization of our scientific theories. Similarly, such reasoning is completely unable to adjudicate between the scientific realist who maintains that the aim of science is approximate truth, and those like van Fraassen who argue that the aim of science is best understood in terms of a more modest epistemic goal.

3.4. Chapter summary

- The demise of logical empiricism had important consequences for the contemporary scientific realism debate. If the language of our scientific theories must be taken at face value, and if we accept the idea that a linguistic framework is too flexible to impose any serious structural constraints upon the objects of our knowledge, then we appear to have a default argument in favour of scientific realism.
- This resulted in a shift of emphasis towards the epistemological credentials of our scientific practice, and the idea that even though

we might not be able to reduce or otherwise eliminate our theoretical vocabulary, it does not necessarily follow that we need to *rely* upon these elements of our scientific theories in order to explain the preconditions of their predictive success.

- The No-Miracles Argument is therefore an attempt to establish that commitment to unobservable entities postulated by our scientific theories is the best explanation for their predictive success. It was originally articulated as an *a priori* appeal to our philosophical intuitions, but such an argument can do little to convince those who possess different philosophical intuitions.

- Consequently, the No-Miracles Argument is usually understood as an *a posteriori* appeal to our most successful empirical methods for adjudicating between competing theories. But in that case, the argument is circular, since it relies upon the reliability of our scientific methods in order to show that our scientific methods are reliable. The most therefore that such an argument can achieve is to show that scientific realism offers an internally coherent philosophy of science.

- More generally, we might also worry about the principle of inference to the best explanation that underlies such reasoning. It is not clear, for example, whether approximate truth really is the *best* explanation for predictive success, or indeed if considerations of explanatory power can be anything more than a heuristic for more important epistemological considerations.

- Part of the problem lies in the fact that many of the arguments in the scientific realism debate are bound up with meta-philosophical claims about how the scientific realism debate should be conducted. This in turn motivates the suspicion that the scientific realism debate is a philosophical pseudo-problem – not so much a pragmatic dispute over our scientific language as Carnap maintained, but a philosophically misguided attempt to go beyond whatever explanations are already explicit in the scientific practice with which we are concerned.

3.5. Further reading

The No-Miracles Argument is a central component of the contemporary scientific realism debate, and is the subject of a voluminous literature. One of the more accessible introductions can be found in Ladyman, J. (2002) *Understanding Philosophy of Science* (London: Routledge). For a more detailed overview, see Psillos, S. (1999) *Scientific Realism: How Science Tracks Truth* (London: Routledge), who as we have seen also offers a limited defence of the No-Miracles Argument as a way of demonstrating the internal coherence of scientific realism. Also recommended is Musgrave, A. (1988) 'The Ultimate Argument for Scientific Realism' in R. Nola (ed.) *Relativism and Realism in Science* (Dordrecht: Kluwer Academic Press), which discusses the distinction between inductive and deductive arguments for scientific realism. A number of other important articles are collected together in Papineau, D. (ed.) (1996) *The Philosophy of Science* (Oxford: Oxford University Press). Much of the more recent discussion of the No-Miracles Argument has centred on the so-called Base Rate Fallacy – this is discussed in detail in Chapter 5.

For more on the selectionist explanation of scientific success, see Wray, K. Brad (2010) 'Selection and Predictive Success', *Erkenntnis* 72: 365–77. The best introduction and discussion of IBE is still Lipton, P. (2004) *Inference to the Best Explanation* (London: Routledge). For further material on the Bayesian approach to the philosophy of science, see Howson, C. and Urbach, P. (1989) *Scientific Reasoning: The Bayesian Approach* (La Salle, IL: Open Court). A good introduction to theories of truth, including the various forms of minimalism, is Kirkham, R. (1992) *Theories of Truth* (Cambridge, MA: MIT Press); more detailed material can be found in Blackburn, S. and Simmons, K. (eds) (1999) *Truth* (Oxford: Oxford University Press).

4

The Pessimistic
Meta-Induction

Following the demise of logical empiricism, the contemporary scientific realism debate evolved from an essentially semantic issue concerning the language of our scientific theories to an epistemological issue concerning the extent to which we are justified in believing those theories to be true. We have seen, however, that this evolution has not been entirely unproblematic. For while this shift abandons the broadly Kantian project of clarifying the ways in which we structure the objects of our knowledge in favour of a more direct interaction with the external world, it nevertheless retains the broadly Kantian methodology of attempting to explain the acknowledged success of our scientific theories, rather than pursuing the more general sceptical inquiry into whether or not such success really is the case. The result is an epistemological investigation into the reliability of our scientific theories that effectively presupposes that these theories are indeed generally reliable. This curious state of affairs in turn helps to explain why the No-Miracles Argument appears to simply beg the question, and why many critics have concluded that the entire scientific realism debate rests upon some kind of meta-philosophical mishap.

The epistemological reformulation of the scientific realism debate may seem then simply to derail any meaningful discussion over the status of our scientific theories, leaving us with little more than a default argument in favour of scientific realism that is nevertheless philosophically quite empty. However, this reformulation of the debate in fact opens up a number of further epistemological considerations. For whether or not the approximate truth of our scientific theories in general offers a good explanation for their predictive success, we can nevertheless certainly find cases of predictively successful scientific theories that we would want to recognize as *definitely false*. The crucial issue then is just how widespread these counter-examples really are – for if it transpires that most of our predictively successful theories are actually false, then not only do we have reasons to doubt the scientific realist's purported connection between success and truth, but we also have positive reasons to adopt an anti-realist position in the philosophy of science.

It is helpful to distinguish between two different styles of argument that the anti-realist might employ to this effect (§4.1). The first is the *Underdetermination of Theory by Evidence*, which points out that for any predictively successful scientific theory, there is an infinite number of empirically equivalent rivals to that theory. The argument then is that since we have no good reason to prefer one of these theories over any of the others – and since each one of these theories makes different theoretical claims about the unobservable structure of the world – we have no good reason to believe that any particular one of these scientific theories is approximately true. Just as with early articulations of the No-Miracles Argument, however, such considerations tend to operate at an extremely abstract level, and often rely upon the mere logical possibility of constructing empirically equivalent rivals to our predictively successful scientific theories. Consequently, most of the contemporary scientific realism debate has focused upon the second argument, known somewhat misleadingly as the *Pessimistic Meta-Induction*. This differs from the former challenge in that it attempts to draw upon the actual history of our scientific practice to show that many examples of predictively successful theories have in fact turned out to be false. It therefore offers a more concrete challenge to scientific realism in that it goes beyond the mere logical possibility of underdetermination and attempts to show that a sufficiently informed appeal to our best scientific practice actually tells against scientific realism.

There are of course a number of ways in which the scientific realist can try to resist this conclusion. The most important strategy, however, has been to draw a sharp distinction between the theoretical claims made by our scientific theories and the various entities to which these claims are supposed to apply. The idea is that while many of the predictively successful scientific theories from the history of science are strictly speaking false – insofar as we now know their theoretical claims to be inaccurate – we can nevertheless show that they were making inaccurate claims *about the same things* as our contemporary scientific theories. The history of science can be seen therefore not as a sequence of unmitigated failures undermining scientific realism, but rather one of continuity and a gradual progress towards ever more accurate scientific theories that ultimately confirm our confidence in their approximate truth. I discuss some of the problems involved in trying to read the right sort of interpretation back into the history of science (§4.2) and consider some of the ways in which these historical considerations have revived interest in a broadly instrumentalist attitude towards our scientific theories (§4.3). The chapter concludes with a summary of the key points discussed (§4.4) and some suggestions for further reading (§4.5).

4.1. Against scientific realism

According to the scientific realist, the approximate truth of our scientific theories is the best explanation for their predictive success. We have already seen reasons why we might doubt this inference, and attended to some meta-philosophical worries regarding the presuppositions that it involves, but let us grant for the moment the cogency of such reasoning. One difficulty facing this argument is that there may well be more than one scientific theory capable of generating the same predictions. Different scientists might offer different explanations for the same observational experiences and therefore defend different claims about the unobservable structure of the world. If each of these theories really is predictively successful, then by the scientific realist's own standards it seems that we should conclude that every single one of them is approximately true – even though they make conflicting claims about what the world is like. To put the point another way, our observational experiences do not logically entail any particular description of the unobservable structure of the world; in the jargon, evidence *underdetermines* theory. But if all of our scientific theories possess any number of equally good alternatives, then we can hardly take the predictive success of one of them as a reason for supposing it to be true, since we could just as easily offer the same argument in support of another. Thus even if we accept the general structure of the No-Miracles Argument, it seems that the most we can squeeze out of it would be a widespread agnosticism about the status of our scientific theories.

We have already encountered some straightforward cases of underdetermination. If a scientific theory Φ is predictively successful, then so too is its instrumentalist reaxiomatization Craig(Φ), which of course disagrees about the existence of any unobservable entities whatsoever. Less controversially, if a scientific theory Φ is predictively successful, then so too is Ramsey(Φ). Indeed, the Ramsey Sentence offers a particularly good way to think about the problem of underdetermination since it shows us that while the predictive success of our scientific theories forces us to believe in *something*, it does not favour any particular interpretation of those existential commitments. But we do not need to engage in any sophisticated semantic analysis to demonstrate the Underdetermination of Theory by Evidence. We simply need to postulate different types of unobservable entities. If quarks allow us to explain some of the more esoteric elements of subatomic interaction, then so too will *smuarks* – where a smuark is understood to be causally very similar to a quark, yet different in some further qualitative respects. More generally, if a scientific theory Φ is predictively successful, then so too is the rival theory Φ*, which simply states that (phi) is true of the universe whenever some observation is being made, but not otherwise (see Kukla, 1993).

It would seem then that the Underdetermination of Theory by Evidence is an ubiquitous phenomenon. But it is the very ease with which such examples are constructed that might make us suspicious of their relevance. All that the above cases show is that for any set of evidence, there will be an indefinite number of rival scientific theories *logically compatible* with that evidence. But we have already seen that for the scientific realist, a good scientific theory needs to do more than simply accommodate the evidence – it should also explain it. Thus the mere fact that Craig(Φ), Ramsey(Φ) and our temporally-disjointed construction Φ* are all logically consistent with the same evidence as our original scientific theory Φ does not necessarily entail that they are all *equally well supported* by that evidence. After all, the Underdetermination of Theory by Evidence is supposed to be an epistemological problem. It is supposed to undermine the scientific realist's confidence in the approximate truth of his scientific theories by showing that we have equally good reason to endorse any number of incompatible alternatives. The examples of under-determination sketched above, however, depend upon nothing more than the *logical* relationship between evidence and theory: they are therefore an attempt to derive an epistemological conclusion from a logico-semantic premise, which is simply a category mistake.

More specifically, we can note that scientific practice involves more than purely deductive reasoning. As we have already seen throughout this book, it also involves a great deal of ampliative reasoning, such as an assessment of the explanatory power of a particular scientific theory or its ability to accommodate our inductive or statistical reasoning. In order to present an interesting challenge, therefore, the anti-realist needs to show that for any predictively successful scientific theory there will be countless rival theories that are not just logically compatible with the available evidence, but that are equally well supported by that evidence. In Larry Laudan's (1990) terminology, he needs to demonstrate deductive *and* ampliative underdetermination – that for any predictively successful scientific theory, there will be countless other predictively successful scientific theories, and that none of our methods of theory choice give us any reasons to choose one over another. If this can be shown to be the case, then the scientific realist really would have no good reason to suppose that any particular scientific theory was approximately true, and his position would collapse.

4.1.1. The Duhem-Quine Thesis

One powerful consideration often advanced in favour of this stronger version of underdetermination is the idea of *confirmational holism*. In essence, this is just the observation that no scientific theory is ever tested in isolation. This may be because we require sophisticated instruments in order to detect the predicted consequences of the scientific theory in question, and must therefore rely upon the theoretical underpinnings of these instruments. Or it might be because we have to make certain assumptions about the domain in which our theory is being tested, which will themselves rest upon the predictions of other scientific theories. To take a simple example, we might think that in order to test a theory of planetary motion, all we need to do is make our predictions and observe the night sky. But we must also rely upon our theory of optics in order to make sure our telescope is functioning correctly, not to mention our theory of human physiology to correct for natural bias. If we are dealing with events over suitably large distances or appropriately high velocities, we might need to factor in relativistic considerations. In addition, we must also take into consideration any external factors that might influence the otherwise smooth motion of the heavens – cataclysmic events on the surface of the planets sufficient to knock them off their orbit, for example – which will presuppose other theoretical assumptions in turn.

The point of all of this is that if our scientific theories are always tested *en masse*, it is consequently no straightforward task to determine the extent to which any particular scientific theory has been confirmed or falsified by the evidence at hand. This difficulty was raised with particular clarity by Pierre Duhem:

> In sum, the physicist can never subject an isolated hypothesis to experimental test, but only a whole group of hypotheses; when the experiment is in disagreement with his predictions, what he learns is that at least one of the hypotheses constituting this group is unacceptable and ought to be modified; but the experiment does not designate which one should be changed. (1914 [1954]: 187)

It is important to note that Duhem himself did not draw any strong conclusions about underdetermination from the fact of confirmational holism; he merely concluded that scientific reasoning involves more than just the logical relationship between theory and evidence, since it will require various other considerations regarding how to interpret the results of any experimental test. The idea, however, has been developed into a more radical thesis by Quine (1951a; see also his 1975), who reasons that if our scientific theories can only ever be assessed as part of a larger theoretical whole, then any scientific theory can be made compatible with any observational experience one likes provided it is embedded in the right theoretical background. If our favourite scientific theory does not predict the right observational experiences, we can simply keep on adding auxiliary assumptions until it does.

This claim is known as the *Duhem-Quine Thesis*, and it goes beyond the simple cases of underdetermination that we have already discussed in two important ways. First, it is a fairly trivial observation that for any set of successful predictions there will be an infinite number of rival theories logically compatible with those predictions. The Duhem-Quine Thesis, however, argues that for any set of successful predictions, *every other* scientific theory that we can formulate can be made logically compatible with those predictions. Given the right adjustments elsewhere in our theoretical background, even those theories that initially conflicted with our observational experiences can be reconciled with the existing facts. So the Duhem-Quine Thesis drives an underdetermination argument with much greater scope than that with which we began. Second, and more importantly, it also purports to be a form of *ampliative* underdetermination. We have already seen in the discussion of the No-Miracles Argument and the defence of IBE that the way in which we evaluate our contemporary scientific theories is significantly shaped by the background theories that we have previously accepted. If we are already committed to a certain type of unobservable entity for example, then any new theory that also postulates such an entity will seem much more plausible than another which denies it altogether, even if both theories are otherwise equally successful. It seems to follow then that not only can any scientific theory be made logically compatible with the available evidence given the right auxiliary assumptions, but that any scientific theory can be made *equally explanatory* of that evidence given the right tweaks elsewhere in our background beliefs. The Duhem-Quine Thesis therefore suggests a form of underdetermination that extends even to the epistemological considerations that we bring to theory choice.

However, as Laudan and Leplin (1991) point out, while we may indeed be able to make one theory just as explanatory as another by making the necessary adjustments in our background beliefs, there is no guarantee that the end result will possess all of the theoretical virtues of its rivals. The adjustments we need to make will undoubtedly produce an overall theoretical system that is considerably less simple and economical than that involving our original scientific theory. Moreover, the confirmation of a scientific theory often extends beyond its direct relationship to the available evidence. Suppose we have a scientific theory Φ_1 that entails two further scientific theories Φ_2 and Φ_3. Any evidence that confirms Φ_2 will retrospectively confirm Φ_1, and any confirmation for Φ_1 will clearly carry over as confirmation for Φ_3. Thus Φ_2

confirms Φ_3, albeit in a somewhat roundabout way. Crucially, this will still be the case if the evidence in question has no direct bearing on Φ_3 – it will be an *indirect* form of support for the theory, one that depends upon the structure of our theoretical background, and is therefore easily lost when adjusting our background beliefs.

We have already encountered an appeal to these broader theoretical virtues in the discussion of eliminative instrumentalism. There we noted that the instrumentalist reaxiomatization was almost necessarily more complex and unwieldy than our original scientific theory. However, given that the whole purpose of eliminative instrumentalism was merely to capture the observational consequences of our scientific theories within a purely obser- vational vocabulary, we noted that such considerations were irrelevant. In the context of underdetermination, however, the claim is that the Duhem-Quine Thesis entails that we never have any reason to suppose that any particular scientific theory is true, since we never have any reason to prefer it over any of its rivals. But this is clearly not the case – in most situations, one predic- tively successful scientific theory will provide a much more satisfying fit with the rest of our background beliefs than any of its logical or explanatory rivals. The important question is whether or not this is a good reason to suppose that that theory is true.

Many scientific realists have indeed argued for precisely this point, maintaining that the various theoretical virtues such as simplicity and scope upon which decisions are made are indeed a guide to the truth (see for example Boyd 1973; McMullin 1987). Unfortunately, however, at this point we find ourselves facing a familiar impasse. Any such argument will rest upon the fact that we often adjudicate between competing scientific theories on the basis of their various theoretical virtues, and that these background theories in turn play an important role in adjudicating between our contemporary scien- tific theories. Consequently, since our contemporary scientific theories are themselves predictively successful, we have good reason to suppose that our background theories are approximately true and that the various theoretical virtues upon which they were adopted are a reliable guide to that truth. The argument of course is just another version of the No-Miracles Argument, this time focusing upon the theoretical virtues of our scientific theories rather than our general inferential principles. The argument therefore has precisely the same weakness as before, since whether or not we suppose that our background theories must be true in order to have a beneficial influence upon any consequent theory-choice – rather than merely useful or systematically fortuitous – will simply depend upon whatever position we already adopt within the scientific realism debate.

4.1.2. *The bankruptcy of science*

In the end then, even the most virulent form of underdetermination has very little to show us about the status of our scientific theories. The main problem is that the argument operates at too great a degree of abstraction. For while it is true that with enough ingenuity one can cook up an unlimited number of possible rivals to any predictively successful scientific theory, all equally capable of satisfying any number of additional epistemological desiderata, there will always be *some* difference between them all that the scientific realist can capitalize upon as the most reliable indicator of approximate truth. A more powerful objection to the sort of reasoning employed by the No-Miracles Argument therefore must look for more concrete considerations. Rather than showing how such an argument would fare in a number of purely hypothetical scenarios, we should instead look at the actual history of our scientific practice for instances that might undermine the central reasoning employed by the scientific realist.

One promising line of thought therefore is to note that whether or not we have good reason to believe that our current scientific theories are approximately true, one thing of which we can be certain is that they have *superseded* a number of earlier scientific theories that we now believe to be false. In fact, once we consider the issue in more detail, the history of science appears to be littered with such failures. This then raises the worry that maybe our scientific reasoning is not as reliable as we previously thought. As Henri Poincaré famously put it:

> The man of the world is struck to see how ephemeral scientific theories are. After some years of prosperity, he sees them successively abandoned; he sees ruins accumulated on ruins; he predicts that the theories in vogue today will in a short time succumb in their turn, and he concludes that they are absolutely in vain. This is what he calls the bankruptcy of science. (1902 [1905]: 160)

The scientific realist argues that because our current scientific theories are predictively successful, we have good reason to suppose that they are approximately true. Yet that is precisely what earlier scientists thought, often on the basis of equally impressive predictive success. But if all of these thinkers have been proven wrong, what reasons do we have to suppose that our epistemological situation is going to be any different?

Poincaré himself did not draw any such sceptical conclusion, arguing instead that the historical record merely shows us something about the structure of our scientific theories and the limits of our scientific investigations (this view is discussed in more detail in Chapter 6). However, many other philosophers have indeed maintained that the history of science does in fact give us good reason to reject scientific realism. This line of thought is usually referred to as the Pessimistic Meta-Induction, but we must be careful here in distinguishing between two different arguments that we might offer on the basis of our historical data. The first seeks merely to show that the positive arguments offered by the scientific realist for the approximate truth of our scientific theories are undermined by the various counter-examples produced by the track-record of our scientific theorizing. Such an argument is neither particularly pessimistic nor is it a meta-induction in any technical sense of the term. The second argument seeks to show that not only do we not have good reason to suppose our current scientific theories to be true, but that the history of science actually furnishes us with good reasons to suppose that they are in fact false. This is, of course, a much stronger conclusion to draw, and is more accurately thought of as a meta-induction, since it attempts to draw an (extremely negative) inductive conclusion *about* the inductive practices that constitute our scientific practice.

There is plenty of room for terminological confusion here, for while it is only the second argument that is accurately described by the name, it is usually the first and more modest argument that philosophers actually mean when they talk about the Pessimistic Meta-Induction (for a recent discussion of different interpretations of the argument, see Mizrahi 2013). This is because the stronger argument is simply incoherent. At a first pass, we should naturally be suspicious of any line of reasoning that attempts to provide an inductive argument as to why we shouldn't trust induction. More specifically, the argument is that since all of our past scientific theories have been shown to be false, our current scientific theories will probably be shown to be false too. The problem, however, is that the only reason we have for believing our past scientific theories to be false is because they disagree with our current scientific theories. We no longer believe in phlogiston because we now believe in the oxidization of metals; the electromagnetic field has replaced the luminiferous ether; and absolute space has succumbed to the fundamental relativity of distinct frames of reference. But if we only believe that our previous scientific theories are false on the basis of our belief that our contemporary scientific theories are true, we cannot *also* use our belief that our previous scientific theories are false to undermine our belief that our contemporary scientific theories are true.

Lipton (2000) provides a helpful illumination of this point. Suppose that we have two competing scientific theories, and perform some crucial test that provides positive evidence in favour of one and simultaneously provides negative evidence against the other. Since the first theory has been confirmed, we have reason to believe that it is true. Since the second theory has been falsified, we have reason to believe that it is false. But then, according to the stronger reading of the Pessimistic Meta-Induction, the falsification of the second theory also tells against the first – after all, the majority of scientific theories have been falsified, and so chances are that this one will be falsified as well. But then the same experiment would provide both direct evidence in favour of a theory and indirect evidence against it. In Lipton's memorable phrase, the argument is a piece of 'judo epistemology' since it attempts to use the success of science against itself (ibid.: 199–200).

The Pessimistic Meta-Induction is therefore to be understood as the more modest proposal that the history of science offers us good reason to reject the positive arguments put forward by the scientific realist. The classic statement of this sort of argument is due to Laudan (1981), who sees the history of science as explicitly undermining the sort of reasoning exemplified by the No-Miracles Argument (similar readings of the argument are given by Psillos 1999: 101–14, and Saatsi 2005). Suppose for the sake of argument that the predictive success of a scientific theory does generally indicate the approximate truth of that theory. It would follow then that our current scientific theories are indeed approximately true as the scientific realist maintains. But our current scientific theories disagree with our earlier scientific theories, positing different types of unobservable entities and different types of causal relationships holding between them. So if our current scientific theories are approximately true, then our previous scientific theories are predominantly false. But each one of these scientific theories was predictively successful at the time. The conclusion is not then that our current scientific theories must be false, but simply that we cannot reasonably maintain that predictive success is a reliable indicator of approximate truth, despite the scientific realist's protestations to the contrary.

This might seem like something of an anticlimax. The point, however, is that rather than simply denying that predictive success is a reliable indicator of truth, or showing how predictive success is insufficiently discriminatory in a range of hypothetical scenarios, the Pessimistic Meta-Induction attempts to show that the link between predictive success and truth is in fact undermined by the scientific realist's own standards. It is therefore a serious challenge for any contemporary defence of scientific realism.

4.2. The uses and abuses of the history of science

It is difficult to deny that many of our current scientific theories offer conflicting accounts of the unobservable structure of the world than that proposed by their immediate predecessors. The principle of relativity has superseded the Newtonian concept of absolute space, just as the Newtonian concept of absolute space superseded the Aristotelian notion of a stationary Earth lying at rest in the centre of the Universe. What is controversial, however, are the precise philosophical consequences that we can draw on the basis of this observation. The issue will depend upon the *number* of such instances uncovered in our historical research and the *severity* of the disagreement involved. A few isolated instances of minor theoretical quibbling will do little to undermine the scientific realist's proposed connection between predictive success and approximate truth, whereas an endless succession of radical conceptual upheaval will by contrast undermine our confidence in the stability of our own scientific theories.

In order then to properly assess the Pessimistic Meta-Induction – and the relevance of the history of science for the philosophy of science more generally – it would seem that we would need to conduct a detailed investigation of each and every scientific theory that has ever been held on a meticulous case-by-case basis. But as valuable as such a project would no doubt be, there are two difficulties with this proposal. The first is simply practical: such an undertaking would require an enormous amount of time to complete, if indeed it could be completed at all. If we are to make any progress on this issue, therefore, we will have to consider some more general strategies for assessing the history of science. Second, and more schematically, there may be something of a methodological tension involved in this kind of emphasis upon individual case studies. The scientific realism debate is fundamentally an abstraction from our everyday scientific practice. It is concerned with whether or not predictive success is *in general* a good indicator of approximate truth, or with whether or not the historical track-record of our scientific theorizing can *in general* tell us anything about our current scientific theories. These sorts of arguments necessarily involve taking a more synoptic view of our scientific practice than that provided by the sort of detailed case studies suggested, and it therefore remains an open question as to whether or not these sorts of arguments will still make sense once we engage in these kinds of highly specific investigations. This, however, is a complex issue, and will be discussed in more detail later (see Chapter 5).

In any case, there are a number of more general strategies that the scientific realist can adopt in attempting to resist the Pessimistic Meta-Induction. On the one hand, he can argue that many of the instances unearthed by the history of science do not in fact offer relevant counter-examples to our current scientific theories. After all, not all scientific theories are created equal, and we would not want to count every crackpot pronouncement that has bitten the dust as evidence against the well-established and experimentally rigorous scientific theories of today. So at the least, we should limit our historical investigations to those past scientific theories deemed sufficiently mature to warrant legitimate comparison with our current scientific theories. On the other hand, the scientific realist can also argue that once we restrict our attention in this way, we see that the remaining historical instances do not in fact disagree with our contemporary scientific theories in any meaningful way. The idea is that while successive scientific theories certainly do conflict with one another on many points of detail, they nevertheless all agree with respect to their fundamental ontology, such as what sorts of unobservable entities exist and what sorts of causal roles they play. If this is the case, then scientific realism is not threatened by the history of science. Given this sort of underlying continuity, successive scientific theories can be seen as simply *refining* our account of the unobservable structure of the world, rather than offering radically incompatible proposals.

I will not have a lot to say about the first strategy. The problem is that while there is clearly an intuitive difference between those genuine historical rivals to our contemporary scientific theories that might credibly fuel the Pessimistic Meta-Induction and those primitive pre-scientific conjectures that do not, any attempt to further specify the relevant criteria tends to be rather vague. In an early example of this view, Ernan McMullin for instance writes:

> The sort of theory on which the realist grounds his argument is one in which an increasingly finer specification of internal structure has been obtained over a long period, in which the theoretical entities function *essentially* in the argument and are not simply intuitive postulations of an 'underlying reality' and in which the original metaphor has proved continuously fertile and capable of increasingly further extension. (1984: 17)

All of which is no doubt true – but we are never given any further details as to when a theoretical entity functions 'essentially' in an argument, or when a metaphor proves to be 'continuously fertile' or 'capable of increasingly further extension'. Some philosophers have suggested that the best way to make these ideas more precise is to distinguish between those past scientific theories that demonstrated *novel* predictive success, as opposed to those that merely successfully accommodated all of the available evidence (Musgrave 1988; Psillos 1999: 104–8). Other philosophers, however, have questioned whether or not there exists an epistemologically relevant distinction to be drawn on the basis of when exactly a particular prediction took place (see Lipton 1990 for a helpful discussion on this point).

In any case, no matter how closely the scientific realist manages to circumscribe the scope of our historical investigations, there will always remain some examples of genuinely successful scientific theories that nevertheless conflict with our contemporary perspective. Even if we are wrong to suppose that the history of science furnishes us with countless numbers of theoretical failures, it nevertheless continues to deliver enough high-profile examples to cause the scientific realist some concern. The emphasis therefore has tended to focus upon the second strategy outlined above, which is to find some way whereby the scientific realist can *concede* that successive scientific theories disagree with respect to their overall picture of the unobservable structure of the world, but nevertheless maintain that enough continuity exists between them all such that the scientific realist's proposed inference from predictive success to approximate truth remains intact.

4.2.1. The reference and description of theoretical terms

One way in which the scientific realist can acknowledge the conflict that exists between successive scientific theories while nevertheless maintaining their underlying continuity is to distinguish between what our scientific theories *say*, and what they say it *about*. More specifically, the idea is that while the descriptive content of our scientific theories may change and often conflict with that offered by their predecessors, the reference of our scientific theories (within a particular domain of application) remains relatively fixed. As our scientific methods improve, we revise our beliefs and come to offer better and more accurate descriptions of the world around us. But it is precisely because we are offering better and more accurate descriptions of *the same things* that the scientific realist can maintain that there exists a continuity between successive scientific theories. On this account, the core elements of scientific realism are preserved, since we can continue to defend the claim that the predictive success of our scientific theories gives us good reason to suppose that the entities postulated by these theories really exist. All that the Pessimistic Meta-Induction shows us is that some of our beliefs about these unobservable entities may be false – but that is perfectly consistent with the idea that our scientific theories are an improvement upon one another, rather than a straightforward rejection of everything that has come before.

An early example of this strategy has been proposed by Clyde Hardin and Alexander Rosenberg (1982). Following the sorts of accounts given by Hilary Putnam (1975b) and Saul Kripke (1980), they argue that the reference of a theoretical term is not given by a specific set of descriptions associated with the theory in question, but is rather fixed by whatever happens to be causally responsible for the various phenomena the theory is attempting to describe. So, for example, while earlier scientists thought of the propagation of light as taking place against the background of a luminiferous ether, and contemporary scientists reject the notion of an ether altogether in favour of vibrations in the electromagnetic field, they are nevertheless in both cases attempting to describe the same phenomenon, that is, the propagation of light. According to Hardin and Rosenberg, therefore, it follows that both scientific theories are in fact referring to the same thing. They write:

> Looking back across the range of theories from Fresnel to Einstein, we see a constant causal role being played in all of them; that causal role we now ascribe to the electromagnetic field. One permissible strategy of realists is to let reference follow causal role. It seems not unreasonable, then, for realists to say that see a constant causal role being played in all of them. (1982: 613–14)

The luminiferous ether and the electromagnetic field have both featured in sufficiently mature, predictively successful scientific theories. They also disagree insofar as one assigns certain properties to the ether – an all-pervasive medium against which the propagation of light takes place – which the other straightforwardly denies. According to Hardin and Rosenberg, however, they do not disagree with respect to their fundamental ontology. Both theories postulate the existence of the same unobservable entity, but merely conceptualize it in different ways.

There is definitely something to recommend in Hardin and Rosenberg's proposal. The problem is whether or not it achieves too much. In his response to their paper, Laudan (1984) argues that the emphasis upon causal role is simply too permissive for an adequate defence of scientific realism, and that on such an account, all manner of radically ill-conceived theories will count as referring. The problem is that Hardin and Rosenberg confuse the case of two theories having the same explanatory *agenda* with that of two theories having the same explanatory *ontology*. He writes:

> To make reference parasitic on what is being explained rather than on what is doing the explaining entails that we can establish what a theory refers to independently of any detailed analysis of what the theory asserts. If, to save his theory of reference, the scientific realist is forced into such voodoo semantics, then realism scarcely seems worth the candle. (1984: 161)

It may be plausible to suppose that the luminiferous ether was really referring to the electromagnetic field, since both attempt to explain the propagation of light. But on Hardin and Rosenberg's proposal, it seems that we should also suppose that when Aristotle discusses how all elements seek their natural place of rest, he was really referring to the curved space-time of relativistic physics: after all, both concepts attempt to explain why heavy objects fall towards the Earth. But if this is all it takes to secure referential continuity, then scientific realism is a trivial thesis. With enough ingenuity, any two scientific concepts could be made to refer to the same entity, no matter how different they might appear.

A more sophisticated version of this strategy is due to Philip Kitcher (1978; see also his 1993), who argues that the terms of our scientific theories do not have a single referent, but rather a *reference potential*. That is to say, the same term can refer to one or more different entities depending upon the context of utterance. On some occasions of use, the reference of a term might be fixed by an associated description, and on other occasions by whatever stands in the appropriate causal relationship to our utterance. To take the classic example, we might both happily refer to the same individual as 'the man drinking the martini', even though the person we are both speaking about is actually drinking champagne (see, for example, Donnellan 1966).

In the case of the history of science therefore, Kitcher argues that we cannot make general pronouncements as to the reference of past scientific theories in the way that Hardin and Rosenberg suggest. This is because the reference of each particular *token* of a theoretical term will vary depending upon the context of its utterance. Consider for example the case of Joseph Priestley and his experimental work concerning dephlogisticated air. While much of what Priestley had to say we now suppose to be true of oxygen, it remains deeply problematic to suppose that this was what Priestley was talking about all along. Some of the properties of phlogiston – that it is emitted by heating and has a negative weight – are so far removed from our understanding of oxygen that securing referential continuity in this way would be just as pointless as securing any referential stability between Aristotle and Einstein. However, once we look at the individual utterances made by Priestley about dephlogisticated air, the story becomes more plausible. As Kitcher puts it:

> Some tokens of 'dephlogisticated air' refer to oxygen, others fail to refer – and, in assigning referents to tokens we can do no better than to appeal to such general principles about reference as the principle of humanity. To decide on the referent of a token, we must construct an explanation of its production. Our explanations, and the hypotheses about reference which we choose, should enable us to trace familiar connections among Priestley's beliefs and between his beliefs and entities in the world. (1978: 535)

In some contexts, for example, Priestley was clearly trying to refer to the substance that is emitted during combustion, and what remains once this substance is removed from the air. Since there is no such substance, these tokens fail to refer. However, in other contexts Priestley was clearly trying to refer to whatever it is that supports combustion, or whose removal from the bell-jar caused his laboratory mice to suffocate. In cases like these, since we know that it is really oxygen with which Priestley is in causal contact when making these utterances, it is reasonable to suppose that this is to what these tokens actually refer.

Kitcher's proposal allows us then to make finer-grained distinctions than that allowed by Hardin and Rosenberg: we secure referential continuity between the fundamental ontology of successive scientific theories, but without committing ourselves to the view that absolutely *everything* that past scientists said was referentially successful. However, as Psillos (1997) points out, while we may well be able to distinguish between the different utterances Priestley made about dephlogisticated air in terms of their respective referents, this would not have been a distinction that he himself would have accepted. As far as Priestley was concerned, when he spoke about dephlogisticated air as what remains after the results of combustion are removed from the air, and when he spoke about dephlogisticated air as what kept his mice alive, he was speaking about the *same thing*. To suggest then that we can distinguish between different referential intentions on the part of Priestley is to read our own conceptual categories back into the history of science. But not only is this methodologically suspect, it again threatens to make referential continuity trivial. For no matter what previous scientists might have said or believed, it will always remain possible for us to isolate some unobservable entity or process that we now believe to exist, and which would have been causally responsible for some of the utterances made by these scientists, even though the scientists themselves had no concept of it whatsoever.

4.2.2. The trust argument

Any attempt to ensure the referential continuity of our scientific theories that does so by ignoring the descriptive content associated with those theories, as well as the dominant beliefs and intentions of the scientists who endorsed them, makes the defence of scientific realism a trivial enterprise. Such a strategy is just far too strong, insofar as it entails that any two scientific theories concerned with a roughly similar range of phenomena must in fact be referring to exactly the same entities. Surprisingly enough, however, such a strategy also turns out to be far too weak. Even if we are satisfied with the idea that conflicting scientific theories can nevertheless refer to the same unobservable entities, this in itself cannot be considered sufficient as a response to the Pessimistic Meta-Induction. It is one of the central components of scientific realism, not just that the various unobservable entities postulated by our scientific theories actually exist, but that many of our beliefs about these entities are approximately true. After all, one can hardly *explain* the predictive success of our scientific theories by arguing that they success-fully refer to some kind of unobservable entity – but that we have no idea which one, nor what it is like. Yet it is precisely this component of scientific realism that appears to be abandoned in both of the foregoing accounts.

This worry has been articulated with particular clarity by Kyle Stanford (2003). Commenting on Hardin and Rosenberg's proposal, he writes:

> But this runs the realist afoul of what we might call the 'trust' argument: after all, if the central terms of past theories are held to be referential *despite* the fact that the theories in which they are embedded repeatedly turn out to be radically misguided, then the historical record seems to entitle the antirealist to her claim that we would be foolish to *trust* either the theoretical accounts of inaccessible domains of nature offered by successful scientific theories or the descriptions associated with their central theoretical terms. And trusting the accounts of such domains and entities given by (some) current theories is just what the realist hoped to convince us to do! (2003: 556)

The same is also true of Kitcher, who only manages to show how the utter-ances of past scientists were referentially successful on precisely those occasions when most of their scientific beliefs about the world were false (ibid.: 557). As Stanford puts it, any such defence would be a pyrrhic victory for scientific realism, one that salvages the position, but only at the expense of abandoning everything that position was hoping to achieve.

All of this suggests a third and final refinement. In order to accommodate the historical evidence driving the Pessimistic Meta-Induction, the scientific realist does need to differentiate between the descriptive content of his scientific theories and their referential success. But he cannot completely divorce the reference of our theoretical terms from the accounts given of them in their respective scientific theories, or else the enterprise becomes both trivial and counterproductive to most of his epistemological aims. The scientific realist must therefore accept that at least *some* of the descriptive claims of his scientific theories play an important role in fixing the reference of our theoretical terms. But provided that not all of the descriptive claims of our scientific theories play such an important role, it may still be possible to defend the referential continuity of successive scientific theories while still acknowledging the way in which these theories disagree on its details.

Psillos (1999: 293–300) advocates such an approach. In contrast to the purely causal accounts of reference inspired by Putnam and Kripke, this would be an instance of the causal-descriptive theories of reference proposed by

Gareth Evans (1973) and David Lewis (1983). When a particular theoretical entity is postulated by a scientific theory, it will usually be in response to a particular problem or in order to explain a particular set of phenomena. The entity may of course play other roles in our theory, and we may have other theoretical beliefs about the entity, but it is these initial motivations that provide what Psillos calls the *core causal description* associated with the entity – those fundamental properties that something must satisfy in order to count as the entity in question. When successive scientific theories postulate new theoretical entities to explain old phenomena, their core causal descriptions will often demonstrate a significant overlap with the core causal descriptions of older theoretical entities. In cases like these, we can say that both scientific theories refer to the same entities. So, for example, it was part of the core causal description of phlogiston that it is emitted during combustion; since this is not part of the core causal description of oxygen, the two terms do not refer to the same entity. By contrast, however, it is part of the core causal description of the luminiferous ether that it was the medium in which light is propagated in such and such a manner; since this does significantly overlap with the core causal description of the electromagnetic field, this is a case of referential continuity.

The issue will of course depend upon how exactly the core causal descriptions of our theoretical entities are specified. If they are too broad for instance – the reference of our terms is whatever is responsible for objects falling, for example – then we are back with the same difficulties with which we began. The advantage of Psillos's account, however, is that this need not be the case, and our core causal descriptions can be set so as to be extremely discriminating indeed. Unfortunately, however, this risks us running afoul of the opposite difficulty of simply reading our own assumptions back into the history of science. For the account to succeed, therefore, it needs to be the case that past scientists not only associated sufficiently discriminating core causal descriptions with their theoretical terms, but also did so in a way that corresponds with our own judgements about which parts of their theories were genuinely important. But this seems unlikely. Just because we can distinguish between the different utterances Priestley made about dephlogisticated air, it does not follow that Priestley himself would have recognized such a distinction; and just because we can distinguish between those descriptions of the ether that are doing the important work and those that are superfluous to requirement, it does not follow that past scientists would have agreed with our evaluation. Indeed, it seems to have been widely assumed that whatever was responsible for the propagation of light must be some kind of material medium – a core causal description explicitly rejected by contemporary theories of electromagnetism (Stanford 2003: 559–60).

But if we cannot guarantee that past historical actors already agreed with us with respect to which bits of their own theories were eventually going to be abandoned, then we seem to be faced with just another iteration of the Pessimistic Meta-Induction. As Stanford writes:

> Thus, even if Psillos can convincingly argue that the *actual* 'core causal description' of the ether does not include claims about its material or mechanical character, he will be forced to concede that the carefully considered judgments of leading scientific defenders of the theory concerning which of the descriptions associated with its central terms must be satisfied by an entity in order for it to play the causal role associated with the term (that is, which features figure in the actual core causal descriptions) have proved to be unreliable. What this suggests, of course, is that we cannot rely on our *own* judgements about which of the descriptions we associate with our own terms are *genuinely* part of their own core causal descriptions, delivering us back into the arms of the trust argument with respect to current theories. (2003: 561)

Maybe the history of science is one of unbroken referential continuity. But at the risk of considerable anachronism, we have to accept that our contemporary scientific theories radically disagree with their immediate predecessors as to which of the core causal descriptions associated with our theoretical terms are in fact true. But unless we have some reason to suppose that our own situation is somehow epistemologically superior to everyone else who has come before, that just means that we can no longer be certain that *our own* core causal descriptions are likely to be true, which is precisely what the scientific realist was trying to establish.

4.3. Unconceived alternatives

Despite initial appearances then, the history of science does not seem to have much to offer the contemporary scientific realism debate. It is of course true that there have been many predictively successful scientific theories in the past that we now believe to be wrong with respect to their central theoretical commitments. It remains, however, an open question as to just how many such instances can be found in the history of our scientific investigations, and the philosophical consequences that can be drawn from this observation. One could attempt to argue that the past failure of what have been our most successful scientific theories makes it likely that our current scientific theories will themselves turn out to be false. This would be a genuine instance of a Pessimistic Meta-Induction, but any such argument is in fact deeply suspect – not only does it require a wider and more varied inductive basis than any plausible reconstruction of the history of science will provide, but it is also straightforwardly incoherent in that it attempts to undermine the inductive practices that drive our scientific investigations through inductive reasoning. The most that the anti-realist can derive from these historical considerations then is that the scientific realist's purported connection between predictive success and approximate truth is not invariably reliable. But this is hardly a radical revelation, and indeed it is something happily endorsed by the contemporary scientific realist who seems himself to be offering a scientific – and thus ultimately defeasible – explanation for the success of science.

Nevertheless, Kyle Stanford (2001; see also his 2006) has proposed what he sees as a new challenge to scientific realism on the basis of its historical track-record. Stanford's starting point is not that previously successful scientific theories have eventually been abandoned as false, but rather the more modest observation that previously successful scientific theories were underdetermined by the available evidence at the time. Specifically, he follows Lawrence Sklar (1981) in arguing that many of our most successful scientific theories were subject to a relatively weak form of underdetermination which he calls *transient underdetermination* – that at the time in question there were alternative scientific theories equally well supported by the evidence (both deductively and ampliatively), although subsequent evidence would eventually offer grounds to choose between them. Stanford's argument for this has nothing to do with the logical structure of our scientific theories, nor considerations of confirmational holism, but merely the fact that working scientists rarely have the time or resources to consider all of the relevant possibilities. It is ultimately a claim about the cognitive limitations of scientists, and is supported by the equally modest observation that some of these unconceived alternatives have in fact been endorsed by subsequent theorists. Stanford writes:

> We have, throughout the history of scientific inquiry and in virtually every scientific field, repeatedly occupied an epistemic position in which we could conceive of only one of a few theories that were well confirmed by the available evidence, while subsequent inquiry would routinely (if not invariably) reveal further, radically distinct alternatives as well confirmed by the previously available evidence as those we are inclined to accept on the strength of that evidence. (2006: 19)

It is this more nuanced historical observation that then drives Stanford's argument against scientific realism. In the past we have repeatedly failed to consider all of the relevant alternatives to our scientific theories. These theories were therefore underdetermined by the available evidence, undermining any reasons we might have to suppose that they were approximately true. Since we have no reason to suppose that our own epistemological situation is any different, we have good reason to suppose that contemporary scientists have similarly failed to consider all of the relevant alternatives to our current scientific theories, and that they too are underdetermined by the available evidence – thereby similarly undermining any reason we might have to suppose that they are approximately true as well.

As can be readily seen, Stanford's Problem of Unconceived Alternatives is an interesting mixture of the traditional Pessimistic Meta-Induction and the challenge of Underdetermination of Theory by Evidence. As such, it offers a number of advantages over both of these other arguments. First, it is an inductive argument from the past underdetermination of our scientific theories to the conclusion that our current scientific theories will also be underdetermined by the available evidence. This is in contrast to the standard Pessimistic Meta-Induction which tries to argue for the probable falsity of our current theories. The difference can be clearly seen when we note that to argue that our scientific theories are mostly false is to raise doubts about the inductive methods upon which they are based, whereas to argue that our scientific theories are mostly underdetermined is merely to raise doubts about how well those methods are applied. It follows then that while the traditional Pessimistic Meta-Induction suffers from trying to offer an inductive argument against induction, the Problem of Unconceived Alternatives only offers an inductive argument against our ability to consider all of the relevant options – it can therefore be used to offer a positive argument against scientific realism in a way that the Pessimistic Meta-Induction cannot.

Of course, any such argument is only as good as the range of instances upon which it is based. But this is the second respect in which the Problem of Unconceived Alternatives appears to improve upon its predecessors. The difference is that while the Pessimistic Meta-Induction is concerned with the status of our scientific theories, Stanford's argument is concerned with the scientists who formulated them. This then blocks the foregoing strategy for restricting the range of our historical counter-examples, for while it may be plausible to maintain that our contemporary scientific theories are somehow more 'mature' than many of their predecessors, such as to undermine any meaningful comparison, it is arguably much more difficult to maintain that contemporary scientists are somehow much better at imagining and evaluating possible alternatives to their scientific theories than those who came before them. As Stanford writes:

Thus, the problem of unconceived alternatives and the new induction suggest not that present theories are no more likely to be true than past theories have turned out to be, but instead that present theorists are no better able to exhaust the space of serious, well confirmed possible theoretical explanations of the phenomena than past theorists have turned out to be. And neither the force of this concern nor the validity of projecting it into the future is in any way mitigated by pointing out that many present theories differ in important and systematic respects from those of the past. (2006: 44)

The Problem of Unconceived Alternatives appears to offer therefore both a wider range of historical instances, and a more coherent inference, against scientific realism than either of the two argument already discussed in this chapter.

4.3.1. The new instrumentalism

Stanford's novel deployment of the history of science against scientific realism does offer a number of advantages over the traditional Pessimistic Meta-Induction. But it is not entirely without its own share of difficulties. The starting point for Stanford's argument is not that previous scientific theories have turned out to be false, but that they were in fact underdetermined — and the basis of this claim rests on the fact that previous scientists invariably failed to consider all of the possible alternatives to their own scientific theories. This certainly provides a less controversial starting point than the usual argument from the history of science, not least because the kind of underdetermination that Stanford has in mind is itself considerably more concrete than the sort of abstract speculations generated via considerations of confirmational holism. But it is also a very peculiar form of underdetermination. It consists of the claim that for the scientific theories in question there was an equally well-supported alternative that *no one at the time had considered*. The issue therefore depends on what Stanford intends by claiming that these theories were equally well supported. If the idea is simply that both theories would have logically entailed the same observational evidence, then the proposal is relatively uncontroversial, but also relatively uninteresting for reasons we have already discussed. The idea must therefore be that these past scientific theories were ampliatively underdetermined by their unconceived alternatives. But this is a much more difficult claim to assess. As Anjan Chakravartty (2008) points out, it amounts to a *counterfactual* assertion to the effect that, if the unconceived alternative had been considered, it would have fitted equally well into the overall theoretical framework that existed at the time. This may be true, but the issue is a complex one and far from uncontroversial. Indeed, one might well suppose that the very fact that this theory was *not* considered in the first place reveals its general incompatibility with the rest of the theoretical framework entertained at the time.

Stanford's argument therefore may not have a less controversial starting point after all. It is also not clear that his argument has any more force against the scientific realist than the traditional Pessimistic Meta-Induction. We have already noted that Stanford's argument targets scientists rather than theories, and so is immune to the sort of response that attempts to show that our contemporary scientific theories are more mature than their predecessors. Nevertheless, it seems that one might instead argue that contemporary scientists are epistemologically better placed than their predecessors to undermine the comparison Stanford wishes to draw. Such an argument need not depend upon the narcissistic notion that contemporary scientists are just more intelligent than past scientists, although presumably some of the differences between contemporary scientific theories and their predecessors must come down to the differences between the scientists who formulated them. But in any case, as Peter Godfrey-Smith (2008) points out, the Problem of Unconceived Alternatives is not a problem about the cognitive limitations of scientists, but of the *scientific communities* in which they worked – and we have plenty of good reason to suppose that with the ever increasing professionalization of scientific research, our contemporary scientific communities are now very different from those which came before, and are arguably much better placed to consider a greater range of relevant alternatives to our current scientific theories.

Finally, we noted that in offering an inductive argument for the underdetermination of our current scientific theories – rather than an inductive argument against the inductive methods on which they are based – Stanford's Problem of Unconceived Alternatives has a methodological advantage over the traditional Pessimistic Meta-Induction. But maybe this is also too quick. As Psillos (2009: 72–5) points out, Stanford's argument is that since past scientists invariably failed to consider all of the relevant alternatives to their theories, we have good reason to suppose that contemporary scientists have similarly failed to consider all of the relevant alternatives to their theories. But this is certainly not the only conclusion we can draw since, as we have already noted, it might be the case that the scientific community is now much better placed to investigate a wider range of possibilities. This raises the question then as to whether or not Stanford himself has considered all the relevant possibilities to his own inference. The situation is then uncomfortably close to that facing the traditional Pessimistic Meta-Induction after all, since if Stanford is correct that we are in general bad at considering all the relevant possibilities, then we should be equally sceptical of his own capacity to do so. The conclusion that Stanford attempts to draw is thus in tension with the argument upon which it is based: rather than an inductive argument against induction, an underdetermined argument in favour of underdetermination.

It may therefore be tempting to conclude that despite the novel way in which Stanford attempts to deploy the history of science, the Problem of Unconceived Alternatives does not in the end have much to add to the existing debate. What is certainly novel, however, are the conclusions that Stanford draws from these considerations. Traditional opposition to scientific realism has attempted to distinguish between those parts of our scientific theories we can believe and those that we cannot – a distinction usually articulated in terms of the different vocabularies in which these claims are expressed. By contrast, Stanford's position is based upon which specific claims of our scientific theories seem to be more or less vulnerable to this risk of underdetermination. Claims about the behaviour of everyday medium-sized objects, for example, have enjoyed enough epistemological stability throughout the history of science to warrant our belief. But crucially, so too have various well-entrenched 'theoretical' claims about certain aspects of the world. So the distinction depends upon whether or not we possess some epistemic access to the claims in question that are either unmediated by any theory or which are based upon theories we have good reason to believe have not been subject to the Problem of Unconceived Alternatives. As Stanford puts it:

> Suppose … that the middle-sized objects of our everyday experience are no less 'theoretical' entities hypothesised to make sense of the ongoing stream of experience than are atoms and genes, notwithstanding their greater familiarity. Then, it is by means of theories in this broadest sense that we come to have any picture at all of what our world is like, what entities make it up, and how they are related to one another. But recall that only some of these theories will be open to the distinctive challenge posed by the problem of unconceived alternatives that I have suggested lies at the heart of any serious objection to scientific realism. (2006: 199–200)

The precise point at which we draw the line will therefore vary from theory to theory, since just because the historical record gives us reason to suppose that a great deal of the claims of one particular scientific theory are likely to be underdetermined by the evidence, it does not follow that the historical record will give us reason to be similarly sceptical of another scientific theory.

It is still an open question as to whether or not this way of distinguishing between the acceptable parts of our scientific theories is going to prove any more tractable than the distinction between our observational and theoretical vocabularies. Psillos (2009: 77–83), for example, has questioned whether there are any scientific claims that meet Stanford's criteria for epistemo-logical respectability. He notes, for example, that one of the most important consequences of scientific theorizing is that even our most intuitive beliefs about the world end up being revised and superseded – such as the idea that the Earth occupies a privileged frame of reference against which all motion can be judged. Moreover, while the distinction between our observational and theoretical vocabularies does not seem to carry any interesting episte-mological significance, it can at least be made precise in a number of ways. It is not clear, however, that the same can be said for Stanford's distinction between those claims suffering from unconceived alternatives and those that have demonstrated sufficient historical stability.

But what Stanford's new instrumentalism does offer, however, is a new approach to the scientific realism debate. As P. D. Magnus (2010) has stressed, Stanford's new instrumentalism is a form of *local* instrumentalism. It does not seek to impose a sweeping generalization stipulating which aspects of our scientific theories we can believe and not believe, but instead investigates which aspects of individual theories are more reliable than others. In many ways this was perhaps inevitable. We noted at the beginning of this chapter that any serious engagement with the history of science would inevitably require a change of focus from the general features of scientific theorizing to the specifics of individual scientific theories taken on a case-by-case basis. In offering a more nuanced engagement with the historical record, the Problem of Unconceived Alternatives motivates an instrumentalist position that does precisely this. In the next chapter we will consider this development in more detail.

4.4. Chapter summary

- The broadly Kantian methodology of the contemporary scientific realism debate threatens to undermine the possibility of any illuminating discussion regarding the status of our scientific theories. Nevertheless, there do remain various epistemological features of our scientific practice that might provide positive reasons to reject scientific realism.
- One issue is that for any successful scientific theory, there will be countless other theories that also logically entail the available evidence. This is known as the Underdetermination of Theory by Evidence. However, not all empirically equivalent scientific theories will be as equally simple, explanatory or as well supported by the rest of our background beliefs, which means that the scientific realist will always have reason to prefer one scientific theory over another.
- A second issue notes that the history of science is full of successful theories that we now consider to be false, which casts doubts upon the reliability of our contemporary investigations. This is known as the Pessimistic Meta-Induction, although there are two different readings of the argument. The first maintains that the history of science gives us good inductive reasons to suppose our current theories are false; the

▶

second merely notes that the history of science offers counter-examples to the supposed connection between predictive success and approximate truth.

- In response, scientific realists maintain that much of the history of science is insufficiently well developed to bear meaningful comparison with our contemporary scientific theories. Moreover, while successive scientific theories may disagree with respect to their overall picture of the world, there is nevertheless enough continuity with respect to the reference of these theories to retain an optimistic disposition towards scientific realism.
- Most of these issues ultimately require a more detailed engagement with the history of science. Kyle Stanford's recent Problem of Unconceived Alternatives is an example of this strategy, which tries to establish a localized form of instrumentalism on the basis of specific historical case studies. While it remains unclear whether or not his argument is any more effective than the traditional challenges to scientific realism, this is part of an interesting new approach to the scientific realism debate discussed in the following chapter.

4.5. Further reading

On the topic of the Underdetermination of Theories by Evidence, Laudan, L. (1996) *Beyond Positivism and Relativism* (Boulder, CO: Westview Press) remains an insightful collection of articles by one of the most important contributors to the debate. A more recent treatment of the topic is Bonk, T. (2008) *Underdetermination: An Essay on Evidence and the Limits of Natural Knowledge* (Dordrecht: Springer), who offers a more technical discussion of some of the issues. Also worthwhile is Butterfield, J. (2012) 'Underdetermination in Cosmology: An Invitation', *Proceedings of the Aristotelian Society* (Supplementary Volume) 86: 1–18, who discusses how considerations of underdetermination can differ in the context of contemporary cosmology.

Many of the issues relating to the Pessimistic Meta-Induction relate to broader concerns in the philosophy of language. Devitt, M. and Sterelny, K. (1987) *Language and Reality: An Introduction to the Philosophy of Language* (Oxford: Blackwell) is an excellent introduction to the topic with a particular focus on the philosophy of science. Out of the many other introductory works available on the philosophy of language, McCulloch, G. (1989) *The Game of the Name: Introducing Logic, Language, and Mind* (Oxford: Oxford University Press) is still highly recommended. Another option for responding to the historical challenge is to take a fragmentary attitude towards reference. This was originally explored in Field, H. (1973) 'Theory Change and the Indeterminacy of Reference', *Journal of Philosophy* 70: 462–81, and more thoroughly in the articles collected together in his (2001) *Truth and the Absence of Fact* (Oxford: Oxford University Press). It should be noted, however, that some of this material is quite advanced.

McAllister, J. W. (1993) 'Scientific Realism and the Criteria for Theory-Choice', *Erkenntnis* 38: 203–22 raises some interesting concerns about how the notion of predictive success upon which most of the foregoing debate rests may depend upon historical context. Finally, just as with the No-Miracles Argument, much of the recent literature on the Pessimistic Meta-Induction has focused on the so-called Base Rate Fallacy — this is discussed in detail in Chapter 5.

There is of course, an obvious advantage to operating at this level of generality, in that it ensures that one's philosophical reasoning premises the maximum relevance for the scientific realism debate. But operating at such a high level of austerity also comes at a price. In order to make the sort of sweeping generalizations about the likelihood of a predictively successful scientific theory being true that traditionally characterizes both the No Miracles Argument and the Pessimistic Meta-Induction, one first of

5

Wholesale and retail arguments for scientific realism

In the previous two chapters, we have examined the main arguments advanced for and against scientific realism, and explored some of their strengths and weaknesses. Despite their obvious differences, it is interesting, however, to note one important feature that these various arguments have in common. In the case of the No-Miracles Argument for example – even on its more restrictive understanding as an attempt merely to demonstrate the overall consistency of the scientific realist's position, as opposed to a positive argument intended to convince the sceptic – the reasoning concerns the reliability of our scientific methods *in general*, rather than attempting to establish the reliability of the specific, individual inferences that we actually make in our day-to-day scientific investigations. Similarly in the case of the Pessimistic Meta-Induction – understood here as a positive argument for anti-realism, and not merely as a strategy for generating counter-examples to the purported link between predictive success and approximate truth – it is maintained that the history of science reveals the instability of our theoretical speculations *in general*, rather than the instability of specific theoretical entities in specific theoretical sub-disciplines. Both arguments therefore operate at an extremely high level of generalization, abstracting away from many of the details of our actual scientific practice.

There is of course an obvious advantage to operating at this level of generality, in that it ensures that one's philosophical reasoning promises the maximum relevance for the scientific realism debate. But operating at such a high level of abstraction also comes at a price. In order to make the sort of sweeping generalizations about the likelihood of a predictively successful scientific theory being true that traditionally characterizes both the No-Miracles Argument and the Pessimistic Meta-Induction, one first of all needs to know something about the overall distribution of truth and falsity amongst the population of scientific theories about which one is talking; and the worry is that not only is such information unavailable to the realist or anti-realist, but it is in fact precisely what their respective arguments were supposed to establish.

More specifically, the concern is that both the No-Miracles Argument and the Pessimistic Meta-Induction as traditionally articulated are guilty of what is known as the *Base Rate Fallacy*. That is to say, both arguments attempt to draw conclusions about the likelihood of a predictively successful scientific theory being true without taking into account the underlying probability of any arbitrary scientific theory being true – a factor that can have an extremely significant result on our overall assessment. This chapter begins then with an introduction to the Base Rate Fallacy and shows how such considerations are relevant to the arguments offered on both sides of the scientific realism debate (§5.1). It then turns to the various ways in which scientific realists have attempted to respond to this problem. The basic idea has been to distinguish between what we might call those *wholesale arguments* for scientific realism that attempt to make global generalizations about the truth of our scientific theories, and are consequently vulnerable to these sorts of worries about base rates, and those *retail arguments* for scientific realism that target individual scientific theories on a case-by-case basis. However, while the underlying idea is clear enough, there remain important questions as to how exactly one is to articulate a local argument for scientific realism, and in particular, how such reasoning is to be distinguished from the first-order scientific practice about which it is supposed to offer a philosophical assessment (§5.2).

While many of these issues are still being enthusiastically debated in the literature, there nevertheless remains the worry that by switching to a series of local arguments about individual scientific theories, one does not resolve the difficulties faced by the scientific realism debate so much as concede that the whole issue was misguided to begin with. I sketch this concern and compare it with similar assessments already voiced in preceding chapters, and suggest that the problem of the Base Rate Fallacy provides a precise formulation of the idea that the scientific realism debate is a philosophical pseudo-question (§5.3). The chapter concludes with a summary of the key issues discussed (§5.4) and some suggestions for further reading (§5.5).

5.1. The Base Rate Fallacy

It will be helpful to begin with a general introduction to the sort of probabilistic reasoning at issue in this chapter. The Base Rate Fallacy is usually illustrated by way of a medical example. Suppose that we are attempting to identify the prevalence of some kind of disease within a particular population by testing for its symptoms. For the sake of concreteness, suppose that we are attempting to identify the prevalence of a particular type of virus by testing for the presence of a particular chemical in the blood. So as to make the example easier to follow, suppose further that this particular virus always causes this chemical to be present in the blood of its host, and that there are no other possible causes for such a chemical to be present. The only complication is that the test we have for this chemical is less than 100 per cent accurate. Specifically, let us suppose that our test is only 95 per cent accurate – meaning here that it will correctly return a positive result in 95 per cent of those cases where the chemical really is present, and incorrectly return a positive result in 5 per cent of those cases where it is in fact absent. We now run the test on an arbitrarily selected member of the population, and the test comes back positive. What is the probability that the individual in question has the virus?

There is a natural temptation to answer that there is a 95 per cent chance that our individual has the virus, and indeed when this test is given to under-graduate medical students, this is often the most popular response. But this is precisely to commit the Base Rate Fallacy, since it does not take into account the underlying probability of the virus being present for any arbitrary member of the population. In actual fact, the question just posed is *impossible* to answer given the information above. This can be illustrated by making different assumptions about the prevalence of the disease. Suppose to begin with that our population consists of 100,000 people, but that the virus is extremely uncommon and only present in 0.1 per cent of them, that is, 100 people. Suppose then that we test everybody. Our test will correctly return a positive result for 95 per cent of the infected population, and incorrectly return a positive result for 5 per cent of the uninfected population. That means that it will correctly identify (0.95 x 100) = 95 of the infected population, and incorrectly identify (0.05 x 99,900) = 4,995 of the uninfected population. The actual probability of an arbitrary member of the population actually having the virus, given a positive test result, will therefore be the ratio of correct positive results to total positive results, which in this case will be 95/5090, a little less than 2 per cent. By contrast, suppose instead that the virus is extremely prevalent throughout the population, and is present in 10 per cent of the population, that is, 10,000 people. Our test will then correctly identify (0.95 x 10,000) = 9,500 people, and incorrectly identify (0.05 x 90,000) = 4,500. The probability of someone having the virus, given a positive test result, will then be 9500/14,000, roughly 68 per cent. As we can see, the probability changes dramatically on the basis of the underlying base rate.

This is not to say, however, that our natural temptations are completely flawed. The point is rather that they often operate on unarticulated presuppositions that may or may not hold. If we don't know the actual base rate probability of an arbitrary member of the population having the virus, it is natural to suppose that it is no more likely than unlikely. That is to say, there is a natural temptation to respond to a situation of ignorance with an assumption of indifference, to presuppose that the underlying probability is more or less 50 per cent. If that presupposition turns out to be correct, our natural temptations are borne out. Suppose that our virus really is present in exactly 50 per cent of the population. When we run our tests, it will correctly return a positive result for (0.95 x 50,000) = 47,500 of the infected population, and incorrectly return a positive result for (0.05 x 50,000) = 2,500 of the uninfected population. In this situation, the probability of an arbitrary member of the population having the virus, given a positive test result, will be 47,500/50,000, which comes out as 95 per cent as originally expected. The Base Rate Fallacy arises then not so much in ignoring the underlying probabilities, but in making what often turn out to be unjustified presuppositions as to the value of those probabilities.

5.1.1. Statistical challenges for the philosophy of science

It is not difficult to see how these issues about underlying base rates apply to the scientific realism debate. Both the No-Miracles Argument and the Pessimistic Meta-Induction are concerned with the extent to which some easily detectable property of our scientific theories such as predictive success can be taken as a reliable symptom of some underlying property like approximate truth. Scientific realists of course maintain that a predictively successful scientific theory is likely to be approximately true, whereas their critics argue that the history of science suggests otherwise. In the same way, however, that we cannot know the likelihood of someone being infected with a virus on the basis of a blood test without knowing the underlying probability of any arbitrary member of that population having the virus, it seems that we cannot know the likelihood of a scientific theory being approximately true on the basis of its predictive success without knowing the underlying probability of any arbitrary scientific theory being approximately true.

There are a number of ways to illustrate this point. As Colin Howson (2000: 52–4) argues, the No-Miracles Argument begins with an assumption concerning the likelihood of an approximately true scientific theory being predictively successful, yet attempts to reach a conclusion about the contrasting likelihood of a predictively successful scientific theory being approximately true. But we cannot infer one probability from the other without knowing the base rate probability of an arbitrary scientific theory being true. Let S express the claim that a particular scientific theory is predictively successful, and T express the claim that the scientific theory in question is approximately true, and P(S|T) the conditional probability of that scientific theory being predictively successful *given that* it is approximately true. The corresponding probability of a scientific theory being approximately true given that it is predictively successful is then given by Bayes' Theorem:

$$P(T|S) = \frac{P(S|T) \cdot P(T)}{P(S)}$$

Since we know that the scientific theory in question is indeed predictively successful, in this case we can set P(S) as being very close to 1. Similarly, we can suppose for the sake of argument that the conditional probability P(S|T) is also very close to 1, since an approximately true theory will generally make successful predictions. For all intents and purposes, therefore, these two probabilities will cancel each other out. What this shows then is that even if we know that our theory is predictively successful, the likelihood of it being approximately true is almost completely swamped by the underlying probability of any arbitrary scientific theory being true.

We can put the same point in a less technical way. Assume for the sake of argument that the scientific realist is right, and that the approximate truth of our scientific theories is indeed the best explanation for their predictive success. We can think about this in terms of different ways of dividing up the population of scientific theories under consideration. If we think about all of the possible scientific theories in our sample space, and then just take those that are indeed approximately true, it will be the case that a vast majority of these theories will also be predictively successful. Conversely, if we consider all of those scientific theories that are false, only a tiny fraction of those theories will be predictively successful.

However, from this it does not necessarily follow that if we look at all of the predictively successful scientific theories that most of them will also be approximately true. Suppose that there are a significantly larger number of scientific theories that are false (that is to say, that the underlying probability of an arbitrary scientific theory being approximately true is very small). In this case, while the *proportion* of false scientific theories that are nevertheless predictively successful will remain low, the overall number of such theories may be very high indeed; and while the proportion of approximately true scientific theories that are predictively successful may remain high, if there were not very many approximately true scientific theories to begin with, they may in fact be significantly outnumbered by the predictively successful theories that are nevertheless false. For the sake of concreteness, suppose that 90 per cent of theories that are approximately true are predictively successful, but that only 10 per cent of theories that are false are predictively successful. Suppose, however, that we are dealing with a sample of 10 approximately true theories and 100 false theories. This will give us a total of (10 x 0.9) + (100 x 0.1) = 19 predictively successful theories – over half of which are actually false. Again then, we see that the crucial consideration is not the likelihood of a predictively successful scientific theory being approximately true, but the underlying likelihood of any arbitrary scientific theory being approximately true. The problem then is that not only is this something that the scientific realist is not in a position to know, but that it was precisely this issue that the No-Miracles Argument was supposed to help us establish. Ultimately then, we find ourselves facing another circularity in the scientific realist's reasoning, since he cannot establish his purported link between predictive success and approximate truth without that link having already been established.

Similar worries can also be seen in the case of the Pessimistic Meta-Induction. We have already seen various objections to the way in which arguments from the history of science fail to adequately distinguish between scientific theories at different times and stages of development, between scientific theories in different domains or even between the different claims made by our scientific theories. These are all examples of the ways in which how we select the relevant population of scientific theories can influence the sort of conclusions we draw about our scientific theories as a whole. More generally, then, even if we grant that many predictively successful scientific theories have in fact turned out to be false, we might worry about how these putative counter-examples are distributed across the history of science.

To begin with, we can note that simply pointing out the large number of ultimately unsuccessful theories in the past does not itself warrant the general conclusion that our current scientific theories will also turn out to be false, since the historical record may in fact be highly selective. This is ultimately a worry about the reference class of our data, and can be illustrated by the fact that it is perfectly consistent for the history of science to furnish us with an overwhelmingly large number of unsuccessful scientific theories, yet for the vast majority of those failures to be confined to the same, narrowly defined domain of inquiry. In such a situation, we would hardly be justified in inferring the probable falsity of any arbitrary scientific theory – let alone the probable falsity of our contemporary scientific theories in general – just because (say) eighteenth-century biology happened to be particularly unstable. This would be an example of what Marc Lange (2002) identifies as a *turnover fallacy*, noting that what the Pessimistic Meta-Induction requires in terms of historical data is not just a large number of unsuccessful former scientific theories, but rather temporally-specific evidence of the fact that at most past moments of time, most of the theories at that time were false (ibid.: 284).

Moreover, as Peter Lewis (2001) argues, even demonstrating the right sort of distribution of ultimately unsuccessful scientific theories will not alone be sufficient to undermine the inference from predictive success to approximate truth. Consider again the situation outlined above, where the number of false scientific theories massively outweighs the number of theories that are approximately true. In the case of the No-Miracles Argument, we used this to show that just because the likelihood of an approximately true scientific theory being predictively successful was high, it did not follow that the likelihood of a predictively successful scientific theory being approximately true was also high, since there may just be a far greater number of false scientific theories. But the example cuts both ways. Suppose that the history of science does indeed show that there are a great many predictively successful scientific theories that nevertheless turn out to be false. This does not show that the *likelihood* of a predictively successful scientific theory eventually turning out to be false is particularly high, since again our considerations may just be skewed by the vast number of false theories, a few of which just happen to be predictively successful.

5.2. Some problems for retail realism

We have seen then that both the No-Miracles Argument for scientific realism, and the Pessimistic Meta-Induction against, can easily be construed as committing a version of the Base Rate Fallacy. It is relatively uncontroversial to accept that a scientific theory that is approximately true is more likely to be predictively successful than a scientific theory that is just straightforwardly false. But in order to maintain that we have good reason to suppose that a predictively successful scientific theory is therefore likely to be approximately true, the scientific realist must make an important assumption about the general distribution of truth and falsity amongst our population of scientific theories taken as a whole. And conversely, even if we accept that the history of science presents us with a large number of predictively successful scientific theories now considered to be false, this will not itself undermine our confidence in the likelihood of our currently predictively successful theories being approximately true in the absence of a similarly important assumption about the overall distribution of truth and falsity.

Recently, P. D. Magnus and Craig Callender (2004) have gone so far as to suggest that this widespread tendency to ignore the base rate probability of an arbitrary scientific theory being true explains the sense of intractability that seems to pervade the scientific realism debate. Neither the No-Miracles Argument nor the Pessimistic Meta-Induction can be considered compelling in the absence of the appropriate base rate probability, yet it is precisely this probability of an arbitrary scientific theory being true that both arguments are attempting to establish. Thus while the scientific realist attempts to impose ever more demanding criteria for considering a scientific theory to be predictively successful in an effort to increase the likelihood of such a theory being approximately true, and while his opponent may offer ever more historical case studies in an effort to raise the ratio of predictively successful theories that have nevertheless turned out to be false, at the end of the day all such considerations are simply swamped by the underlying base rate probability of any arbitrary scientific theory being true – something over which realists and anti-realists can only trade their brute intuitions.

In their paper, Magnus and Callender go on to distinguish between what they call *wholesale arguments* and *retail arguments* for scientific realism. The former proceed along sweeping statistical lines and are therefore vulnerable to precisely those worries relating to the Base Rate Fallacy, while the latter are concerned with 'specific kinds of things such as neutrinos' (2004: 321) and are consequently immune to such objections. They recommend that since we cannot hope to make progress attending to the philosophical status of our scientific theories considered in general, the scientific realism debate should instead be concerned with a series of retail arguments concerning the approximate truth of individual scientific theories. The challenge, however, is to specify what exactly a retail argument for (or against) scientific realism might look like. Unfortunately, Magnus and Callender do not themselves have a great deal to say on this issue, noting merely that retail reasoning in the philosophy of science is the attempt to answer questions about, for example, the reality of atoms 'by referring to the same evidence scientists use to support the atomic hypothesis' (ibid.) – yet without understanding such evidence as part of a more general claim regarding the reliability of our scientific methods. But here we seem to face something of a dilemma. For on the one hand, a retail argument must obviously avoid operating at such a level of generality that we find ourselves contending with the problem of base rates all over again. Yet on the other hand, it seems like a retail argument must offer some kind of generalization or abstraction from our scientific practices in order to provide a philosophical assessment of their reliability. Any retail argument in the scientific realism debate must therefore walk a fine line between being so general that it collapses into a wholesale philosophical argument about the reliability of our scientific methods, or being so specific that it fails to offer any kind of philosophical argument about our scientific methods at all.

5.2.1. First-order and second-order evidence

According to the traditional understanding of the contemporary scientific realism debate, we can distinguish between two different types of evidence that can be offered in support of a scientific theory. The first type of evidence consists of the sort of arguments offered by scientists for adopting a particular scientific theory. This will include various considerations of predictive power and explanatory depth, as well as the other theoretical virtues of simplicity, scope and coherence with the rest of our theoretical worldview. Let us call this the *first-order scientific evidence* in favour of adopting a scientific theory. The second type of evidence is the sort of philosophical assessment we might offer about the evidence offered by scientists. We might, after all, accept that a particular scientific theory is extremely well supported by the evidence and offers any number of other advantages, yet still conclude that the theory is false since – for example – we think that our scientific methods are historically unreliable, or because we think the language of our scientific theories needs to be reinterpreted, and so on and so forth. Let us call this the *second-order philosophical evidence* that the scientific realism debate has traditionally been understood to provide. The dilemma in trying to formulate a retail argument for scientific realism can then be understood as the challenge of making our second-order philosophical evidence more theory-specific, without thereby simply collapsing into the first-order scientific evidence that it is supposed to assess.

In response to this concern, Psillos (2009: 75–7; see also his 2011a) argues that we should think of the scientific realism debate not as an attempt to legislate over the appropriateness of our first-order scientific evidence, but rather as an attempt to *balance* the often-competing evidence that we may have regarding the approximate truth of a scientific theory. To offer a retail argument for scientific realism can therefore be understood as the attempt to marshal various first-order scientific considerations in favour of a scientific theory that might thereby *override* any second-order philosophical considerations we might have against it. Consider again the case of the Pessimistic Meta-Induction. This is a second-order philosophical argument against the approximate truth of any particular scientific theory, on the basis that we have good historical evidence to suppose that our first-order scientific evidence is generally unreliable. One way in which philosophers have responded to this challenge is to carefully distinguish between the different scientific theories that this argument attempts to lump together. We might argue, for instance, that while certain theoretical posits and unobservable entities have been repeatedly consigned to the dustbin of history, the predictive success of *this particular* scientific theory only depends upon *these particular* theoretical posits and *those particular* unobservable entities – specific instances of our first-order scientific evidence that do not form part of the evidence for the Pessimistic Meta-Induction. Since our first-order scientific evidence for the theory in question is essentially unique, there can be no inductive basis for a general pessimism over their historical stability, and our second-order philosophical argument is undermined.

This is of course a similar line of reasoning to that which is found in Stanford's neo-instrumentalism, as discussed in the previous chapter. In that case, Stanford argued that there were good first-order reasons for rejecting the claims of particular scientific theories – on the basis of whether or not the scientists in question were able to consider all of the relevant alternatives to the theory – and maintained that these could override the second-order evidence that the scientific realist might offer for supposing that our scientific theories are true. The situation is, however, complicated by the fact that Stanford also wishes to draw a *general* conclusion from these considerations, and argues that we have good inductive grounds to suppose that most of our scientific theories will suffer from this kind of transient underdetermination, which would be just another instance of a wholesale argument.

In any case, the general idea is that a retail argument for scientific realism need not collapse our second-order philosophical evidence into our first-order scientific evidence; rather, we are to maintain the distinction between the specific considerations presented by scientists, and the abstract generalizations offered by philosophers, but to reconsider the relationship between the two – specifically, that while a general reflection over the reliability and historical track-record of our scientific reasoning may influence our assessment of our first-order scientific evidence, so too can the specific details of our first-order scientific evidence influence what sort of general philosophical reflections are deemed legitimate.

Yet while the above strategy makes clear the way in which our first-order scientific evidence might influence our second-order philosophical reflections, it still remains unclear how one might try to formulate a *positive* retail argument for scientific realism on this basis. In the case of the No-Miracles Argument, for example, Psillos argues that we can distinguish between one version of the argument as a piece of reasoning that concerns any arbitrary scientific theory, and one version of the argument as applied to a specific scientific theory, and to maintain that while the former does indeed depend upon our overall population of predictively successful scientific theories, the latter only depends upon features particular to the scientific theory in question – as Psillos puts it, 'the approximate truth of each and every theory will *not* be affected by the number (or the presence) of other theories … approximate truth, after all, is a relation between the theory and its domain' (2009: 65). But this only raises more questions than it answers. As we have already seen (see Chapter 3), Psillos specifically presents the No-Miracles Argument as an attempt to further justify the scientific realist's position – if only in terms of demonstrating its internal consistency – by showing that the initial philosophical claim that approximate truth was the best explanation of predictive success was an instance of a *general* inferential pattern that our first-order scientific evidence shows to be reliable. But if we are now to distinguish between different instances of the No-Miracles Argument as applied to different scientific theories, and to sharply differentiate between the individual details of those scientific theories, then it is no longer clear that there will be a general inferential pattern that our first-order scientific reasoning can be said to exemplify.

The problem is in fact even worse than it might at first appear. In Psillos's account, we are recommended to sharply individuate both the content of our scientific theories *and* the inferential methods by which we arrived at such theories. In the example involving the Pessimistic Meta-Induction, the predictive success of a scientific theory was to be attributed to specific theoretical posits and unobservable entities, in order that there can be no general inductive assessment of their historical stability. In the case of the No-Miracles Argument, by contrast, the reasoning by which we arrived at these theories was to be taken as thoroughly context-specific so as to avoid any worries relating to the general reliability of these methods and the base rate probability of an arbitrary scientific theory being true. But if all that is the case – if both our methods of reasoning and the content of our scientific theories are to be taken as thoroughly particular – then there will be absolutely nothing in general that the scientific realist can say about the approximate truth of our scientific theories, and thus nothing in the way of second-order philosophical evidence with which our first-order scientific evidence can interact. Rather than articulating a way in which our first-order scientific evidence can directly influence our second-order philosophical evidence, Psillos in fact rules out the possibility of there being any second-order philosophical evidence at all.

5.2.2. *Material postulates*

A more promising proposal for thinking about how we might try to proceed in the scientific realism debate without committing the Base Rate Fallacy is due to Juha Saatsi (2010), who distinguishes between what he calls *form-driven* arguments for scientific realism, and *content-driven* arguments for scientific realism. The distinction is more or less equivalent to that of Magnus and Callender's distinction between wholesale and retail arguments, yet it is primarily concerned with the structural features of the argument in question, rather than its intended scope. A form-driven argument is primarily concerned with the abstract principles of reasoning employed by the argument in question, whereas by contrast a content-driven argument will be primarily concerned with the specific instances to which that reasoning is applied. By way of illustration we can note that the traditional articulation of the No-Miracles Argument is both a wholesale argument in that it concerns the reliability of our scientific methodology considered in general, and a form-driven argument in that it is concerned with the reliability of IBE as an abstract piece of reasoning.

More specifically, a content-driven argument for scientific reasoning will be concerned with what John Norton (2003) calls the *material postulates* of that argument, that is, the assumptions of uniformity upon which the argument depends. The idea is best illustrated in the case of induction, where rather than attempting to resolve the formidable question as to whether or not any kind of extrapolation to the future is a reliable method of inference, we might instead try to make some progress attending to the somewhat more tractable issue as to what *sorts* of extrapolations are going to be more reliable than others. So, for example, we might argue that the more instances we have, the more likely it is that the inference will hold, even if we cannot be sure that any particular inference will be reliable. Or alternatively, we might argue that the most important consideration is that our inductive basis be suitably varied, or that it only consist of natural kinds or some other philosophically privileged entities. None of this will solve the problem of induction, but it may well put us in a position to distinguish between those inductive inferences that *might* work if induction is indeed reliable, and those inferences that are going to be completely hopeless either way. Similarly, then, in the case of the scientific realism debate, rather than attempting to establish whether or not IBE is a generally reliable method of inference, or whether or not it can be given a non-circular justification sufficient for convincing the sceptic, the philosopher of science should instead be concerned with uncovering those particular features of a scientific theory that will make one instance of IBE better than another.

We can think of Saatsi's proposal then as an attempt to find a third way between the two extremes of offering a philosophical argument for scientific realism that is so general it falls foul of the Base Rate Fallacy, and offering a philosophical argument for scientific realism that is so specific it fails to offer any philosophical assessment of our scientific practices. The idea is that the distinction drawn above between our first-order scientific evidence and our second-order philosophical evidence may not be as clear cut as we initially thought, and that there exists in fact some genuinely philosophical aspects to our first-order scientific evidence, in this case concerning the material postulates upon which that evidence depends. As Saatsi sees it, while an approximately true scientific theory must have somehow latched onto the right sorts of material postulates, it will not always be explicit how exactly those material postulates guided the scientific reasoning that led to the adoption of that theory, or indeed the nature of those material postulates. Hence:

> If a scientist appeals to a theory T because it is the simplest and the most
> unifying, and hence the most explanatory perhaps, it is a task for the

philosopher to make explicit how these contextual judgements reflect the particular material facts, given the scientific background knowledge of the domain in question. Only once material postulates have been made trans-parent can we compare them with the particular assumptions underwriting some commensurate inductions to the observable. (2010: 26)

The picture then seems to be something like the following. We begin with the usual first-order scientific evidence for adopting a particular scientific theory. The philosopher of science then considers the material postulates underlying this evidence – for example, those features of the world that the scientist assumes to be uniform when making his inference – to see if they really are the right sort of assumptions upon which such an inference can be based. This, however, does not constitute a second-order philosophical assessment of the reliability of our scientific practice as a whole, but is rather concerned with the specifics of the scientific theory in question. It is a piece of *first-order philosophical evidence*, something that is distinct from our first-order scien-tific evidence, yet without operating at the level of generality that involves knowledge of the underlying base rates.

The question, however, concerns the extent to which this assessment of our material postulates offers a genuine philosophical contribution to our assessment of that theory. The problem is that whereas Psillos emphasized the importance of our first-order scientific evidence to the extent that it undermined the possibility of any second-order philosophical assessment, Saatsi seems to make the opposite mistake of *underestimating* our first-order scientific evidence in order to produce a philosophical need that does not exist. The assessment of our material postulates is already part and parcel of our first-order scientific practice. When scientists come to accept a particular scientific theory, one of the things that they take into account will be the sorts of assumptions of uniformity upon which the theory depends. Indeed, most of these assumptions will themselves be the result of previously accepted scientific theories. Our acceptance of the atomic theory of matter, for example, crucially depends upon the assumption of Brownian motion in gases, a material postulate for which, in turn, various first-order scientific evidence has been offered in support. Checking the material postulates upon which our inferences depend is indeed an important task; it just doesn't appear to be a distinctively philosophical one.

If Saatsi is right and if the scientific realism debate really does constitute a distinctive philosophical contribution to the question concerning the approx-imate truth of our scientific theory, there must be some other considerations *over and above* our first-order scientific evidence for accepting our material postulates to be sound. It is difficult, however, to see what these might be. One option would be to offer arguments for the claim that any inferences made on the basis of this or that material postulate are generally reliable. This would offer a level of abstraction unavailable to our first-order scientific evidence. The problem of course is that this would be making a second-order philosophical assessment of our first-order scientific evidence, and then we are back with the problem of base rates all over again. Just because our current scientific theories are successful and depend upon a particular class of material postulates, it does not follow that any arbitrary inference based upon that class of material postulates will be reliable – just as with the traditional argument from predictive success to approximate truth, there may be an enormous number of *unsuccessful* inferences based upon those material postulates that our limited sampling overlooks.

5.2.3. *On the reality of molecules*

Both Psillos and Saatsi attempt to provide a very general account of what a retail argument for scientific realism might look like, either in terms of balancing our first-order scientific evidence and our second-order philosophical evidence, or in terms of making explicit the material postulates upon which our first-order scientific evidence depends. It is in part precisely because these accounts are so abstract that it has been so difficult to see how exactly their proposed understanding of a retail argument is to be distinguished from the first-order scientific reasoning with which it is supposedly concerned. In response, some philosophers have suggested that we might make better progress in working from the opposite direction – that we should begin with our first-order scientific evidence and seek to uncover extremely specific arguments for localized forms of scientific realism through the careful reconstruction of particular episodes in the history of science.

For example, both Wesley Salmon (1984) and Peter Achinstein (2002) have argued that the experimental work of Jean Perrin in the nineteenth century on the confirmation of Avogadro's number constitutes not only reasons for accepting the atomic hypothesis of matter, but in addition, compelling reasons to believe that atoms really exist. In their opinion, it was a piece of first-order scientific evidence for accepting a particular scientific theory that was somehow so compelling that it simultaneously constituted a piece of second-order philosophical evidence: it answered both the practical question of which scientific theory we should adopt in the process of our scientific investigations, and the philosophical question of how that theory should be interpreted and what our attitude should be towards its theoretical posits. If this is indeed the case, then we do not need to engage in any abstract worries about first-order and second-order evidence or the material postulates of our scientific theories in order to articulate a retail argument for scientific realism;

we simply need to look at our most successful instances of scientific practice and extrapolate from there.

The general idea is that at the time of Perrin's experiments, there were entrenched philosophical and methodological reasons for denying that our scientific investigations could tell us anything about the unobservable world. Contemporary scientists were for the most part committed to a broadly instrumentalist view of their scientific theories, largely under the influence of Ernst Mach (see Chapter 2). What Perrin did, however, was to calculate the number of molecules in a mole of gas via thirteen distinct experimental techniques, including considerations based upon Brownian motion, alpha particle decay, x-ray diffraction, black-body radiation and electrochemistry. Given the prevailing instrumentalism, there was no particular reason to suppose that all of these quite unrelated experimental investigations would deliver the same result, yet they all demonstrated a remarkable degree of agreement. So surprising was the result, that not only did Perrin confirm Avogadro's number for a range of distinct techniques, but he convinced the scientific community to abandon their instrumentalist commitments and accept the existence of atoms as the only explanation for why all of these different experiments should deliver exactly the same result.

It is certainly the case that Perrin's work did have an enormous impact upon the background philosophical convictions of his contemporaries. However, it is far from clear whether or not there is a distinctive kind of argument for scientific realism to be found within these considerations. Indeed, we have already encountered precisely this kind of reasoning in some of the early articulations of the traditional No-Miracles Argument when it was suggested that scientific realism is just philosophically more plausible than any of its instrumentalist rivals (see Chapter 3). There we explicitly considered the situation where the scientific realist was able to explain a complex series of phenomena – like the effects of a magnetic field on the patterns produced in a cloud chamber – in terms of the existence of various unobservable entities, whereas the eliminative instrumentalist could only accept the 'cosmic coincidence' that all of these observational experiences continued to hang together in the right sort of way. We also noted, however, that the strength of such reasoning depended upon one's presuppositions concerning the purpose of a scientific theory, and of what makes one explanation better than another.

So if the idea is supposed to be that Perrin's work demonstrated the explanatory power of accepting the existence of atoms, then this is neither a new argument for scientific realism nor a particularly good one. The point, however, is presumably more to do with the number and diversity of different experimental techniques, and their remarkable degree of conformity, rather than simply the explanatory power offered by accepting the existence of atoms. But what sort of argument is this? It would seem to be an instance of

IBE, that the *best explanation* for the widespread agreement of our different experimental techniques is that they are all investigating one and the same unobservable entity. But again, this just takes us back to familiar territory, for we have already seen that the reliability of IBE is precisely one of the issues that divides scientific realists from their opponents, and which cannot be considered compelling in the absence of any second-order philosophical considerations as to why we should accept such an inferential principle.

Ian Hacking (1985), for example, has offered a number of arguments for scientific realism on the basis of the reliability of our experimental techniques and sophisticated scientific instruments. He has argued that it is implausible to suppose that any beliefs we acquire about atoms or other unobservable entities are somehow less justified than our beliefs about our observational experiences just because they must be mediated through complex experimental techniques. Hacking argues that the human eye can also be considered as a kind of sophisticated instrument that one must learn to use before its results can be considered reliable; and that for the practising scientist with many years of experience using a scientific instrument, any observations made with the device are as direct and unmediated as normal vision. But more importantly, Hacking also argues that the persistent agreement that exists between all of the various different scientific instruments that we use gives us good reason to suppose that they are generally reliable. He gives the example of observing a microscopic object that has been prepared through some independent process. In such cases, he writes:

> I know that what I see through the microscope is veridical because we *made* [the object in question] to be just that way ... moreover, we can check the results with any kind of microscope, using any of a dozen unrelated physical processes to produce an image. Can we entertain the possibility that, all the same, this is some gigantic coincidence? (1985: 146–7)

In the same way then that Salmon and Achinstein conclude that the agreement between Perrin's different calculations of Avogadro's number *ipso facto* gives us good reason to believe in atoms, so too does Hacking conclude that the correlation between our diverse scientific instruments provides a philosophical argument for accepting the existence of whatever unobservable entities they manage to detect.

We should, however, be careful in how we interpret these results. In particular, we should not underestimate the difficulty and ingenuity involved in conducting a successful experiment, or in producing an image or representation through a scientific instrument. As van Fraassen (1985: 298) has argued in response to Hacking, the persistent agreement of diverse scientific instruments and experimental techniques need not be considered particularly surprising – or in need of any deep, philosophical explanation – once one takes into account how all of these instruments and experiments rely upon one another for calibration. The considerations raised by Salmon, Achinstein and Hacking would be more compelling if every single experiment or instrumental observation really did record the same result all the time. But this is manifestly not the case, since our experiments often go wrong and our scientific instruments break down and malfunction. Moreover, it is often the case that the only grounds we have for supposing that the experiment worked, or that our scientific apparatus was functioning correctly, is when they agree with other experimental outcomes and scientific instruments that we already suppose to be reliable. But if that is the case, then examples like that of Perrin lose much of their force, since if our primary reason for supposing that one particular experimental technique for calculating Avogadro's number is reliable is that it agrees with another experimental technique for calculating that value, then we can hardly *appeal* to the fact that all these techniques agree as an independent argument for their individual reliability.

This is not to say that van Fraassen is right, or that Salmon and Achinstein are misguided in using the case of Perrin as an argument for scientific realism. The point is that whatever the merits of this case, it does not constitute a *retail argument* for scientific realism, and it does not avoid the problem of the Base Rate Fallacy with which we began. As the exchange between Hacking and van Fraassen makes clear, the issue over the significance of experimental correlation is nothing more or less than the traditional scientific realism debate in microcosm. The scientific realist traditionally maintains that the predictive success of our scientific theories gives us good reason to suppose that our scientific methods are generally reliable, whereas his opponent replies that the predictive success of our scientific theories is hardly surprising since any unsuccessful scientific theory would never have survived long enough to be under consideration. Similarly, Salmon, Achinstein and Hacking maintain that the widespread agreement between our scientific instruments and experimental techniques gives us good reason to trust their results, whereas van Fraassen maintains that such agreement is hardly surprising, since it is only those scientific instruments and experimental outcomes that agree with one another that we are willing to treat as reliable.

5.2.4. Back to the base rates

The case of Perrin does not then differ from the familiar wholesale arguments that make up the traditional scientific realism debate. To put the point in simple terms, we can happily agree with Salmon and Achinstein that the best explanation for Perrin's results is that atoms really do exist, but nevertheless reject IBE as a compelling method of inference. The underlying problem is that a piece of first-order scientific evidence does not in itself simultaneously constitute a piece of second-order philosophical evidence. Rather, it will depend upon how we choose to *interpret* that first-order scientific evidence – for example, whether we think that the best way to understand Perrin's result is in terms of the diverse investigation of one and the same kind of unobservable entity, or whether we think it makes more sense to understand Perrin's work as the ingenious correlation of variously unrelated predictive tools. There may of course be good arguments for preferring one of these interpretations over another, but it is simply implausible to suppose that our scientific practices wear their philosophical implications on their sleeve. If that was the case, then there would never have been a scientific realism debate in the first place, since we would have been able to answer all of our philosophical questions about the nature of science by simply observing scientists going about their day-to-day business (for an explicitly anti-realist interpretation of Perrin's experiments, see van Fraassen 2009).

Moreover, not only does the case of Perrin fail to offer any real progress with respect to the problem of trying to articulate a retail argument for scientific realism, the reason that it can seem so compelling is in fact best *explained* in terms of the Base Rate Fallacy that it is supposed to resolve. We have already seen that the predictive success of a scientific theory only implies something about its approximate truth relative to a particular context: for while it may be extremely unlikely for a false scientific theory to be predictively successful, if our overall population contains a sufficiently large number of false theories, the probability of any particular predictively successful scientific theory being approximately true will be pretty low. The situation is in fact the same when we come to consider the widespread agreement of our different experimental techniques or scientific instruments. It may well be extremely unlikely for a series of inaccurate experiments or faulty scientific instruments all to come up with the same result as one another, but it will again depend upon the overall context – for if our overall population contains a sufficiently large number of inaccurate experiments and faulty scientific instruments, there is a good chance that some of them will deliver the same (although erroneous) result.

So the reasoning offered by Salmon and Achinstein is just another instance of the Base Rate Fallacy, just as with other traditional arguments for scientific realism. The difference, however, is that when we come to consider the diverse range of methods that Perrin actually employed, we instinctively feel that this must go some way towards exhausting the relevant possibilities. We do not know the underlying base rate probabilities, and we do not know how many inaccurate experimental methods there might be that would also deliver the same result – but we nevertheless feel that by comparing techniques based upon alpha particle decay, x-ray diffraction, black-body radiation and all the rest we are thereby considering a more representative sample of our overall population, and that therefore we can have a greater degree of confidence that the base rates in question are relatively high. Perrin's case is therefore one that *seems* to both offer a wholesale argument for scientific realism and to simultaneously reassure us about the underlying base rates, which is why it can strike us as both strongly compelling and as indicating its own philosophical interpretation. Unfortunately, of course, all of this is simply false. If we do not know the size of our overall population of experimental techniques, we cannot know that any particular sample is more representative than another, and the same old problem remains.

5.3. Arguments concerning scientific realism (Part II)

The contemporary scientific realism debate has been traditionally conceived of as an attempt to provide a second-order philosophical assessment of our first-order scientific practices. In the case of the No-Miracles Argument, this has consisted of showing that since our scientific methods are generally reliable, we have good reason to suppose that our scientific theories are approximately true. In the case of the Pessimistic Meta-Induction, by contrast, this has consisted of showing that since our scientific methods are historically unreliable, we do not have good reason to suppose that our scientific theories are approximately true. In both cases, however, these considerations crucially depend upon certain assumptions about the overall nature of the population of scientific theories in question – assumptions that the philosopher of science is not in a position to know, and which the various arguments in the scientific realism debate are in fact intended to establish. This state of affairs helps to explain the sense of intractability that has pervaded the contemporary scientific realism debate, and provides a general framework for thinking about the charges of circularity that have been levelled against some of its central arguments, since no matter how compelling the case to be made for either the No-Miracles Argument or the Pessimistic Meta-Induction, any such consideration will be simply overwhelmed by the underlying issue of whether or not any arbitrary scientific theory is likely to be approximately true.

Recent developments in the contemporary scientific realism debate have therefore begun to explore the possibility of offering a philosophical argument about the status of our scientific theories that does not depend upon these underlying considerations. These have all attempted to rethink the relationship between our first-order scientific practices and our second-order philosophical assessments. Psillos, for example, argues that we should focus upon the ways in which the specific details of our first-order scientific practices can influence our second-order philosophical assessments, while Saatsi maintains that there are some distinctively philosophical elements to our first-order scientific practices with which the scientific realism debate can be concerned. These proposals are still programmatic, yet in their present form threaten to eliminate the scientific realism debate altogether, for in shifting our attention to an almost exclusive focus upon the specific details of our first-order scientific evidence, there does not appear to be anything left for the philosopher of science to contribute. By contrast, Salmon and Achinstein have suggested that some instances of our first-order scientific evidence are so compelling that they simultaneously provide their own philosophical assessment – yet in this case, the problem is the opposite one of simply smuggling a second-order philosophical assessment into our interpretation of the facts, and not giving the details of our first-order scientific practices a proper examination.

5.3.1. Naturalism and normativity

The difficulties involved in trying to articulate a retail argument for scientific realism can again be traced to the way in which the debate has developed from its historical origins. We will recall that in the early half of the twentieth century, the scientific realism debate was primarily concerned with the logic-semantic structure of a scientific theory – with whether or not our theoretical discourse was to be taken at face value and thereby entailing ontological commitment to various unobservable entities, or if it was to be somehow reinterpreted or eliminated as a purely syntactic device. This of course had its own origins as a way of reconciling a broadly Kantian approach to investigating the status of our scientific theories with the modern realization that the objects of our knowledge are too revisable to be based upon the unchanging structure of our cognition. On such a linguistic construal, however, the intended scope of the scientific realism debate was extremely easy to circumscribe, since one could happily *appeal* to our actual scientific practice to adjudicate between competing semantic claims without thereby *engaging* in that practice: the open-ended nature of scientific research, for example, weighed heavily against any attempt to explicitly define our theoretical vocabulary in terms of our observational vocabulary. Given this somewhat peculiar focus, it was possible to both investigate the necessary preconditions for the predictive success of our scientific theories and to allow these investigations to be closely guided by our actual scientific practice, without any risk of circularity.

Yet with the demise of logical empiricism, the contours of the scientific realism debate shifted to a more epistemological orientation. The idea that our linguistic frameworks could somehow partly construct the objects of our knowledge – or that our scientific theories crucially depended upon the prior specification of various coordinate definitions – was undermined by Quine, who noted that the flexible inter-translatability of these frameworks meant that they could not in fact make any substantial contribution to these objects. Yet while the last remaining elements of Kant's philosophical framework were finally abandoned, his overall methodological convictions remained; and it is here that the crucial distinction between our first-order scientific evidence and our second-order philosophical assessment of that evidence began to blur. The idea that the philosopher of science somehow has access to a deeper or more profound source of knowledge, on the basis of which he can sit in judgement over our first-order scientific practices, is one that remains firmly rejected by the contemporary scientific realism debate. Indeed, if there is one thing that all parties to the debate do agree upon, it is that any investigation into the status of our scientific theories must proceed in conjunction with a suitably naturalist methodology. That is to say, any argument in the scientific realism debate must acknowledge the fact that our philosophical investigations are *continuous* with our empirical investigations, and do not constitute some higher court of appeal.

Yet it is precisely this continued endorsement of a broadly Kantian approach, in the absence of any distinctively Kantian tools or framework, that has led the scientific realism debate into its current impasse. If the philosophy of science does not constitute an independent source of reasons and arguments concerning the approximate truth of our scientific theories as the naturalist contents, then our second-order philosophical reflections can only differ in degree from the first-order scientific practice with which they are concerned. But the most obvious way in which to understand this difference is in terms of the generality at which these two kinds of consideration operate – our second-order philosophical arguments proceed via the same sort of considerations as those that constitute our first-order scientific practice, but merely offer a more abstract consideration of the same issues. Yet it is of course this difference, between the *specific* first-order evidence assembled by practicing scientists, as opposed to the *general* second-order evidence assembled by the philosopher, that has been explicitly undermined by worries relating to the Base Rate Fallacy. The fact is that in making our philosophical assessments continuous with our scientific practices, we cannot help but build into those scientific practices the very philosophical intuitions that we are attempting to uncover, as evidenced by the differing assumptions concerning the underlying base rates that seem to frame the contemporary debate.

It is interesting to note, however, that unlike other pronouncements of the death of scientific realism, this particular result appears to be entirely self-generated. We have already seen that Carnap took the debate over the existence of electrons and neutrinos to be a philosophical pseudo-problem, arguing that one simply took a pragmatic decision as to whether or not one wished to use a language that included terms like 'electron' or 'neutrino', and declared this to be as close as one could get to explicating an otherwise intractable metaphysical muddle. We have also seen that Fine and Blackburn have taken the debate to be based upon a misunderstanding of the concept of truth, and that once we realize that there is no philosophically substantive notion of a scientific explanation being true over and above that already implicit in our first-order scientific practices, the entire debate dissolves as a philosopher's fantasy. But both positions are controversial, and rest upon philosophical assumptions that one may come to hold or reject quite independently of one's views in the philosophy of science. In order to endorse Carnap's meta-ontological dissolution of the scientific realism debate, one must also endorse a series of further claims regarding the meaning of an existential claim and the distinction between the analytic and the synthetic. Similarly, if one had good reason to suppose that the concept of truth was philosophically substantive after all, then one would be utterly unconvinced by the diagnoses offered by Fine and Blackburn. The situation regarding the Base Rate Fallacy, however, is different. The problem seems to be that in maintaining both that the philosophy of science should be concerned with individual scientific theories rather than general methodological pronouncements, and that the philosophy of science should be understood as continuous with our scientific methods and not as contributing a distinctive source of normative evaluation, is that there is simply nothing left for the philosophy of science to do. The two strictures taken together threaten to squeeze the scientific realism debate into providing nothing more than the superfluous repetition of the first-order scientific reasoning that it was supposed to evaluate.

In short, then, the Base Rate Fallacy provides a precise, formal diagnosis of the problems underlying the contemporary scientific realism debate. It is a diagnosis that we can see lurking in the background of Carnap's insistence that the entire scientific realism debate is nothing more than a disagreement over language, since if we have no independent way of knowing the underlying base rate of an arbitrary scientific theory being approximately true, the debate really does amount to little more than a choice between realists and anti-realists over the most expeditious way of setting up the issue. Similarly, it is a diagnosis that does justice to Fine's and Blackburn's analysis that realists and anti-realists are simply adding superfluous philosophical baggage to an independently coherent picture of scientific practice – for without knowing the underlying base rate probability of an arbitrary scientific theory being approximately true, the No-Miracles Argument and Pessimistic Meta-Induction can only proceed by making unwarranted stipulations about this fact. But it is also a diagnosis that does not presuppose any further philosophical framework, but follows simply from the historical evolution of the contemporary scientific realism debate

5.4. Chapter summary

- The contemporary scientific realism debate is ultimately concerned with calculating the likelihood of a scientific theory being true, given that it is predictively successful. However, any such calculation will depend upon the base rate probability of an arbitrary scientific theory being true – something that we are not in a position to know.

- Both the No-Miracles Argument and the Pessimistic Meta-Induction are therefore guilty of committing the Base Rate Fallacy. For while explanatory considerations may increase the likelihood of a predictively successful theory being true – and while historical considerations may by contrast decrease it – such issues will be simply swamped by the underlying ratio of true theories to false theories in our overall sample space.

- These difficulties give a precise sense to the intractability that has plagued the contemporary scientific realism debate. They also motivate a change of focus from the sort of *wholesale arguments* that consider the reliability of our scientific methods in general to a series of *retail arguments* concerning the approximate truth of individual scientific theories.

- Unfortunately, it is difficult to specify what exactly a retail argument for or against scientific realism might look like. It has been suggested that it is a way of balancing our first-order and second-order arguments, making explicit the material postulates of our scientific inferences, or of identifying those first-order scientific arguments that are so compelling that they entail philosophical consequences.

- None of these suggestions have proved persuasive. The problem is that if the scientific realism debate is committed to being methodologically continuous with our scientific practices, yet also prohibited from offering any generalizations over that practice, it is difficult to see how the philosophical assessment of science can be distinguished from the first-order activity of scientists – or whether there remains any scientific realism debate at all.

5.5. Further reading

Many of the best discussions of the Base Rate Fallacy, and other common probabilistic errors in everyday reasoning, are to be found in the cognitive psychology literature. Unsurprisingly, some of this work can become highly specialized at times, but there still remains much that is of value to the philosopher of science. One of the most important works is Kahneman, D., Slovic, P. and Tversky, A. (1982) *Judgements Under Uncertainty: Heuristics and Biases* (New York: Cambridge University Press), which collects together a number of useful articles. For further work focusing on the Base Rate Fallacy in particular, see Cohen, L. Jonathan (1981) 'Can Human Irrationality Be Experimentally Demonstrated?', *Behavioral and Brain Sciences* 4: 317–70 for a philosophically stimulating, if controversial, approach to the topic, and Koehler, J. (1996) 'The Base Rate Fallacy Reconsidered: Descriptive, Normative, and Methodological Challenges', *Behavioral and Brain Sciences* 19: 1–53 for a more up-to-date account.

The role of the Base Rate Fallacy in the scientific realism debate is still a relatively underdeveloped field. Howson, C. (2000) *Hume's Problem: Induction and the Justification of Belief* (Oxford: Clarendon Press) is still the best place to start; see also his (2013) 'Exhuming the No-Miracles Argument', *Analysis* 73: 205–11 for a reply to some recent attempts to circumvent the problem. Menke, C. (2014) 'Does the Miracle Argument Embody a Base Rate Fallacy?', *Studies in History and Philosophy of Science* 45: 103–8 suggests that some of the probabilistic difficulties can be avoided by considering specific fields of scientific research rather than individual theories. Also recommended is Psillos, S. (2011b) 'On Reichenbach's Argument for Scientific Realism', *Synthese* 181: 23–40, which considers an alternative argument for scientific realism that explicitly acknowledges the need for assigning prior probabilities to the approximate truth of our scientific theories.

6

Structural realism

The previous three chapters in this book have discussed the principal considerations that have framed the contemporary scientific realism debate, specifically the No-Miracles Argument in favour of believing our scientific theories to be approximately true, and the Pessimistic Meta-Induction in support of a more cautious assessment. In both cases, however, we have found these arguments to be seriously flawed, since they effectively presuppose the very conclusions that they are supposed to establish – a flaw that can be rendered precise in terms of a widespread tendency to ignore the underlying base rate probabilities upon which both arguments fundamentally depend. We have also canvassed a number of diagnoses of how the contemporary scientific realism debate has managed to end up in such an ignominious state of affairs, including various meta-philosophical assessments regarding the meaning of an existential question and the status of our concept of truth. However, once we take a more synoptic view of the origins of the contemporary debate, a more modest explanation presents itself. Since its inception, the philosophical question over the approximate truth of our scientific theories has always been distinguished from the more general epistemological debate in terms of its distinctive methodology. The scientific realism debate is not concerned with whether or not we can have any knowledge of the external world, but with what we must presuppose in order to explain the manifest success of our scientific theories. This is a question that Kant attempted to answer in terms of the structure of our cognitive faculties, and which the logical empiricists attempted to answer in terms of the structure of our language. Nevertheless, in the face of technical difficulties with these approaches, the contemporary scientific realism debate evolved into a series of arguments concerning whether or not our scientific methods are indeed reliable. It is no surprise, therefore, if such arguments appear to either beg the question given the epistemological presuppositions of the debate, or simply collapse back into the general issue of scepticism against which they were supposed to be distinguished.

In this chapter and the next, we will therefore consider two approaches to the contemporary scientific realism debate that remain closer in spirit to the original formulation of the challenge: structural realism and constructive empiricism. According to the structural realist, the predictive success of our scientific theories only gives us reason to suppose that they are approximately true with respect to the structure of the external world. Unlike the case with full-blown scientific realism, however, this is not based upon any general epistemological considerations regarding the reliability of our scientific methods – that the claims our theories make about structure are more reliable than the other claims they make, for instance – but rather upon considerations relating to the nature of scientific representation. It is in this respect that the arguments for structural realism are closer in spirit to those offered by Kant than they are to those explored in the previous three chapters. Indeed, one of the principal considerations advanced in favour of structural realism is that it provides a way to finesse the issues raised by the No-Miracles Argument and the Pessimistic Meta-Induction altogether.

We begin in this chapter with some of the historical background to structural realism, as found in the work of Bertrand Russell and Henri Poincaré, who both defended something like Kant's distinction between the objects of our knowledge and the things-in-themselves (§6.1). For Russell, this is because the nature of our scientific knowledge is best understood as a claim about the abstract, logico-mathematical relationships that hold between the objects of the external world, rather than specific claims about those objects themselves. According to Poincaré, it is only by distinguishing between the broadly structural elements of our scientific theories about which we can have knowledge, and the specific claims about the unobservable entities of the world about which we cannot, that we can best make sense of the historical progress of scientific inquiry.

Both lines of thought have exerted a considerable influence over contemporary structural realists, although the results have been far from uniform. In the second part of this chapter, we will therefore consider some of the different kinds of structural realism that have been proposed, and in particular the distinction between *epistemic* structural realism and *ontic* structural realism (§6.2). According to the former, we can only have knowledge of the structure of the external world, although there are presumably non-structural elements to the world about which we must remain in ignorance. According to the latter, structure is the only thing that actually exists. We will discuss some of the difficulties relating to these views, and the problems involved in articulating the right account of structure. In response to the latter concern, the most recent literature on this issue reintroduces another character from the history of the scientific realism debate, and has explicitly appealed to the device of forming the Ramsey Sentence of a scientific theory in order to make precise its underlying structure. I discuss some of the developments surrounding this particular technique, and their consequences for the scientific realism debate in general (§6.3). The chapter concludes with a summary of the key issues discussed (§6.4) and some suggestions for further reading (§6.5).

6.1. From scepticism to structuralism

One way to think about structural realism is to see it as lying somewhere between full-blown scientific realism and some of the familiar forms of eliminative instrumentalism that we encountered earlier. According to the scientific realist, the best explanation for the predictive success of our scientific theories is that they are approximately true, and that we can therefore take our scientific theories as providing us with reliable knowledge about those parts of the external world that lie beyond our observational experiences. According to the eliminative instrumentalist, by contrast, our scientific theories are nothing more than tools for organizing our observational predictions, and are therefore unable to tell us anything at all about the unobservable world. The structural realist occupies a position somewhere between these two extremes. On this view, we have good reason to suppose that our scientific theories are approximately true, but only in certain respects: they provide reliable knowledge about the *structure* of the unobservable world, but do not tell us anything more about the various entities and processes of which this world consists. The view therefore goes beyond eliminative instrumentalism in that it accepts that we have *some* knowledge about the unobservable world, but falls short of traditional scientific realism in that it severely restricts the scope of this knowledge.

Once we understand structural realism in this way, it becomes possible to distinguish between two different argumentative strategies that have been offered in its support. Following Psillos (2001), let us call these the *upward path* and the *downward path* respectively. The upward path is essentially an attempt to show that the eliminative instrumentalist should strengthen his position into something approaching structural realism. It begins from a minimal set of assumptions about our epistemological situation, and argues that even these frugal beginnings justify a degree of confidence in what our scientific theories tell us about the structure of the unobservable world – while nevertheless stopping short of endorsing a traditional formulation of scientific realism. The downward path by contrast is essentially an attempt to show that the scientific realist should weaken his position into something approaching structural realism. The idea here is that while something like eliminative instrumentalism is certainly far too extreme, moderate qualifications to scientific realism in the face of reasonable sceptical challenges lead us to endorse the structural realist's more modest point of view.

Structural realism can therefore be seen as something of a compromise between realism and instrumentalism. Nevertheless, this way of putting things threatens to obscure an important aspect of the position. For while issues relating to both the No-Miracles Argument and the Pessimistic Meta-Induction do feature in many of the considerations advanced in its favour, structural realism is not simply a way of trying to reconcile these two lines of thought. The upward path for structural realism does not attempt to show that our scientific methods are generally reliable with respect to the structure of the unobservable; and the downward path for structural realism does not attempt to argue that our scientific methods are historically unreliable with respect to their non-structural content. There is no issue relating to the underlying base rate probabilities of a scientific theory being approximately true with respect to the structure of the unobservable world. As we shall see, most of the arguments advanced in favour of structural realism are primarily concerned with some straightforwardly Kantian issues relating to the nature of scientific representation. Structural realism is therefore not so much an attempt to reconcile the No-Miracles Argument and the Pessimistic Meta-Induction, but rather an attempt to move beyond these sterile considerations and return to the key issues framing the scientific realism debate.

6.1.1. Knowing the structure of the world

One of the most well-known examples of the upward path for structural realism is due to Bertrand Russell, although it should be noted that these arguments were advanced as part of a larger philosophical project that does not neatly correspond to our present interests regarding the scientific realism debate. It is nevertheless an argumentative strategy that many have endorsed in the context of structural realism. Russell begins with an extremely sparse conception of our epistemological situation. Specifically, he argues that we never directly perceive the physical objects around us, but are only ever acquainted with our *sense-data* – colours, smells and textures – from which we can only infer the existence of the physical objects in question. So, for example, Russell (1912: 8–11) argues that we never directly perceive the desk in his study, but only our individual sense-data of the desk, since that is the only way to explain the fact that different people at different times and under different lighting conditions will come to very different conclusions about its colour. The distinction of course recalls Kant's contention that we never directly perceive the things-in-themselves, but only the external world as it appears through the filter of our senses. Moreover, just as Kant argued that we can come to know certain *synthetic a priori* truths by examining the contribution made by our cognitive faculties, so too does Russell contend that even though we only ever have direct knowledge of our sense-data, we have good reason to suppose that these sense-data are caused by physical objects, and that they thereby encode a great deal of information about those objects. It is therefore possible to have indirect knowledge about the external world by investigating the nature of our sensory impressions.

Russell's argument rests upon a basic metaphysical assumption, namely that any differences that we can discern in our sense-data must ultimately be caused by differences in the objects responsible for them. For historical reasons, Psillos (2001: S14) calls this the *Helmholtz–Weyl Principle* after the German physicists Hermann von Helmholtz and Hermann Weyl who both endorsed this principle in their theoretical work. On the basis of this principle, Russell concludes that whatever relationships we find to hold between our sense-data must derive from a corresponding set of relationships that hold between the physical objects themselves. He concludes therefore that:

> there is a roughly one-one relation between stimulus and percept [which] enables us to infer certain mathematical properties of the stimulus when we know the percept, and conversely enables us to infer the percept when we know these mathematical properties of the stimulus. (1927: 226–7)

So, for example, from the fact that one set of sense-data is invariably followed by another, or that when one set of sense-data begins another abruptly ceases, we can infer a corresponding pattern of behaviour concerning the physical objects themselves.

It should be immediately noted, however, that any such indirect knowledge of the external world will be extremely abstract. It is tempting to suppose for example that even though we can never know the colour of any of the furniture in Russell's office, we would nevertheless be able to infer (say) that the desk really was darker than the chair on the basis that our sense-data of the desk were darker than our sense-data of the chair. This, however, is not the case, since there is nothing about the Helmholtz–Weyl Principle that guarantees that the relationships that hold between physical objects will be *qualitatively* similar to the relationships that hold between their respective sense-data. In fact, all that we can infer in this instance is that since the relationship of one sense-datum being darker than another is an asymmetrical relationship, the physical objects in question must also stand in some kind of asymmetrical relationship, otherwise a change in one will not accurately correspond with a change in the other – but from this we cannot infer anything at all about what this relationship is actually like, or indeed that it bears any resemblance to our notion of one thing being darker than another. Our indirect knowledge of physical objects will therefore be confined to the most general logico-mathematical relationships that hold between them; as Grover Maxwell (1971: 18–19) put it in a more recent articulation of Russell's view, we cannot know anything about the first-order relationships that hold between objects, but only the higher-order properties of those relationships, such as whether or not they are reflexive, transitive or symmetric.

This may not seem like a great deal of knowledge. But in fact, the situation is even worse than we might have at first imagined. The problem is that the Helmholtz–Weyl Principle is actually too weak to even deliver the meagre amount of structural knowledge outlined above. As Psillos (2001: S15) points out, the Helmholtz–Weyl Principle as currently stated only works in one direction. It states that if there is a change in our sense-data, then there must be a corresponding change in the physical objects behind these sense-data. But it does not guarantee the converse relationship, namely that every change in the physical objects will correspond to a change in our sense-data. To get a sense of this situation, it is sufficient to imagine that the structure of the physical objects is significantly more complex than the structure of our sense-data, and that there are various properties and relationships holding between the physical objects of the external world that our sense-data are too coarse-grained to differentiate, such as shades of colour that the human eye is simply unable to detect. In this sort of scenario, it would still be the case that any change in our sense-data would correspond to a change in the physical objects standing behind them, but there might also be changes in the physical objects that are too subtle to register in our sense-data – and if that is the case, then investigating the structure of our sense-data cannot give us reliable knowledge about the structure of the external world, since it would seriously underdetermine all of the relevant possibilities. In technical terms, the Helmholtz–Weyl Principle merely guarantees that the structure of our sense-data will be *embeddable* within the structure of the external world, whereas what we really require is for the two to be *isomorphic* to one another.

In order for Russell's project to work, therefore, we need to augment the original Helmholtz–Weyl Principle, and to assume not only that there can be no change in our sense-data without a corresponding change in the physical objects responsible, but also that there can be no change in these physical objects without a corresponding change in our sense-data. In effect, this amounts to the stipulation that no matter how complex the structure of the external world turns out to be, it cannot outstrip our capacity to understand that complexity, which is an extremely strong assumption to make – especially from the perspective of a position that was supposedly attempting to *establish* how much knowledge we have about the external world. Roman Frigg and Ioannis Votsis (2011: 237) have suggested that we might have good evolutionary grounds to support such an assumption. They argue that unless changes in the external world corresponded to a change in our sense-data, it would be miraculous that creatures like ourselves manage to successfully navigate our environment and survive. But this is not a compelling argument, since evolutionary pressures tend to select for pragmatic utility over representational accuracy, and there is no particular reason to suppose that every form of excess structural content in the external world will impinge upon our reproductive survival.

Russell's upward path for structural realism therefore faces a dilemma, for while the Helmholtz–Weyl Principle is plausible, it is too weak to provide any indirect knowledge about the structure of the external world, yet any attempt to improve it will require an unwarrantedly strong assumption about the nature of the world we are trying to investigate. Nevertheless, the idea that our knowledge of the external world is predominantly structural has continued to exert a strong influence over the contemporary philosophy of science. Although he does not himself defend structural realism, van Fraassen (1997), for example, has argued that since most of our scientific representations are mathematical in nature, our scientific knowledge must be predominately structural – the point being that while a mathematical description of an object will be able to specify the various relationships in which that object stands, it will be unable to provide us with any qualitative details about what that object is like. Such a line of thought differs from Russell's, however, in that it attempts to restrict our scientific knowledge to claims concerning the structure of the external world, rather than attempting to build up to such knowledge on the basis of a more modest starting point. It would therefore better motivate a downward path to structural realism, which has generally been the preferred strategy adopted by structural realists.

6.1.2. The best of both worlds

The principal considerations advanced in support of structural realism have generally sought to impose various limitations upon full-blown scientific realism, and to argue that our knowledge of the unobservable world only stretches as far as its structure. Probably the earliest articulation of this downward path to structural realism is due to Poincaré, who, as we have already seen, advanced this understanding of our scientific theories in the context of the Pessimistic Meta-Induction (see Chapter 4). The idea roughly is that while the history of science does indeed demonstrate the continuous replacement of our scientific theories, there nevertheless remains a significant degree of continuity between successive scientific theories sufficient to undermine any undue scepticism. Specifically, Poincaré argues that successive scientific theories tend to preserve the mathematical equations and other structural relationships of their predecessors, and moreover, that it is these more formal elements of our scientific theories that are responsible for their predictive success. He writes:

> If we look more closely [at the history of science], we see that what thus succumb are the theories properly so called, those which pretend to teach us what things are. But there is in them something which usually survives. If one of them taught us a true relation, this relation is definitely acquired, and it will be found again under a new disguise in the other theories which will successively come to reign in place of the old. (1902 [1905]: 182)

As stated, therefore, Poincaré's position would appear to be of the same form as some of the responses that we have already considered – that in order to undermine the Pessimistic Meta-Induction, we are to distinguish between the essential and inessential elements of our scientific theories; and whereas someone like Kitcher will draw this distinction between the referential and descriptive content of our scientific theories, Poincaré draws it between the mathematical and non-mathematical content of those theories.

This is certainly one way in which we can understand structural realism, but it fails to do justice to Poincaré's own motivations. The point is not that our scientific theories attempt to describe the non-structural features of the unobservable world, but that we have good historical reasons to suppose that this aspect of our scientific practice is generally unreliable. For Poincaré, we cannot know anything about the unobservable world as a matter of philosophical principle: it is the realm of the Kantian things-in-themselves, which can only be known through the mediation of our senses, or more specifically, through the mathematical framework of our scientific theories. It follows then for Poincaré that our scientific theories do not in fact even *attempt* to describe the non-structural features of the unobservable world, and consequently that any complaint or concern about how the non-structural content of our scientific theories changes over time is simply misplaced. As Poincaré put it:

> The aim of science is not things themselves, as the dogmatists in their simplicity suppose, but the relations between things; outside those relations there is no knowable reality. (1902 [1905]: 25)

The point then is not that the Pessimistic Meta-Induction shows us that we must revise our understanding of our scientific theories, but rather that a proper understanding of our scientific theories shows that the Pessimistic Meta-Induction never even arises.

Poincaré's downward path to structural realism therefore puts the position into closer contact with the work of Kant and Reichenbach than it does with the amended scientific realism of Psillos and Kitcher. The mathematical equations of our scientific theories can be thought of as part of our contribution to the objects of our knowledge, in the same way that Kant understood the forms of our sensibility, and Reichenbach understood the role of our coordinate definitions. That is why we can know the structure of the unobservable world – insofar as that structure is mirrored in our mathematical framework – but nothing else about that world.

More recently, Poincaré's emphasis upon the mathematical structure of a scientific theory has been taken up in the contemporary scientific realism debate by John Worrall (1989). The starting point for Worrall is again based upon the history of science, and as a way of trying to locate some form of continuity in successive scientific theories. He takes as a case study the development in our concept of light as a vibration in some all-pervasive luminiferous ether to our current understanding in terms of the electromagnetic field. According to Worrall, what remains common between all of these successive scientific theories are the differential equations used to describe the propagation of light, even though they disagree on how those equations are to be interpreted. He writes:

> There was an important element of continuity in the shift from Fresnel to Maxwell – and this was much more than a simple question of carrying over the successful empirical content into the new theory. At the same time it was rather less than a carrying over of the full theoretical content of full theoretical mechanisms (even in 'approximate' form). And what was carried over can be captured without making the very far-fetched assumption of Hardin and Rosenberg that Fresnel's theory was 'really' about the electromagnetic field all along. There was continuity or accumulation in the shift, but the continuity is one of form or structure, not of content ... Roughly speaking it seems to say that Fresnel completely misidentified the nature of light, but nonetheless it is no miracle that his theory enjoyed the empirical predictive success that it did; it is no miracle because Fresnel's theory, as science later saw it, attributed to light the right structure. (1989: 117)

As Worrall goes on to note, this is a diagnosis that Poincaré himself also offered in the case of our scientific theories about light.

Despite initial appearances, however, it is again important to note that Worrall's structural realism is not intended as merely a way of reconciling the No-Miracles Argument and the Pessimistic Meta-Induction. This is made more explicit in Worrall's later writings, where he acknowledges the difficulties associated with both of these arguments. According to Worrall (2007), we should see the No-Miracles Argument and the Pessimistic Meta-Induction as providing general *intuitions* that should guide our philosophical reasoning: the predictive success of our scientific theories does need to be accounted for one way or another, and the history of science imposes some important constraints on the sort of account that we might give. In that sense, Worrall's structural realism can be seen as part of a downward path from full-blown scientific realism. Yet Worrall also argues that neither the No-Miracles Argument nor the Pessimistic Meta-Induction can be developed into a satisfactory argument, and he cautions us against expecting either one to answer our philosophical questions about scientific practice. In simple terms, then, Worrall's articulation of structural realism cannot really be understood as a way of reconciling the No-Miracles Argument and the Pessimistic Meta-Induction, since he does not believe that either argument plays a significant role in the philosophy of science. Indeed, the principal motivation behind Worrall's structural realism seems to be that he just thinks it provides the most satisfactory way of understanding the history of science, independently of any further philosophical motivation.

6.2. The varieties of structuralism

We have seen so far that structural realism occupies a halfway position between traditional scientific realism and eliminative instrumentalism insofar as it advocates a limited knowledge of the unobservable world. We have also seen that in terms of its underlying methodology, the position is comparable to Kant's formulation of the issue, since it is primarily motivated by considerations of the nature of our scientific theories and the way in which they represent the world, rather than general epistemological considerations concerning their reliability. The plausibility of the position, however, depends crucially upon what the structural realist means when he talks about the structure of the unobservable world. In the case of Russell, for instance, this structure was understood in terms of the most general logico-mathematical properties of the various relationships holding between the objects of the external world, although this result was severely constrained by the way in which Russell attempted to derive his structural knowledge from our more immediate experiences. In the case of Poincaré and Worrall, this structure was understood in terms of the much broader notion of the actual mathematical equations involved in our scientific theories, although this result in turn is based upon a limited number of historical illustrations. It is important therefore for the structural realist to provide a more precise account of how exactly our scientific knowledge is supposed to stretch beyond our observational experience if we are to properly assess his position.

Moreover, there is something of a dilemma facing the structural realist in this respect. If one's account of structure is too specific, such as in terms of particular mathematical equations as suggested by Poincaré and Worrall, then it will be easy enough to identify concrete instances of when one scientific theory preserves the structural content of another, and to thereby justify the claim that structural realism offers a satisfactory interpretation of the history of science. However, in giving such a specific account of structure, one also seriously restricts the scope of one's philosophical position. On such a reading, structural realism would be inapplicable to any scientific theory or discipline that lacked the required degree of mathematization, such as those areas of the social and biological sciences that proceed upon predominately statistical analysis, or indeed pretty much any area of science other than the last few hundred years of mathematical physics. By contrast, if one's account of structure is too abstract, such as in the case of Russell, then it will be easy to extend structural realism to cover almost any branch of human knowledge. The problem of course is that the thesis threatens to collapse into triviality, since it is difficult to imagine how anything could fail to be accurately described in terms of relationships that were symmetrical, transitive or reflexive. The structural realist therefore needs to provide an account of structure that is both detailed enough to show us something interesting about our scientific theories, but broad enough to apply to a sufficient number of cases.

6.2.1. Revisiting the historical record

As Worrall (1989: 120–1) himself concedes, the transition between Fresnel and Maxwell is an unusually good illustration of structural realism, since in this instance the mathematical formalism is exactly preserved. This, however, is not generally the case. Leaving to one side the issue as to whether or not a focus upon mathematical equations is too narrow to support a philosophically interesting articulation of structural realism, the fact nevertheless remains that even amongst our more highly mathematized scientific theories, the preservation of structure is rarely so transparent. This leads Worrall to make an important qualification to his account. The claim is now not so much that successive scientific theories retain the exact same mathematical equations, but that the mathematical structure of previous scientific theories is retained as a *limiting case* of the mathematical structure of their successors. That is to say, the mathematical framework of our scientific theories is retained, but modified through successive scientific theories so as to approach an ever greater degree of generality.

On the whole, this is a perfectly reasonable qualification. If our scientific theories really did preserve *precisely* the same mathematical equations of their predecessors, it is hard to see how we have managed to make any scientific progress at all. But there is an important difference between amending the mathematical framework of a scientific theory so as to range over more variables or to offer more detailed predictions, and amending the mathematical framework of a scientific theory so as to cover a completely new range of phenomena. Consider again the transition between Newtonian Mechanics and Relativistic Mechanics that motivated so much of the contemporary scientific realism debate. For Newton, space and time were absolute, and so if we wanted to calculate the time taken for a particular event to take place, it was a reasonably straightforward procedure. For Einstein, by contrast, space and time are relative, and so any such calculation must take into account the effects of time dilation that occur when the velocities involved are sufficiently large. This leads to very different results in the two cases: roughly speaking, the faster an object is moving, the longer everything takes. The question then is whether or not an instance like this can be seen as the preservation of mathematical structure in the way that Worrall suggests. For on the one hand, the equations that one uses in a Newtonian context look very different from the equations used in a Relativistic context. Yet on the other hand, there is a sense in which Einstein's equations simply extend Newton's equations – in the case where the velocity of an object is zero, the effects of time dilation disappear and the two sets of equations are indeed equivalent. It will therefore depend on further assumptions about what we mean by structure. Worrall thinks that this convergence at low velocities is sufficient to show that Newtonian Mechanics is indeed a limiting case of Relativistic Mechanics; by contrast, Michael Redhead (2001) argues that since both sets of equations depend upon very different parameters, the fact that they agree in this particular instance is irrelevant.

So even an extremely concrete specification of structure in terms of mathematical equations raises further interpretative issues, since if structural realism is supposed to provide a satisfactory interpretation of the history of science, it needs to show that these mathematical equations are generally preserved through successive scientific theories despite the fact that they are usually modified and extended to accommodate new phenomena. Conversely, the structural realist also needs to show that no *non-mathematical* content is also preserved in these cases – and again, a closer look at the history of science raises difficulties for this claim as well. In the case of Fresnel and

Maxwell, for example, Psillos (1999: 157–9) argues that not only were the mathematical equations describing the propagation of light preserved, but also some of the theoretical assumptions that guided their derivation. As Psillos sees it, Fresnel depended crucially upon a mechanical assumption that the amplitude of a lightwave is somehow proportional to the density of the medium in which it travels, and a general principle concerning the conservation of energy. These assumptions are not structural in any reasonable sense of the term, and are certainly not part of the mathematical formalism of Fresnel's theory. But they were necessary for Fresnel's understanding of his equations, and, most importantly, were also taken over by Maxwell in his subsequent understanding of light as an electromagnetic wave. According to Psillos, therefore, the mathematical equations were only preserved alongside a broader theoretical package of how those equations were to be interpreted. If that is the case, then the most satisfactory interpretation of the history of science goes some way beyond that suggested by the structural realist.

6.2.2. The structure and content of a scientific theory

Both of the issues raised above are of course controversial and require a much more detailed investigation into the historical case studies in question for a proper evaluation. They nevertheless help to illustrate a more general worry about the difficulties in distinguishing between the structural and non-structural content of a scientific theory, and in particular, the way in which knowledge of the former can in fact often presuppose knowledge of the latter. One way to put this point is to note that the structural realist must in some sense be committed to more than simply the mathematical symbolism in his scientific theories. After all, to be committed to nothing more than the mere mathematical symbolism of his scientific theories would make structural realism just another form of eliminative instrumentalism. So it seems then that the structural realist cannot just be committed to the mathematical content of his scientific theories, but also to some kind of *interpretation* of that content. But the natural way to interpret the mathematical content of our scientific theories is in terms of the various unobservable entities and processes that it supposedly describes; and if that is the case, then our scientific theories tell us about more than just the structure of the unobservable world.

The issue is somewhat subtle, and so it is best to proceed slowly. A more concrete version of this worry is offered by Psillos (1995; see also his 1999: 151–5), who notes that if our scientific theories really did consist of nothing more than a set of uninterpreted mathematical equations, then they would not be able to give us any knowledge about the unobservable world at all, structural or otherwise. This is because a mathematical equation is essentially a conditional statement. It tells us how one variable depends upon another, but until we specify what those variables are, the equation as a whole has no way of making contact with the real world. It follows then that if the structural realist thinks that the mathematical equations of his scientific theories do tell us *something* about the unobservable world – rather than merely about how our observational experiences hang together – then this can only be because our interpretation of those mathematical equations also tells us something about the unobservable world. In Psillo's view, then, we can only have structural knowledge about the unobservable world if we also have non-structural knowledge of that world.

In response, however, Ioannis Votsis (2007: 63–5) complains that Psillos has conflated two different senses in which we might provide an interpretation of our mathematical equations. He argues that there is of course a minimal sense in which the structural realist must provide an interpretation of his mathematical equations, in that of providing precise numerical values for the variables. In order to do so, the structural realist must therefore specify which sorts of observational experiences and experimental outcomes are to be used as providing the raw data in these instances. None of this, however, presupposes any non-structural knowledge of the unobservable world, since there is nothing about this sort of minimal interpretation that requires us knowing what it is that these experimental outcomes are measuring. One does not have to assume that one is measuring vibrations in a luminiferous ether or an electromagnetic field in order to look at a meter reading and plug the right numbers into a differential equation. Or to put it another way, a minimal interpretation of our mathematical equations does presuppose that there is *something* about which these equations are supposed to provide structural knowledge, but it does not require us to know any further non-structural details about what it is.

Such a response has some merit, but it remains unclear whether or not we can really draw the sort of distinction that Votsis has in mind here. In order to work, it must be the case that a robust interpretation of our mathematical symbolism really does go above and beyond that which is offered by the sort of minimal interpretation that Votsis suggests. There must be a sense in which talk of the luminiferous ether or the electromagnetic field really does constitute a meaningful difference from talk of an unknown *something* that is nevertheless sufficiently concrete to allow us to assign numerical values to the variables of our equations. Yet as Psillos (1999: 155–7) goes on to note, it is difficult to see just what this might be. Of course, we associate all sorts of qualitative descriptions and conceptual ideas to the notion of a luminiferous ether or an electromagnetic field – Lord Kelvin once wobbled a bowl of jelly in a public lecture in order to illustrate the way in which light was supposed to propagate through the ether – but the point is that none of this is part of our *scientific* description of the world. As Psillos writes:

> To say what an entity *is* is to show *how this entity is structured*: what are its properties, in what relations it stands to other objects, etc. An exhaustive specification of this set of properties and relations leaves nothing left out. Any talk of something else remaining uncaptured when this specification is made is, I think, obscure. I conclude, then, that the 'nature' of an entity forms a continuum with its 'structure', and that knowing the one involves and entails knowing the other. (ibid.: 156–7)

To argue for a sharp distinction between the structure and the nature of an entity is to hark back to the medieval distinction between form and substance. But on the modern scientific view, to talk about the nature of an entity is just to specify the various causal relationships – expressed in terms of mathematical structure – by which it interacts with other entities.

This all leaves us then in something of a bind. In order for the mathematical equations of our scientific theories to express structural knowledge of the unobservable world beyond that countenanced by the eliminative instrumentalist, they must be given some kind of interpretation. Votsis argues that some interpretations are less troublesome than others, since we can distinguish between a bare minimal interpretation that simply assigns values to our variables, and a robust interpretation that seeks to add qualitative detail to the entities in question. But the distinction is problematic, since it is unclear whether or not such a metaphysically robust or qualitative account of objects was ever part of our modern scientific worldview. To put the point in more simple terms, if structural realism does not commit us to everything that our scientific theories say about the unobservable world, then we should be able to identify those parts of our scientific theories about which we are to remain ignorant. But since our contemporary scientific theories no longer talk about the *qualities* or *essences* of unobservable entities as something over and above their causal relationships, it is not clear which parts of our scientific theories these are.

6.2.3. The metaphysics of structure

The difficulties above have all concerned the way in which the structural realist attempts to determine the structural content of his scientific theories. They are essentially epistemological problems, and reflect the fact that when we interact with a scientific theory – such as using it to make predictions – we tend to treat the theory as a whole, and subsequently have difficulties in distinguishing between those parts that do the important work. But the fact that we have difficulties identifying the structural content of a scientific theory does not mean that such a distinction cannot be drawn, and in fact motivates an alternative formulation of structural realism that has been gaining increasing currency in the literature. This was originally proposed by James Ladyman (1998), who argues that:

> We should seek to elaborate structural realism in such a way that it can diffuse the problems of traditional realism, with respect to both theory change and underdetermination. This means taking structure to be primitive and ontologically subsistent. (1998: 420)

The idea is that rather than taking structural realism to be an epistemological thesis about how much of our scientific theories we should believe, we should take it to be a metaphysical thesis about the nature of the world. Let us call these two positions *epistemic structural realism* and *ontic structural realism* respectively. According to the ontic structural realist, the reason that we should only believe what our scientific theories say about structure is because structure is the only thing that actually exists – structure is primitive and ontologically subsistent – and thus that is all that our scientific theories talk about anyway.

This is certainly a radical thesis, and it is worth pausing to understand just how ontic structural realism attempts to resolve the problems facing epistemic structural realism. Essentially, the idea is that rather than attempting to distinguish between structure and content ourselves, we should allow the world to do the hard work for us. For the epistemic structural realist, our scientific theories describe an external world of entities and processes, and we then decide which bits of those theoretical descriptions meet some further epistemological criteria of reliability, historical continuity, and so on and so forth – on this view, structural realism is something that we impose upon the world, and the onus is on us to find an epistemological principle that does this in the right sort of way. For the ontic structural realist, by contrast, our scientific theories describe a world that is itself fundamentally structural. There is therefore a fact of the matter as to which parts of our scientific theories correctly represent these parts of the world, and the purpose of our scientific theorizing is simply to provide ever more accurate descriptions of these structures. On this view, structural realism is something that the world imposes upon us. To be clear, articulating structural realism as a metaphysical thesis does not in itself make it any easier for us to distinguish the structural content of our scientific theories. What it does, however, is to guarantee that such a distinction is at least possible. For the epistemic structural realist, scepticism over our ability to distinguish between structure and content threatens to undermine the very essence of the position. But for the ontic structural realist, who maintains that structure is a feature of the world rather than of our descriptions, this merely indicates our own inability to grasp an objective feature of the world.

In essence, then, ontic structural realism finesses the difficulties raised for epistemic structural realism by endorsing an additional metaphysical commitment. This is of course a common strategy in philosophy, and its success depends upon the perceived cost-benefit analysis of endorsing such a commitment. In the case of ontic structural realism, this consists of the claim that structure is primitive and ontologically subsistent. But there are a number of different ways in which we might understand this claim. On its most radical reading, this is the idea that structure is the only thing that exists, and that there are no such things as objects or individuals in the traditional sense at all. Slightly less radical would be the claim that structures are the only things that exist, but that objects and individuals can be said to somehow *supervene* on these structures in a derivative manner. The least radical proposal – and the one favoured by most ontic structural realists – would be to acknowledge the existence of both structures and objects, but to maintain that structures are the more basic and are therefore capable of existing independently of these objects. On such a view, objects and individuals can be eliminated from our scientific theories since they do not perform any useful function.

Regardless of how exactly the thesis is articulated, however, there is a basic oddity at the heart of ontic structural realism. In our usual way of thinking, it is the objects and individuals that are ontologically fundamental; a structure is usually understood as an *abstraction* from the individuals and properties that it describes. We can think of objects existing without any structure, but we can make no sense of a structure without any objects. But for the ontic structural realist, this relationship is reversed. For some, this is simply incoherent. Psillos (2001), for example, writes:

> But I am not sure whether we can even make sense of this primitive structural identity. And if we introduce individuals as 'heuristic' devices whose sole role is 'the introduction of structure' (only to be 'kicked away' later on), we need to justify why they are just 'heuristic devices' if the *only* road to structure is through them. I conclude that it's hard to see how the ontological revisions [ontic structural realism] suggests is possible. (2001: S22–S23)

Moreover, as Anjan Chakravartty (2003) notes, individual objects play an important explanatory role in many other areas of our lives. On our traditional understanding of causation, for example, it is because objects have properties at one time, and different properties at another, that we would say that a change has occurred. But this is not something that the ontic structural realist can accommodate, since a world of structures appears to be something that is fundamentally changeless. The issue, however, is a difficult one to decide. For while Psillos and Chakravartty are certainly correct that ontic structural realism rests upon a radical thesis about the nature of the world that we may have difficulty understanding, the whole point of ontic structural realism is of course to advocate a radical new understanding of the nature of the world. Such a criticism therefore either indicates the obvious absurdity of ontic structural realism, or merely begs the question against it.

More recently, the main arguments in favour of ontic structural realism have been concerned with interpretative issues in the philosophy of physics. It is claimed, for example, that a proper understanding of quantum mechanics requires us to abandon our classical understanding of the world as consisting of individuals and objects in favour of a structuralist ontology. There are therefore independent reasons to adopt ontic structural realism, which trump the misgivings raised above. The arguments here obviously go far beyond the scope of this present book, but in simple terms they rest upon the fact that certain intuitive principles of identity do not straightforwardly apply at the quantum level. In classical mechanics and everyday life, our notion of identity and objecthood is governed by considerations such as Leibniz's Principle of the Identity of Indiscernibles – if two objects have all of the same properties, then they are identical; or alternatively, if two objects are not identical, then they must have at least one property that is different. This includes spatial and relational properties, and is illustrated by the fact that we can easily distinguish between a situation where object a has a particular property and object b does not, and the situation where object b has that property and object a does not. But in quantum mechanics, there are certain entangled systems where this distinction cannot be represented: we know that only one of the objects has the property in question, but there is absolutely nothing in our theory that can distinguish between the two possibilities that exist in the classical case. In such a situation, then, we have two objects that are completely indiscernible, but which are yet clearly not identical (see French and Redhead 1988). The conclusion seems to be then that we must abandon Leibniz's Principle and our traditional understanding of objecthood in the case of quantum mechanics.

In the case of quantum mechanics, then, there does seem to be a case to be made that it is the *structure* of a quantum system that is more fundamental than the objects it contains, since many of these objects are not characterized sufficiently to meet our traditional understanding of objecthood. It also raises an interesting methodological consideration similar to the one explored in the previous chapter – that in order to fully assess the range of positions in the contemporary scientific realism debate, we must also attend to the details of particular scientific theories and specific scientific disciplines. This is not necessarily the same thing as offering a retail argument for structural realism, but merely recognizes the fact that our philosophical reasoning can be profitably guided by the results of the scientific theories with which they are concerned. Needless to say, however, such considerations are extremely controversial, and while a lively field of research, do not yet settle the issue concerning ontic structural realism.

6.3. Ramsey Sentence realism

Associating the structure of a scientific theory with its mathematical content threatens to give structural realism too narrow a scope of application, limiting the position to only the more recent developments in physics and with nothing to say about the rest of our scientific practices. It also raises difficulties about how exactly we are to interpret this mathematical content, for on the one hand, too little detail would fail to differentiate structural realism from eliminative instrumentalism, while on the other hand, too much detail commits the structural realist to knowledge of the unobservable that goes beyond its structure. In his more recent work, therefore, Worrall has begun to articulate the structure of a scientific theory in terms of the familiar device of constructing its Ramsey Sentence (this idea is first discussed in Worrall and Zahar 2001).

As we discussed earlier (see Chapter 2), the Ramsey Sentence of a scientific theory is constructed by replacing its theoretical terms with the appropriate number of existentially quantified variables. So for example, in the case where our scientific theory is attempting to define the theoretical property of temperature (Tx) in terms of a particular experimental set-up and outcome (O_1x and O_2x respectively), our original scientific theory will be of the form:

$$\forall x \, [O_1x \supset (O_2x \supset Tx)]$$

while its Ramsey Sentence will be of the form:

$$\exists X \forall x \, [O_1x \supset (O_2x \supset Xx)]$$

where again we note that since we are quantifying over predicates rather than variables, the sentence as a whole will be expressed in a second-order language. As can be easily seen, associating the structure of a scientific theory with its Ramsey Sentence provides a straightforward solution to the problems mentioned above. To begin with, we can note that any scientific theory will admit of a corresponding Ramsey Sentence, regardless of its degree of mathematical sophistication. Such an account therefore allows one to be a structural realist about any domain of our scientific investigations. There is also no further issue regarding the interpretation of a Ramsey Sentence, since it is constructed precisely to make explicit the various relationships that hold between the objects of our scientific theories, but without telling us anything else about what these objects themselves are like.

But if the appropriate interpretation of a mathematical equation threatens to commit the structural realist to too much knowledge of the unobservable world, the Ramsey Sentence of a scientific theory threatens to commit him to too little. We have already seen that the Ramsey Sentence of a scientific theory is easier to satisfy than its original scientific theory. The worry is that it may in fact be far too easy to satisfy. This problem was first raised by Max Newman (1928) with respect to Russell's view on structuralism, and later raised in the context of the scientific realism debate by William Demopoulos and Michael Friedman (1985). Consider again our extremely simply example of a Ramsey Sentence outlined above. This tells us that there is some property X such that, if an object in our domain undergoes the appropriate experimental procedure (O_1x) and produces the appropriate experimental outcome (O_2x), then that object also has that property (Xx). But logically speaking, to say that there is some property X is just to say that there is some set of objects whose members can be grouped together on the basis of some criteria. So what our Ramsey Sentence really tells us is that there is some way of grouping objects together into a set such that, if an object in our domain undergoes an experiment and produces the appropriate outcome, then we can include that object amongst this set. But without any further constraints on how such groupings can be formed, the existence of such a set of objects is mathematically trivial – provided that there are enough objects in our domain, we can construct any number of different sets that we please simply by stipulating how these objects are to be grouped together (for a detailed proof of this result, see Ketland 2004).

Another way to put the point is to remember that while the Ramsey Sentence of a scientific theory commits us to the existence of different properties, it very specifically does not tell us what these properties are like. So while our original scientific theory may tell us that if an object successfully undergoes the appropriate experimental procedure it can be included amongst the set of objects that all have the same temperature, the Ramsey Sentence of that scientific theory only specifies that there is *some* set of objects amongst which it can be included. But since we are now no longer constrained to construct our sets on the basis of genuine physical properties, we can just as easily construct them on the basis of some abstract mathematical relationship. It might belong to the set of the first five things we can think of, or some other arbitrary lexicographical device – and if that is the case, then the existence of any such set will be guaranteed provided that enough objects exist. On first impressions, then, the Ramsey Sentence of a scientific theory seems to commit us to the observational content of that theory, and the structure of the unobservable content of that theory. On closer inspection, however, all that the Ramsey Sentence really commits us to is the observational content of our theory and a claim about how many objects exist, which does not amount to very much structural knowledge at all.

This problem is known in the literature as *Newman's Objection*, and in very simple terms it notes that the structural knowledge provided by the Ramsey Sentence of a scientific theory is so limited – amounting to nothing more than a cardinality constraint on the domain of quantification – that any such articulation of structural realism collapses into a form of eliminative instrumentalism. The obvious response therefore is for the structural realist to try to impose some additional constraints upon the way in which we construct the Ramsey Sentence of a scientific theory. As we outlined it above, the main problem is that if the second-order quantifiers of a Ramsey Sentence can be satisfied by any arbitrary set of objects, then it does not in fact tell us very much about the structure of the unobservable world. Borrowing an idea from Lewis (1983), therefore, the structural realist might stipulate that only certain sorts of sets are legitimate. We might argue, for example, that some groupings of objects are more natural than others, and that only those sets that individuate genuine physical properties can satisfy the structural commitments of a Ramsey Sentence. Notice that this still falls short of full-blown scientific realism, since the proposal is not to specify what theoretical property each and every second-order variable actually picks out, but rather to draw a general distinction between two different classes of properties and to stipulate that only one of them is relevant to the task at hand. This would certainly resolve Newman's Objection, since on this proposal it would no longer be possible to satisfy the Ramsey Sentence of a scientific theory with mathematically trivial sets of objects, and so our structural commitments would indeed go beyond a mere claim about the number of objects that exist. The problem, of course, is how to *justify* this fundamental distinction between genuine and non-genuine properties. The worry is that while this sort of constraint would not result in the Ramsey Sentence of a scientific theory telling us more about the unobservable world than its structure, it seems that the structural realist would need to possess some independent knowledge about the unobservable world in order to justify this distinction.

A more promising proposal has been offered by Joseph Melia and Juha Saatsi (2006). Their proposal is not to amend the way in which we interpret the Ramsey Sentence of a scientific theory, but to amend the way in which it is constructed. The idea is that our scientific theories do not simply express relationships between different unobservable objects, but that they also implicitly suggest that such relationships are necessarily true. That is to say, they seek to express something like the laws of nature that describe the external world, not simply accidental regularities. So to return to our earlier example, our simple scientific theory about the experimental outcomes of temperature is better expressed in the form:

$$\Box \forall x \, [O_1 x \supset (O_2 x \supset Tx)]$$

where the $\Box$ is to be read as the one-place modal operator 'it is necessary that ...' Consequently, the Ramsey Sentence of this theory will be of the form:

$$\Box \exists X \forall x \, [O_1 x \supset (O_2 x \supset Xx)]$$

which now tell us not just that there is some set within which we can group any object that successfully produces the appropriate experimental outcome, but that in every possible world there is such a set. This provides additional formal constraints upon how we construct the various sets that satisfy the Ramsey Sentence, yet without engaging in any further discussion about their interpretation. Unfortunately, further discussion of this issue will involve further details relating to how we understand our modal logic, which again lies outside the scope of this book (see Yudell 2010 for a criticism of this approach). Needless to say, finding ways to articulate the Ramsey Sentence of a scientific theory in such a way as to resolve the challenge posed by the Newman Objection remains very much a live topic in the scientific realism debate.

6.3.1. A Kantian finale

We began this section by identifying a basic dilemma for the structural realist concerning the way in which he identifies the structure of our scientific theories. If the account is too specific, such as in the case of identifying the structure of our scientific theories with their mathematical content, then structural realism will only apply to a limited range of our scientific investigations. Yet if the account is too general, such as in the case of identifying the structure of our scientific theories with their respective Ramsey Sentence, then structural realism threatens to become trivial. In particular, we have seen that unless we impose further restrictions upon how we construct the Ramsey Sentence of a scientific theory, the most that it can tell us about the structure of the unobservable world is the size of its domain, which is really not very much at all.

The underlying problem with all of this is that, while structural realism does of course draw some of its inspiration from Kant and his emphasis upon how our scientific theories represent the external world, it is not intended as a purely retrogressive step in the contemporary scientific realism debate. In Worrall's view at least, structural realism is also supposed to *supersede* the traditional concerns of the No-Miracles Argument and the Pessimistic Meta-Induction by providing an account of our scientific theories that can satisfy both of these intuitions. Yet if the structural realist only believes what our scientific theories say about the structure of the unobservable world, and if what our scientific theories say about the structure of the unobservable world is limited to a claim about the size of its domain, then it is hard to see how this additional desideratum can be met. To put the same point another way, while the structural realist rejects the No-Miracles Argument as a faulty piece of reasoning, he nevertheless agrees that a satisfactory account of our scientific theories must go some way towards explaining their predictive success. This is something that his commitment to structure is supposed to provide, over and above the more parsimonious commitments of the eliminative instrumentalist – yet if those structural commitments are nothing more than a cardinality constraint, it is hard to see what advantages structural realism might possess in this respect.

It is certainly true that in associating the structure of a scientific theory with its Ramsey Sentence, the structural realist does not seem to possess a great deal of knowledge about the unobservable world. It also seems to be the case that any attempt to extend that structural knowledge will end up presupposing precisely the sort of non-structural knowledge about the unobservable world that the structural realist rejects. But there is another way to approach this issue. In order for the Ramsey Sentence of a scientific theory to provide too little structural knowledge, it must be the case that there is more structural knowledge that is somehow available. But as Worrall (2007; see also his 2009) now sees it, this is simply not the case. The problem then is not so much that the structural realist fails to provide enough structural knowledge about the unobservable world, but rather that his critics are working with an implausible account of how much there is to know.

Worrall's argument here echoes many of the concerns with which we began this book. He argues that we only ever have access to the unobservable world through a variety of descriptions, be they linguistic descriptions or the more formal representations provided by our scientific theories. This is because we never have direct access to the unobservable world, but only to the way in which we detect it through whatever experimental techniques are at our disposal. Moreover, we can never independently check the reliability of these experimental techniques, since that would involve us somehow standing outside of our representational practices. As Worrall puts it:

> We fool ourselves if we think that we have any independent grip on what [the extensions of our original theoretical predicates] are aside from whatever it is that satisfy the Ramsey-Sentence. (2007: 152)

Most importantly, however, it follows on this view that we can never hope to increase the structural content of a Ramsey Sentence by restricting the sorts of sets over which it can quantify. In order to demand that we only ever quantify over natural properties, or sets of objects that satisfy the appropriate modal relationships, we must first of all have some knowledge of those properties. But if all our knowledge is mediated through our descriptions and representations as Worrall maintains, then we would only ever be able to grasp those properties insofar as they were themselves expressed in terms of yet another Ramsey Sentence – in which case, these properties will be unable to provide any meaningful constrain upon our original Ramsey Sentence, since they too will be subject to the same problem of mathematical triviality all over again.

The argument is of course heavily Kantian, only now it is the unobservable objects of our scientific theories that are to be considered things-in-themselves, forever lying beyond the reaches of our immediate experience. It is in fact Poincaré's view all over again, only with the structure of our scientific theories articulated in terms of their respective Ramsey Sentence, rather than in terms of their mathematical equations. Worrall's most recent articulation of structural realism is therefore an explicit return to the roots of the contemporary scientific realism, a Kantian view of the world expressed through the technical resources developed by the logical empiricists.

6.4. Chapter summary

- Structural realism is the view that our scientific theories are approximately true with respect to the structure of the unobservable world. It therefore occupies a position somewhere between traditional scientific realism and eliminative instrumentalism – we have some knowledge of the unobservable world, but only in a highly limited respect.
- In contrast to both scientific realism and eliminative instrumentalism, however, structural realism is not motivated by considerations relating to the No-Miracles Argument and the Pessimistic Meta-Induction, but in fact seeks to overcome them. It is rather primarily motivated by

considerations of how our scientific theories represent the external world and the most plausible method of interpreting the history of science.

- The principal difficulty facing structural realism, however, is to provide a clear distinction between the structure and content of a scientific theory that is both broad enough to cover a wide range of different scientific theories, but not so broad as to render the position trivial. This leads to a distinction between *epistemic* structural realists, who see the distinction in epistemological terms, and *ontic* structural realists, who believe that the fundamental ontology of the world is in fact structural.
- The most recent articulations of structural realism have sought to understand the notion of structure in terms of the Ramsey Sentence of our scientific theories. However, given that the Ramsey Sentence of a theory is only committed to the existence of abstract mathematical sets, the notion of structure that remains on such an approach amounts to little more than a cardinality constraint on the domain of quantification.
- In many ways, however, structural realism offers a more direct continuation of the scientific realism debate as originally formulated by Kant. In the work of Poincaré and Worrall at least, it maintains that we can never have knowledge of things-in-themselves, but only those objects of our knowledge as mediated through the structural framework of our scientific theories.

6.5. Further reading

There are many excellent texts on the history of philosophy relating to the themes discussed in this chapter. One of the best introductions to Russell's philosophy is Hylton, P. (1990) *Russell, Idealism, and the Emergence of Analytic Philosophy* (Oxford: Oxford University Press). For more on Poincaré, see Zahar, E. (2001) *Poincare's Philosophy. From Conventionalism to Phenomenology* (La Salle, IL: Open Court). For a more general overview of the historical background to structural realism, see Gower, B. (2000) 'Cassirer, Schlick and "Structural" Realism: The Philosophy of the Exact Sciences in the Background to Early Logical Empiricism', *British Journal for the History of Philosophy* 8: 71–106.

The best introduction to ontic structural realism, and its location within the philosophy of science in general, is Ladyman, J. and Ross, D. (2007) *Every Thing Must Go: Metaphysics Naturalised* (Oxford: Oxford University Press). Other variations on structural realism include Chakravartty, A. (2007) *A Metaphysics for Scientific Realism: Knowing the Unobservable* (Cambridge: Cambridge University Press), which is articulated alongside a dispositional account of properties. For a good discussion of the role of representation in scientific practice, and an empiricist twist on the traditional structural realist position, see van Fraassen, B. C. (2008) *Scientific Representation: Paradoxes of Perspective* (Oxford: Oxford University Press).

The Newman Objection, and the various responses that have been offered in the literature, are discussed in Ainsworth, P. (2009) 'Newman's Objection', *British Journal for the Philosophy of Science* 60: 135–71. Finally, for a broadly structural realist approach to issues beyond the philosophy of science, see Lewis, D. (2009) 'Ramseyan Humility', in D. Braddon-Mitchell and R. Nola (eds) *The Canberra Programme* (Oxford: Oxford University Press), 203–22.

7

Constructive empiricism

Throughout the discussion in this book, we have seen how the various positions offered in the scientific realism debate have tended to fall into one of two competing categories concerning the function of our scientific theories. On the one hand, we can think of them as tools primarily concerned with the systematization and prediction of observational experience; while on the other hand, we can think of them as aiming to provide accurate descriptions of the external world which can thereby help us to *explain* our observational experience. These two functions of course are not mutually exclusive, but the more one emphasizes the practical purpose of prediction, the less one is motivated to endorse the existence of various unobservable entities.

For the logical empiricists in the early half of the twentieth century, this contrast was made in terms of the language of our scientific theories. If our theoretical terms could be shown to have a meaning only insofar as they could be explicitly defined within our observational vocabulary, then it would follow that they played no role in explaining how our scientific theories manage to be predictively successful. Technical difficulties with this approach led not only to the rejection of logical empiricism, but to a change of focus from the logico-semantic structure of our scientific theories to an epistemological investigation concerning their warrant and justification. Nevertheless, we saw in the previous chapter how the broadly Kantian idea that we can only grasp the objects of our knowledge insofar as they are in part constructed by our own contribution to experience has been updated and preserved in the structural realism of Poincaré and Worrall. Similarly, there are other ways in which to articulate the emphasis of prediction over explanation that do not depend upon the reduction or reaxiomatization of our theoretical vocabulary. According to Bas van Fraassen (1980: 12), science aims to give us theories that are empirically adequate, where a scientific theory is empirically adequate provided what it says about the observable phenomena is approximately true. This position is known as constructive empiricism, and the idea then is that while our scientific theories are still held to deliver much less than the scientific realist maintains, this distinction has absolutely nothing to do with the language of our scientific theories – indeed, van Fraassen happily accepts that our theoretical vocabulary is not only to be taken at face value, but that it also plays an indispensable role in our scientific theorizing. Rather, the crucial distinction concerns the particular entities and processes with which our scientific theories are concerned, rather than the words and phrases we use to describe them.

Constructive empiricism therefore offers a way to articulate the idea that the primary function of our scientific theories is to systematize and predict our observational experiences, but without the semantic preoccupations that derailed logical empiricism. I will begin in this chapter by clarifying in greater detail the contrast between logical empiricism and constructive empiricism (§7.1). According to van Fraassen, the problems with logical empiricism all stem from an inadequate technical framework, which sees a scientific theory as consisting of a *set of sentences* or other linguistic devices. By contrast, the constructive empiricist argues that we should understand a scientific theory as a *set of models*, and that it is this updated framework that provides the resources necessary for the task at hand. The most important issue, however, remains the way in which we are to distinguish between the observable and unobservable entities upon which the position depends (§7.2). For the constructive empiricist, this is held to be an empirical question, to be investigated by our best scientific methods, rather than our *a priori* philosophical speculations. This, however, raises further difficulties of its own, and in particular the worry that the constructive empiricist will often find himself in the uncomfortable situation of having to use his scientific theories in order to determine which parts of those very theories he is entitled to believe.

In his more recent work, however, van Fraassen has sought to articulate constructive empiricism within a broader epistemological context that emphasizes the role of choice and decision within our understanding of rationality (§7.3). This has important consequences for how some of the objections to constructive empiricism are to be answered, and for how we are to understand the scientific realism debate in general. I assess some of the strengths and weaknesses of this framework, and how it relates to our broader question concerning the apparent intractability of the scientific realism debate. The chapter concludes – as always – with a chapter summary of the key issues discussed (§7.4) and some suggestions for further reading (§7.5).

7.1. Saving the phenomena

For the logical empiricists, a scientific theory is to be thought of as consisting of a set of sentences expressed within a formal language. This is perhaps most clearly seen in the case of the eliminative instrumentalist and the way in which he sought to provide a reaxiomatization of our scientific theories couched entirely within our observational vocabulary. We begin by listing all of the axioms of our scientific theory, deducing all of the logical consequences of those axioms, eliminating those that include any theoretical terms and then using these to construct a new list of axioms with a particular syntactic structure. All of this is of course explicitly committed to the idea that a scientific theory can be expressed as a set of sentences, that is, in terms of its axioms and theorems. Similarly, any attempt to provide an explicit definition of our theoretical terms also presupposes that our scientific theories can be expressed as a set of sentences within a particular language with a particular vocabulary.

This is known as the *syntactic account of theories*, and the most important consequence of this view for our present purposes is the fact that the only information a scientific theory can give us about an entity will be in terms of the various linguistic predicates that it is supposed to satisfy. We have of course already seen the limitations associated with this approach, and that in particular there is no way that this kind of framework will capture anything of epistemological significance, since with a little ingenuity we can just as easily describe the same entity in terms of the various predicates that it *does not* satisfy (see Chapter 2). For someone like Carnap, perhaps, this was not a serious difficulty, since he was only concerned to show on technical grounds that our scientific theories did not perform the sort of function attributed to them by the scientific realist. For the constructive empiricist, by contrast, the problem remains a significant one, since it is a central part of his position to show that there is indeed an important epistemological distinction to be drawn between the different claims made by our scientific theories.

This is, however, not the only way to think of our scientific theories. According to the *semantic account of theories* a scientific theory is to be thought of as consisting of a set of models. On this account, there are two different pieces of information that a scientific theory can give us about an entity: the various predicates or relationships that it satisfies, and *whereabouts in the model* it appears. The advantage of such an account is that it allows the constructive empiricist another method of individuating the entities of his scientific theories, one that is independent of the various predicates used to describe them. He can simply specify the entities in which he is interested in terms of the particular region or substructure of his model in which they are embedded. Of course, this in itself does not guarantee that the desired distinction between observable and unobservable entities can be drawn, but it does at least finesse the problem facing a syntactic account of theories whereby any entity can be equally well described in both our observational and theoretical vocabularies.

This predominately technical observation, however, neatly segues into a second important idea underlying van Fraassen's constructive empiricism. Rather than attempting to explicitly define or otherwise eliminate the unobservable content of his scientific theories, van Fraassen argues that we can distinguish between two different epistemological attitudes that we can hold towards the claims of our scientific theories – that while we *believe* what our theories say about the observable phenomena, we merely *accept* what they say about the unobservable phenomena. This is essentially a distinction between those claims of our scientific theories that we find credible and those that we are willing to adopt because we find them useful. This combination of a semantic account of theories, alongside the distinction between acceptance and belief, offers an updated articulation of the instrumentalist point of view within the epistemological context of the contemporary scientific realism debate. We consider both of these components in more detail below.

7.1.1. *The syntax and semantics of observability*

According to the constructive empiricist, the aim of science is to produce theories that are empirically adequate, where a scientific theory is said to be empirically adequate precisely if it is accurate with respect to the observable phenomena. In contrast to the logical empiricists, however, this distinction between the observable and the unobservable is not something that can be captured by the language of our scientific theories. Rather:

> To present a theory is to specify a family of structure, its *models*; and secondly, to specify certain parts of those models (the *empirical substructures*) as candidates for the direct representation of observable phenomena. (van Fraassen 1980: 64)

In its most simple terms, a model is just an ordered pair, consisting of a set of objects in a domain and a set of relationships defined over those objects. The objects in question could be physical objects, such as the coloured balls and sticks often used to represent complex molecules in chemistry, although in most cases they will just be sets of numbers and other mathematical objects. A substructure of a model is a subset of our overall domain, along with whatever relationships still hold for the objects in question.

The crucial point is that, since the objects of a scientific theory can now be individuated independently of their theoretical description, we can also appeal to whatever external criterion we please in order to specify the domain of our empirical substructure. Again van Fraassen:

> To delineate what is observable … we must look to science – and possibly to that same theory – for that is also an empirical question … I regard what is observable as a theory-independent question. It is a function of facts about us *qua* organisms in the world. (ibid.: 57–8)

The idea then is that we can actually look to our best scientific theories about human physiology and the propagation of light to draw our distinction between observable and unobservable entities. These theories will tell us that some objects (tables, chairs, etc.) are large enough and sufficiently opaque for unaided human observation, and that some other objects (electrons, quarks, etc.) are not. We can use these results to independently specify the observable subdomain of our scientific theories, and consequently to read that distinction *back into* the structure of our scientific theories, without relying upon any of our problematic theoretical descriptions.

The additional flexibility offered by a model-theoretic approach to our scientific theories can be further illustrated by the following consideration. Both Michael Friedman (1982: 278) and Jeff Foss (1984: 86) have objected that while the constructive empiricist may well be able to appeal to an empirical criterion of observability, in contrast to the logical empiricist's linguistic criterion, he is nevertheless still unable to differentiate between the entities of his theories. The argument runs that since the constructive empiricist believes whatever his theories say regarding the observable phenomena, and since many of these theories will attribute unobservable properties to these phenomena, it follows that the constructive empiricist will also end up believing in various unobservable phenomena after all. So, for example, the constructive empiricist will believe whatever his theories say about tables and chairs, since these are uncontroversially observable phenomena. However, some of our scientific theories make quite high-powered theoretical claims about these phenomena, such as the fact that tables and chairs are made up of subatomic particles. So it follows then that the constructive empiricist believes that tables and chairs are made up of subatomic particles. But if that is the case, then the constructive empiricist must believe that there are such things as subatomic particles, which is clearly a belief about unobservable phenomena. The point then is that while it may be the case that a model-theoretic approach allows the constructive empiricist to individuate between the observable and unobservable phenomena in a way that is unavailable to the linguistic approach, it seems that he still cannot hold a belief about one without thereby holding a belief about the other.

What this objection fails to appreciate, however, is precisely the distinction between observable entity and theoretical description that lies at the heart of the model-theoretic approach. If the constructive empiricist believes what his scientific theories say about tables and chairs, and if his scientific theories say that tables and chairs are composed of subatomic particles, then the constructive empiricist is certainly committed to believing that tables and chairs *can be described as* being composed of subatomic particles. But this will only commit him to the existence of subatomic particles if these entities themselves also appear within the empirical substructure of his scientific theories, which presumably they do not. The distinction may seem arbitrary, but as a logical point it is perfectly sound – merely describing an entity as composed of subatomic particles does not in itself entail the existence of subatomic particles, unless we are working within a framework that lacks the expressive resources to distinguish between the entities that exist and the descriptions we attribute to them. Such an objection would therefore hold against the logical empiricists and their linguistic approach, but does not hold against the model-theoretic approach of the constructive empiricist (see Muller 2004).

The semantic account of theories therefore provides precisely the kind of technical resources that the logical empiricists seemed to lack. Indeed, at certain points in his account, van Fraassen goes so far as to argue that the widely acknowledged failure of logical empiricism can be attributed entirely to its reliance upon a flawed understanding of a scientific theory. He writes:

> The syntactically defined relationships are simply the wrong ones … It is hard not to conclude that those discussions of axiomatisability in restricted vocabularies, 'theoretical terms', Craig's theorem, 'reduction sentences', 'empirical languages', Ramsey and Carnap sentences, were one and all off the mark – solutions to purely self-generated problems, and philosophically irrelevant. The main lesson of twentieth-century philosophy of science may well be this: no concept which is essentially language-dependent has any philosophical importance at all. (van Fraassen 1980: 56)

This is a characteristically provocative assertion by van Fraassen, and one which bears closer examination. One worry we might have is that while we have seen the shortcomings of both explicit definition and eliminative reaxiomatization, we have also seen that the Ramsey Sentence offers a way around many of these difficulties. Indeed, we have also seen that the best way to understand the underlying structure of a Ramsey Sentence is as a claim about the existence of various *sets of objects* – which then begins to sound a lot like the sort of semantic account of theories that van Fraassen has in mind. So while thinking about a scientific theory as consisting of a set of models certainly helps to make clear how some of the difficulties with logical empiricism can be overcome, it may not be as revolutionary as initially suggested.

7.1.2. Acceptance and belief

The distinction between a syntactic and semantic account of theories may therefore not be quite as important as we originally supposed. By contrast, however, the distinction between acceptance and belief is both novel and crucial to the articulation of constructive empiricism. According to van Fraassen, we should only believe what our scientific theories say about the observable phenomena. But we do not thereby abandon, eliminate or thereby attempt to reinterpret the unobservable content of our scientific theories. On the contrary, van Fraassen not only agrees that these projects face insurmountable technical difficulties, but also argues that they are completely unnecessary. Instead, the constructive empiricist happily endorses the unobservable content of our scientific theories, is willing to use them at face value in making predictions and offering explanations and relies upon them to construct future research projects and to design novel experimental techniques. As van Fraassen puts it, to accept a claim involves:

> [A] commitment to confront any future phenomena by means of the conceptual resources of this theory. It determines the terms in which we shall seek explanations. If the acceptance is at all strong, it is exhibited in the person's assumption of the role of explainer, in his willingness to answer questions *ex cathedra* ... There are similarities in all of this to ideological commitment. A commitment is of course not true or false: the confidence exhibited is that it will be *vindicated*. (van Fraassen, 1980: 12)

None of this, however, necessarily involves believing those claims to be true.

It is a frequent complaint, however, that once one takes into account the substantial epistemological commitment that seems to be involved in accepting the claims of a scientific theory, it is difficult to see how this is supposed to be contrasted with regular belief. Paul Horwich (1991), for example, has argued that it is natural to try to understand both acceptance and belief as some kind of mental state, and that they can therefore be at least partly characterized in terms of their functional role. But if that is the case, argues Horwich, then accepting a scientific theory sounds a lot like believing that theory to be true. He writes:

> If we tried to formulate a psychological theory of the nature of belief, it would be plausible to treat beliefs as states with a particular kind of causal

role. This would consist in such features as generating certain predictions, prompting certain utterances, being caused by certain observations,
entering in characteristic ways into inferential relations, playing a certain
part in deliberation, and so on. But that is to define belief in exactly the way
[van Fraassen] characterises acceptance. (1991: 3)

Horwich concludes therefore that since acceptance and belief are characterized by the same causal role, they must in fact be the same mental state.
Consequently, the constructive empiricist's distinction between acceptance
and belief is illusory – in which case, despite all of the effort in distinguishing
between observable and unobservable phenomena, constructive empiricism
simply collapses into scientific realism after all.

Despite the importance of the distinction, van Fraassen himself rarely
discussed the difference between acceptance and belief. However, van
Fraassen (1985: 276–81) has argued that there may be reasons for accepting
a proposition or theory that are not reasons for believing that proposition
or theory, and vice versa. More specifically, he argues that one comes to
accept a scientific theory on what are predominantly pragmatic grounds
– for example, that a particular scientific theory is easy to use, simple to
understand or neatly coheres with the rest of one's scientific worldview. By
contrast, we come to believe a scientific theory on largely evidential grounds,
such as how likely it seems that the theory is true. Crucially, these considerations can come apart. To take a simple example, the more claims that a
scientific theory makes about the world, the more useful that theory is, and
thus the more reason we have to accept it. However, the more claims that a
theory makes about the world, the more chance it has of saying something
false, and thus the less reason we would have to believe it. As a limiting case,
then, a tautology such as (p v ¬p) would be *maximally believable* in the sense
that there would be no way for it to be false, yet *minimally acceptable* in the
sense that it tells us practically nothing about the way the world is.

This then is a response that can directly engage with Horwich's argument,
for if van Fraassen is right, and the causes of belief are to be differentiated from the causes of acceptance, then by Horwich's own functionalist
standards the two attitudes must be distinct. Horwich (1991: 7–8), however,
simply dismisses this line of thought. According to Horwich, van Fraassen's
distinction between the pragmatic and the evidential underdetermines the
case at hand – that while our mental lives may indeed be governed by both
instrumental and evidential considerations as van Fraassen suggests, this
in itself is insufficient to establish that we are dealing with two distinct
attitudes. In Horwich's view, then, all that van Fraassen has shown is that our
decision to *believe* a proposition or theory will depend upon both its likeliness
and its loveliness, considerations that can pull apart for sure; and none of this

is sufficient to establish a principled distinction between the two contrasting attitudes of acceptance and belief.

The issue over acceptance and belief is therefore controversial to say the least, and still very much an open question in the literature. One possible way to think about the distinction, however, is in terms of the contrast between a voluntary and involuntary action. The idea is that accepting a scientific theory must be voluntary, since it is primarily concerned with an agent's actions, and involves an element of choice, of weighing up the various pros and cons of endorsing one theoretical framework over another. By contrast, believing a scientific theory is an involuntary action. This is based upon Bernard Williams' (1973) argument that it is conceptually necessary that one just cannot choose what one believes. To take his oft-quoted argument:

> One reason [that one cannot believe at will] is connected with the characteristic of beliefs that they aim at truth. If I could acquire a belief at will, I could acquire it whether it was true or not. If in full consciousness I could will to acquire a 'belief' irrespective of its truth, it is unclear that before the event I could seriously think of it as a belief, i.e., as something purporting to represent reality. (1973: 148)

The argument is not watertight. For one thing, it concerns what an agent knows about his own mental state, which does not rule out the possibility of acquiring a belief at will and immediately forgetting that this was the case (Bennett 1990). It also doesn't do much to show how the two attitudes of acceptance and belief differ in their functional role, and so while these considerations may show that such a distinction is logically possible, it won't help to convince someone like Horwich that it is actually the case. Nevertheless, this remains a potentially fruitful line of inquiry for future work on the topic.

7.2. Observables and unobservables

According to van Fraassen, constructive empiricism is the view that science aims to give us theories that are empirically adequate, where a theory is empirically adequate provided that it correctly represents the observable phenomena. We have also already seen that in contrast to the logical empiricists, the constructive empiricist's distinction between observable and unobservable phenomena is a fact about the phenomena themselves, not the language we use to describe them. As van Fraassen puts it:

The human organism is, from the point of view of physics, a certain kind of measuring apparatus. As such it has certain inherent limitations – which will be described in detail in the final physics and biology. It is these limitations to which the 'able' in 'observable' refers – our limitations *qua* human beings. (1980: 17)

What this means is that in order for the constructive empiricist to determine whether or not a scientific theory is empirically adequate, he must first of all appeal to our best scientific theories concerning such matters as the behaviour of light and the intricacies of human physiology to tell him which consequences of that theory concern entities that we can directly observe.

One immediate issue arising from this account is that the distinction between observable and unobservable phenomena will be vague. As Maxwell (1962) originally argued in the context of logical empiricism:

There is, in principle, a continuous series beginning with looking through a vacuum and containing these as members: looking through a windowpane, looking through glasses, looking through binoculars, looking through a low-power microscope, looking through a high-power microscope, etc., in the order given. The important consequence is that, so far, we are left without criteria which would enable us to draw a non-arbitrary line between 'observation' and 'theory'. (1962: 7)

In a sense, then, this is the trade-off between logical empiricism and constructive empiricism. If we attempt to draw a distinction within the language of our theories – between the observational terms and the theoretical terms – the distinction can be made as sharp as we like, since we can clearly stipulate for each and every term of our language which category it falls into. The problem, of course, is that it is difficult to see what epistemological relevance such a distinction may possess. By contrast, by distinguishing between the phenomena themselves, the constructive empiricist can draw a distinction with immediate epistemological relevance. The problem, however, is that since nature is never as well behaved as our linguistic descriptions, there will always be borderline cases of whether or not a particular phenomenon is observable.

The fact that the distinction is vague, however, is not necessarily a problem. For all the difficulties involved in drawing the distinction, there will still remain uncontroversial instances of observable phenomena (such as tables and chairs) and uncontroversial instances of unobservable phenomena (such as quarks and neutrinos). Nevertheless, unobservable phenomena can still be detected in various ways, through experimentation and the use of sophisticated scientific instruments, and the question remains as to whether or not this still constitutes a relevant epistemological distinction. We have already seen some discussion of the role of instruments in our scientific theories in the case of Perrin (see Chapter 5). The argument was that the beliefs we acquire through the use of instruments are just as reliable as the beliefs we acquire through the use of our unaided senses. The problem here generalizes in a number of interesting ways, as we shall see below.

7.2.1. A concern about counterfactuals

One important issue here is that in order to draw a distinction between the observable and unobservable phenomena that lies at the heart of his position, the constructive empiricist must appeal to certain counterfactual conditionals. This is because a scientific theory is empirically adequate provided it gets it right about what we *could* observe under the appropriate circumstances, and not simply with what we have already observed in the past. So, for example, the moons of some distant planet are still a paradigmatic case of an observable phenomenon, even if they are so far away from us that they have never actually been observed. Similarly, a long-extinct dinosaur should also count as an observable phenomenon even though it perished long before the existence of mankind. It follows then that the constructive empiricist will be committed to various counterfactual conditionals, such as the claim that *if we were* to travel far enough into outer space in a rocket-ship, *then we would* be able to observe the moons out of the window, or that *if we were* to travel back in time, *then we would* be able to directly observe the enormous and terrifying dinosaur just before it eats us.

By contrast, there are various unobservable phenomena like electrons or quarks that are presumably unobservable no matter what – the constructive empiricist is therefore committed to denying the counterfactual possibility of us shrinking ourselves to the point where we could observe such phenomena directly, or building some kind of device that could make them bigger, or anything else that might change their observational status. But as Paul Churchland (1985: 39–40) argues, this just seems arbitrary. The idea of shrinking ourselves to a size where we could directly observe electrons may seem sufficiently outlandish, but it is far from clear why it should be considered any more outlandish than travelling back in time to look at dinosaurs. Even the case of the distant moons can begin to stretch credibility when we note that even if physical constraints about the speed of light and the heat-death of the universe ensured that we could *never* put ourselves in a position to make a direct observation, the constructive empiricist would still classify those moons as observable.

In response, the constructive empiricist can argue that the distinction between observable and unobservable phenomena is an empirical distinction, and that our best scientific theories concerning the propagation of light and the physiology of the human eye have a lot to tell us about the various parameters that determine whether something can be observed. We know, for example, that the size of the object in question and the way in which light is scattered from its surface are extremely important for whether or not it can be directly observed. Similarly, we also know that where exactly in time and space the observational event takes place is not a relevant consideration. Thus the constructive empiricist does have good reason to suppose that the moons of a distant planet are observable, since even if we could never travel that far into outer space, there is nothing about the observational event itself that suggests that our eyes would stop working or that light would behave differently. By contrast, however, the constructive empiricist has equally good reason to suppose that electrons and quarks can never be considered observable, since our scientific theories tell us that the sort of physical trans- formation entailed by the shrinking scenario envisaged above is *precisely* the sort of variation that will have a significant effect upon our sensory modalities.

Perhaps a better way to put the objection then is to consider those individuals who might draw the distinction between observable and unobservable phenomena in a very different manner. In Churchland's (1985: 43–4) example, we are invited to consider a race of extra-terrestrials with electron microscopes for eyes. The idea is that these individuals can make direct observations of subatomic particles, and so would endorse a significantly broader notion of observability than the one that we have been considering. The question then is how the constructive empiricist should respond to these creatures if we were to meet them. On the one hand, it seems that he cannot concede that the aliens make direct observations of microscopic phenomena since the causal mechanism employed by these aliens to observe microscopic phenomena is *ex hypothesis* exactly the same as the causal mechanism employed by human scientists working in the lab. The only salient difference is the epistemologically irrelevant one that the aliens have their electron microscopes permanently affixed to their face. So if using an electron microscope does not render an object observable for us, then neither can it render an object observable for the aliens. Yet on the other hand, why is it that human beings can determine what is observable and unobservable, whereas other creatures are deemed to be simply mistaken in their assessments? The aliens in question certainly *act* as if they are making such observations, and to discount their evidence simply on the grounds that they are weird looking and come from another planet is both chauvinistic and without any epistemological justification.

Thus just as the constructive empiricist seems to endorse some counterfactual conditionals while rejecting others that appear to be no less epistemologically outlandish, so too does he seem to pick and choose at random the circumstances under which we are allowed to endorse the reliability of a particular causal mechanism. However, as van Fraassen (1985: 256–8) points out, there is something of an equivocation in Churchland's argument. Suppose that we do encounter such a race of instrumentally augmented aliens. We would be faced with two possibilities. The first possibility is that we include these individuals within our epistemic community. Were this to happen, our notion of observability would be extended accordingly, since some of us would now be able to make direct observations of microscopic phenomena. So far, so good. The second possibility is that we refuse to include these individuals within our epistemic community, in which case our notion of observability would remain the same. Yet in refusing to consider such individuals as members of our epistemic community, the constructive empiricist again avoids any charge of epistemic inconsistency. The basic point is that if we do not consider these aliens as part of our epistemic community, it simply begs the question to suppose that their causal connections to the world are reliable. From an epistemological point of view, we have no reason to treat these instrumentally augmented aliens any differently from any other electron microscopes or pieces of scientific apparatus encountered in the laboratory.

Ultimately then, Churchland's objection rests upon conflating these two possibilities. He invites us to imagine a situation where we assume that the aliens have some kind of reliable causal connection to the world, while nevertheless refusing to count them as members of our epistemic community. But that is simply to beg the question in favour of scientific realism, since unless we already *presuppose* that electron microscopes are reliable, we have no reason to grant any credence at all to the behaviour of these alien beings. But for the constructive empiricist, the reliability of electron microscopes is precisely the question that is at issue. It follows then that the only circumstances in which the constructive empiricist would be forced to take our instrumentally augmented neighbours at their word would *ipso facto* be circumstances in which he would be forced to reconceptualize the borders of our epistemic community. Whatever else one may think about it, there is at least nothing *inconsistent* about the constructive empiricist's attitude to such extra-terrestrial individuals.

7.2.2. The limits of observability

Let us suppose that the preceding objections can be successfully answered by the constructive empiricist, and that there is a principled distinction to be drawn within our scientific theories between the observable and unobservable phenomena. Unfortunately, it does not necessarily follow that this will be a distinction to which the constructive empiricist can appeal. The worry is that there may be a tension between the constructive empiricist's claim that we should only believe what our scientific theories say about the observable phenomena, and his reliance at the same time upon those very same scientific theories to determine what counts as observable. In particular, there is no guarantee that the parts of our scientific theories that the constructive empiricist *needs* to believe in order to draw his distinction will coincide with those parts of his scientific theories that he *can* believe if his view regarding the aim of science is correct. This is the concern raised by Musgrave (1985), who argues that if the constructive empiricist is going to draw a principled distinction between the observable and unobservable phenomena, he will need both to correctly identify the observable phenomena as observable *and* correctly identify the unobservable phenomena as unobservable. In the latter case, though, this will clearly involve believing claims about unobservable phenomena – for example, claims of the form 'x is unobservable' – which is of course precisely the sort of claim that the constructive empiricist cannot believe. So if there is a principled distinction between the observable and unobservable phenomena, this is not something of which the constructive empiricist can consistently avail himself.

In response, van Fraassen again suggests that the problem lies in how we understand the structure of a scientific theory. He writes:

> Musgrave says '[x] is not observable by humans' is not a statement about what is observable by humans. Hence, if a theory entails it, and I believe the theory to be empirically adequate, it does not follow that I believe that [x] is not observable. The problem may only lie in the way I sometimes give rough and intuitive rephrasings of the concept of empirical adequacy. Suppose T entails that statement. Then T has no model in which [x] occurs among the empirical substructures. Hence, if [x] is real and observable, not all observable phenomena fit into a model of T in the right way, and then T is not empirically adequate. So, if I believe T to be empirically adequate, then I also believe that [x] is unobservable if it is real. I think that is enough. (van Fraassen, 1985: 256)

The idea then is that Musgrave's objection presupposes a syntactic account of theories, as evidenced by the demand that the constructive empiricist give us some account of how he can believe certain *statements* about unobservable phenomena. On a semantic account of theories, by contrast, the problem never arises, since all that the constructive empiricist needs to believe is that our best scientific theories fail to include a particular phenomenon amongst its relevant substructures.

In more recent work, Muller and van Fraassen (2008) make this idea a little bit more perspicuous. They argue that in order to believe that something is unobservable does not commit the constructive empiricist to believing more than what his scientific theories say regarding the observable phenomena, since such a belief will logically follow from all of our beliefs about the observable phenomena *along with* the belief that this list is exhaustive. To take a slight variation on the example above, suppose that the constructive empiricist accepts a scientific theory that classifies entities as either being an electron or as being observable, and suppose further that there is no possible model of that theory in which the two categories overlap. It follows then that if the constructive empiricist believes that this theory is empirically adequate – and therefore believes that all of the actual observable phenomena are represented as such in some model of that theory – then since he also knows that nothing that is classified as being an electron is also classified as being observable, then he knows as a matter of logic that electrons are unobservable. In very simple terms then, since the constructive empiricist can provide necessary and sufficient conditions for being an observable phenomenon, and since anything which is not an observable phenomenon must therefore be an unobservable phenomenon, it looks as if the constructive empiricist can draw his distinction between the observable and the unobservable after all, entirely from the observable side of the line.

This response certainly has some merit, but as Muller and van Fraassen (2008: 201–4) themselves note, it can only get the constructive empiricist so far. The problem is that our beliefs about whether or not something is observable have an intrinsically modal component. For example, the claim that electrons are unobservable is a law-like statement, and thus supports various counterfactual conditionals such that if there were to exist an additional electron, then it would also be unobservable, and so on and so forth. But this goes beyond the constructive empiricist's notion of empirical adequacy, which only demands that a scientific theory correctly classify all of the observable phenomena in the actual world.

In order to bridge this residual gap, Muller and van Fraassen propose an amendment to the constructive empiricist's basic epistemic policy. They stipulate that when it comes to matters of observability, exhaustive beliefs concerning the empirical adequacy of one's scientific theories are automatically to be given the widest possible modal scope. Thus if our theories classify an entity or process as (actually) unobservable, then we are simply to believe that entity or process to be (necessarily) unobservable. The sheer awkwardness of this policy can be seen when we reflect on the fact that it presumably does not hold for any other of our classificatory categories. None of the scientific theories that I believe to be empirically adequate classify any entity as being both a sphere with a diameter greater than 10 miles, and as being made entirely out of gold. I therefore believe that there are no actual golden spheres with a diameter greater than 10 miles. Crucially, though, I don't believe this combination to be *impossible* in the same way that I discount the possibility of a *uranium* sphere with a diameter greater than 10 miles (it would reach critical mass and explode), or indeed in the same way that I discount the possibility of an observable electron. Muller and van Fraassen's considered response to Musgrave's objection therefore rests upon assigning a privileged status to what the constructive empiricist's accepted scientific theories say about observability, which, while not necessarily *ad hoc*, certainly lacks any independent motivation. Observability, although obviously of enormous importance to the constructive empiricist, is in all other respects a perfectly straightforward scientific concept, to be investigated and determined by our accepted scientific theories like any other scientific concept.

7.2.3. *The metaphysics of modality*

We have seen then that in order to draw a satisfactory distinction between the observable and the unobservable, the constructive empiricist is committed to believing various counterfactual conditionals. We have also seen that it seems to be somewhat arbitrary as to which counterfactuals the constructive empiricist believes, both as a response to the objection raised by Churchland and as a response to the objection raised by Musgrave. But there is also a more general difficulty here relating to the constructive empiricist's endorsement of counterfactual conditionals. As James Ladyman (2000) argues, part of the motivation for constructive empiricism is the desire to present a parsimonious picture of our scientific practice, one stripped of the ontological commitments and metaphysical speculation that define scientific realism. In particular, van Fraassen explicitly denies that our counterfactual conditionals describe some objective modal feature of the world, since this would be precisely the kind of unobservable phenomenon that the constructive empiricist rejects. But if that is the case, Ladyman argues, then the truth-value of any counterfactual conditional is rendered entirely arbitrary, and the distinction between observable and unobservable phenomena that is so central to constructive empiricism carries no philosophical weight at all.

We can think of this problem as a general dilemma for the constructive empiricist. In order to draw his distinction between observable and unobservable phenomena, the constructive empiricist is committed to believing some of the modal consequences of his scientific theories, such as the claim that the moons of a distant planet *would be* observable were we to travel suffi- ciently far into outer space. The question then for the constructive empiricist is whether or not this is an objective modal fact. For on the one hand, if the constructive empiricist maintains that these counterfactual conditionals do have objective truth-conditions – for example, in terms of what is the case at other possible worlds – then he is admitting that his scientific theories tell us about a lot more than just the observable phenomena. They would also tell us about possible worlds, non-actual possibilia, laws of nature or whatever else is taken to provide the objective truth-conditions of our modal statements. This would be a very strange position for the constructive empiricist to find himself in. As Ladyman puts it:

> It would be bizarre to suggest that we do not know about electrons merely because they are unobservable, but that we do know about non-actual possibilia. If we were to believe what our best theories say about modal matters, then why not believe what they say about unobservables, too? (2000: 855)

However, if the constructive empiricist defends some non-objectivist account of his counterfactual truth-conditions, he appears to be left with far too arbitrary a distinction with which to do any useful philosophical work. The constructive empiricist either ends up believing *so much* that he undermines his position, or *so little* that he is unable to establish it in the first place.

The objection may, however, be a little too quick. As Monton and van Fraassen (2003) have argued, it may be possible for the constructive empiricist to provide an account of our counterfactual conditionals that is both robust enough to ground the distinction between observable and unobservable phenomena, yet without invoking the sort of problematic commitments that Ladyman suggests. What Monton and van Fraassen propose is in essence the traditional empiricist strategy of reducing our modal statements to the structure of our language, although in this case articulated in terms of the models of our scientific theories. The basic idea is that since the details of the various contexts from which our modal discourse is to be evaluated will be determined by the models of our various accepted scientific theories – and since as empiricists we should refrain from reifying these models to the status of full-blown possible worlds – it follows that our modal discourse is indeed made true or false by the models of our accepted scientific theories. As van Fraassen put it in an earlier statement of the view:

> Guided by the scientific theories we accept, we freely use modal locutions in our language. Some are easily explicated: if I say that it is impossible to observe a muon directly, or to melt gold at room temperature, this is because no counterpart to such events can be found in any model of the science I accept. (1980: 201)

Similarly then, Monton and van Fraassen (2003: 410–11) argue, the truth-value of most other counterfactual conditionals will follow as a matter of logic *relative* to certain background assumptions and scientific theories held fixed by the speaker. To take one of their examples, the counterfactual conditional that if I had looked in the drawer I would have found the letter is true as a matter of logic *relative* to the tacit premise that the letter is in the drawer (alongside numerous other premises such as that my eyes are working properly, and that the letter doesn't suddenly disappear, and so on and so forth). This is the sense in which Monton and van Fraassen argue that most counterfactual conditionals lack objective truth-values and are to be considered as context-dependent. The context in which a counterfactual conditional is asserted will be given in terms of the various background theories and implicit premises held by the speaker; and when a counterfactual conditional is true, it is true because background theories, together with the antecedent of that counter-factual, logically entail the consequent. Thus counterfactual conditionals do have truth-values – but since these are relative to a context, and since the relevant context will frequently change, Monton and van Fraassen conclude that these modal truth-values are not objective modal truth-values.

The crucial element in all of this of course concerns the slippery notion of context, since the counterfactual conditionals in which the constructive empiricist is interested will have one truth-value relative to one context and quite another truth-value relative to another. For example, a context within which we allow the physiology of the human eye to be kept fixed, yet which allows my spatio-temporal location to vary, will classify one set of phenomena as being observable; while a context within which my spatio-temporal location is kept fixed, yet which allows the sensitivity of my optic nerves to be vastly increased, will classify an entirely different set of phenomena as being observable. According to Ladyman (2004: 762), this is where the real problem with the account lies. He puts the problem as follows: on what grounds can Monton and van Fraassen maintain that if I were to travel deep into outer space then I would observe the moons of Jupiter? How can they justify privi-leging this counterfactual conditional over the opposing claim that if I were to travel deep into outer space, then I would not observe the moons of Jupiter on account of them suddenly becoming invisible? Similarly, why suppose that if I were to travel back in time then I would observe the markings upon a particular species of dinosaur, and not that if I were to travel back in time then said species of dinosaur would disappear or change its appearance? In the context of possible worlds, this amounts to a question about the *similarity-ordering* of the possible worlds in question. In the context of models, it is the question as to why it is that when selecting the appropriate model of my accepted scientific theories for evaluating counterfactual conditionals about travelling into outer space, I should choose one that keeps the various facts about the shape, size and constitution of the moons of Jupiter constant, rather than a model that allows these parameters to vary. Unless Monton and van Fraassen can provide some non-arbitrary account of this, the truth-values of their crucial counterfactuals will remain indeterminate.

The obvious solution of course would be for Monton and van Fraassen to claim that the constructive empiricist can justify privileging one model over another on the grounds that he has reason to believe that the regularities described by our accepted scientific theories describe objective features of unobservable reality – that is, laws of nature. But such a response is clearly unavailable to van Fraassen who is as adamant in his rejection of laws of nature as he is in his rejection of objective modality. On this account, to privilege one model of a theory over another, on the grounds that it is nomologically similar to the actual world (that is, preserves the laws of nature that are said to exist at the actual world), is merely to privilege one model of a theory over another on the grounds that it satisfies more of our *conventions* about how to represent the world. Ultimately, then, Monton and van Fraassen's meta-linguistic account makes the truth of a counterfactual conditional dependent upon certain conventional, pragmatic decisions of the scientific community about how they are to represent the world. In particular, counterfactual claims about what we would have observed had the circumstances been different are also dependent upon certain conventional and pragmatic decisions of the scientific community about how they are to represent the world. The problem then, of course, is that it would seem that the constructive empiricist's distinction between the observable and the unobservable has to be far more substantive than *that*. A distinction based upon little more than our aesthetic sensibilities about modelling, however, really does seem entirely arbitrary.

7.3. The new epistemology

Throughout the preceding discussion, we have seen that the main complaint levelled against constructive empiricism is that it lacks adequate episte-mological justification. In particular, it has been repeatedly claimed that the central distinction between observable and unobservable phenomena is quite arbitrary, since there are no good reasons to endorse the counter-factual observability of distant moons but not the counterfactual observability of quarks and neutrinos. It has also been objected that there are no good reasons to allow observability to take the widest possible modal scope when discussing the concept of empirical adequacy, and that more generally, the constructive empiricist has no good reason for endorsing the truth of any counterfactual conditional whatsoever. It may of course be possible to respond to each of these challenges in turn, but it is also important to note that they all share a particular epistemological framework. Specifically, they all presuppose that rationality is a *rule-based* activity: that in order to be justified in one's beliefs, there must be some invariable principle of inference that necessitates holding those beliefs. But this is not the only way to think about rationality, and nor, according to van Fraassen, is it the best way to think about it.

As an initial orientation to what van Fraassen proposes, consider the general problem of scepticism. There are roughly speaking two different approaches that one can take to this problem (van Fraassen 1989: 170–1). The first strategy is to concede that our everyday beliefs do stand in need of justification in the face of the sceptic's challenge, and consequently attempt to find some more secure footing upon which to build our edifice of knowledge. The second strategy by contrast rejects the sceptical challenge as posing an unrealistic and unreasonable demand. The idea here is that we already find ourselves out and about in the external world guided by a set of beliefs that we otherwise have no particular reason to question, and that therefore the onus is upon the sceptic to provide more concrete considerations for rejecting what we already believe.

The contrast between these two approaches helps to illustrate what van Fraassen has in mind with his alternative epistemological framework. The first response to the sceptical challenge parallels the traditional, rule-based concept of rationality. In attempting to answer the sceptic directly, those who favour this strategy are implicitly endorsing the idea that what one should believe is (merely) what one can provide sufficient reasons for believing. Similarly, in criticizing the constructive empiricist's distinction between observable and unobservable phenomena on the basis of their counterfactual equivalence, his critic is also endorsing the idea that what one should believe is (merely) what one can provide sufficient reasons to believe. Both are instances of a restricted, rule-based understanding of rationality.

By contrast, however, the second response to the sceptical challenge parallels the new epistemological framework that van Fraassen advocates. In refusing to engage with the sceptic directly, those who favour this strategy are implicitly endorsing the idea that what one is justified in believing is more than just what one can defend in the face of the sceptical challenge – rather, the idea is that one is justified in believing anything that we do not have positive reasons to *disbelieve*. As van Fraassen puts it:

> What it is rational to believe includes anything that one is not rationally compelled to disbelieve. And similarly for ways of change: the rational ways to change your opinion include any that remain within the bounds of rationality – which may be very wide. *Rationality is only bridled irrationality.* (1989: 171–2; original emphasis)

According to van Fraassen, then, our epistemological practices are as much an issue of pragmatics and values as they are of rules and evidence. On this account – which van Fraassen calls *epistemic voluntarism* – the counterfactual equivalence of observable and unobservable phenomena would be of no consequence to the constructive empiricist, since just because we *can* infer the science-fiction-based observability of quarks and neutrinos, it does not follow thereby that we *must* infer their observability. It is therefore a highly permissive understanding of rationality, with significant consequences for how we understand the scientific realism debate in general.

7.3.1. The English and Prussian models of rationality

Another good way to illustrate van Fraassen's notion of epistemic voluntarism concerns the generation of hypotheses. In both scientific practice and our everyday lives, we must often form opinions about the world that go beyond our available evidence. The conservative view on this issue is that one should only allow those hypotheses that are positively supported by our current evidence. The more liberal attitude is that one should allow any hypothesis that is not explicitly ruled out by our current evidence. The first option again relates to the kind of rule-based epistemology that underlies much of the scientific realist's objections to constructive empiricism. Thus when the scientific realist complains that the constructive empiricist is endorsing one kind of counterfactual inference in one case, while refusing to endorse the same kind of counterfactual inference in another, he is presupposing that there is a single canon of inferential practice that must be followed at all times. Similarly, the second option relates to van Fraassen's more permissive conception of rationality. Thus when the constructive empiricist rejects the claim that we must always draw the same sorts of counterfactual conclusions from the same sorts of evidence, he is endorsing the claim that what we should believe cannot be completely dictated by the disinterested application of a set of rules.

In allowing all those hypotheses that have not been explicitly ruled out, those who favour this approach are agreeing with William James (1948) that our epistemological practices are intimately connected to our epistemological values. James argues that the goal of our reasoning cannot simply be the acquisition of as many true beliefs as possible, since then we would simply end up believing *everything*; and nor can the goal be understood simply as the avoidance of error, since then we would end up believing *nothing* at all. Rather, the goal of our reasoning is to find some happy balance between the pursuit of truth and avoidance of error – but since there can be no algorithm for that, whatever way we seek to balance these competing desires will ultimately come down to a matter of personal preference.

These two themes – that we are justified in our beliefs so long as we have no specific reason to doubt them, and that whatever inferences we draw will be determined as much by our epistemological values as the available evidence – conform to what van Fraassen refers to as the Prussian and English models of rationality (van Fraassen 1989: 171). The Prussian model is a bottom-up approach and focuses upon what one is *allowed* to do. This is the model underlying scientific realism, which maintains that there are certain beliefs that are deemed to be justified, and that there are certain inferences that are deemed to be reliable, and that everything else – such as the constructive empiricist's arbitrary attitude to counterfactuals – is thereby irrational. By contrast, the English model is a top-down approach and focuses upon what one is *forbidden* to do. This is the model underlying constructive empiricism, which maintains that there are certain beliefs which are necessarily false and there are certain inferences which are straightforwardly invalid, but that anything else – such as picking and choosing one's preferred counterfactual conditionals – is all that we could ever hope to achieve in terms of being rational.

By way of illustration, let us consider again the issue of IBE and its role in the scientific realism debate. As Psillos (1996) notes, the constructive empiricist's belief that a scientific theory is empirically adequate is one that goes well beyond the available evidence, just as the scientific realist's belief that a scientific theory is true goes well beyond the available evidence. After all, a theory is empirically adequate if it is one that gets it right about *all* of the observable phenomena – past, present and future. Consequently, the constructive empiricist can only infer that his scientific theories are empirically adequate on the basis of the available evidence, just as the scientific realist can only infer that such a theory is true. It follows then, Psillos argues, that the constructive empiricist cannot object to IBE as a matter of principle, since his own philosophy of sciences depends upon just such a method of reasoning. Rather, the constructive empiricist must object to the particular *way* in which the scientific realist employs IBE. The idea presumably is that there is more risk involved in inferring the approximate truth of a scientific theory than there is in inferring its empirical adequacy, since while the latter only leads to the postulation of more observable entities, the former ties us into a whole new domain and postulates radically different types of entities. The problem, however, is that this appears to be a distinction without a difference: both types of inference involve a degree of epistemic risk, and if the constructive empiricist is justified in believing his theories to be empirically adequate, then he is equally justified in believing them to be approximately true.

Psillos's argument is of course a generalization of the sorts of objections encountered above, and it is tempting to interpret van Fraassen here as distinguishing between two different types of IBE. But in contrasting IBE to the truth with IBE to the empirically adequate, van Fraassen is not intending to introduce an alternative method of reasoning. Rather, IBE to the empirically adequate is intended as a *counter-example* to the claim that the only possible interpretation of our everyday scientific reasoning is as an inference to the truth of our best explanation (Ladyman et al. 1997: 313–14). The basic argument for scientific realism often proceeds by citing the successful application of IBE in the construction of scientific theories, arguing specifically that these are instances of an inference to the truth of our best explanations, concluding that inference to the truth of our best explanations is a reliable method of reasoning and then employing such an inference to move to scientific realism in general. As we have seen, however, we cannot automatically assume that the successful application of IBE is an instance of inference to the *truth* of our best explanations, since the same inferential phenomena admit of countless other interpretations (see Chapter 3)

However, once we focus on this idea of generating counter-examples to what the scientific realist claims, rather than advocating an alternative epistemological strategy, we can understand how exactly van Fraassen can continue to endorse his own instances of IBE while apparently criticizing the practice in general. What van Fraassen wants to undermine is not the practice of IBE in general, but understanding such a method of reasoning as a *rule*, that is, a principle that one is always obliged to follow. What remains then is rather a *choice* to use the principle as widely or as narrowly as your desire for truth and aversion for error demand. This may license belief in the truth of one's scientific theories, or it may only license belief in their empirical adequacy; the only thing that one must avoid is to suppose that one's own policy makes rational demands upon others. As van Fraassen puts it:

> Someone who comes to hold a belief because he found it explanatory, is not *thereby* irrational. He becomes irrational, however, if he adopts it as a rule to do so, and even more if he regards us as rationally compelled by it. (van Fraassen 1989: 142)

7.3.2. Taking a stance in the philosophy of science

These considerations concerning epistemic voluntarism relate to van Fraassen's broader understanding of how one should proceed in philosophy, and of the scientific realism debate in general. In particular, van Fraassen argues that we should not think of scientific realism or constructive empiricism as the adoption of a certain doctrine or a specific set of beliefs, but rather as a particular 'stance' that one adopts towards scientific inquiry, metaphysical speculation and any other putative source of knowledge.

Tying this point together with the previous discussion, we can note that the positive and negative arguments for epistemic voluntarism sketch an episte- mological picture whereby to make an epistemic judgement is to undertake certain commitments, and where our canons of inferential practice are to be considered permissible rather than obligatory. And so with empiricism in general, rather than the embracing of a doctrine or a set of core beliefs, empiricism is to be seen as the adoption of an epistemic policy or set of commitments; rather than adherence to a set of principles, it is a tendency to privilege experience, advocate scientific practice and avoid metaphysical speculation. In particular, the 'empirical stance' can be especially well characterized in terms of one's views regarding explanation. According to van Fraassen, two central features of empiricism are the rejection of certain *demands* for explanation – and thus a willingness to stop the explanatory regress at an earlier stage than one's more metaphysically inclined opponent – and dissatisfaction with certain *types* of explanation, in particular those that proceed by the postulation of additional entities.

There are a number of reasons for van Fraassen's insistence on this point, but the most important is that he thinks it is incoherent to attempt to characterize empiricism in terms of a specific doctrine (van Fraassen 2002: 41–4). Suppose that such a characterization was available, something like the claim that experience is the only source of knowledge, or that we can only believe what our scientific theories say regarding observable phenomena. Such a statement would have to satisfy two basic desiderata: it would have to motivate or otherwise underlie the empiricist's criticism of the supposedly excess speculation characteristic of the scientific realist, while at the same time remaining immune to that criticism. But these two requirements can pull apart, as we can see by considering the status of this characterization. It cannot be taken to be true *a priori*, for then the empiricist would be embracing just the sort of metaphysical speculation that he supposedly rejects. He would be in the unfortunate position of offering an abstract philosophical argument against the desirability of engaging in abstract philosophical argument. Yet neither can our characterization of empiricism be taken to be true *a poste- riori*, as an empirical claim that itself needs to stand before the tribunal of experience, since then the empiricist's opposition to realism becomes just one more scientific conjecture, open to reasonable dispute and legitimate disagreement, and therefore incapable of underlying a general philosophical framework. To characterize empiricism as a specific doctrine therefore leads to incoherence. The solution, according to van Fraassen, is to reject the idea that a philosophical position like empiricism or realism can be characterized as a particular doctrine or set of beliefs. There is no statement that one must believe in order to be an empiricist. Rather, the position consists of a certain *attitude* towards our putative sources of knowledge, a certain view concerning the making of epistemic judgements and a certain policy towards our methods of reasoning.

To recast scientific realism and constructive empiricism in terms of a general epistemic stance towards our scientific practices obviously has important consequences for how we should understand the scientific realism debate. On such an account, it is no longer compelling to note that the constructive empiricist has no grounds for endorsing some counterfactual conditionals but not others, since this is just part of his general stance towards observability. Similarly, it is also no longer compelling to note that the scientific realist can only offer arguments in favour of his position that in fact presuppose that scientific realism is true, since again this is just part of his general stance towards our scientific reasoning. More generally, it no longer makes sense to complain that realists and empiricists adopt otherwise unsupported opinions about the base rate probability of an arbitrary scientific theory being true, since – again – this will just be part of their general epistemic stance. Indeed, provided that one can show that one's overall framework is logically consistent and does not lead into self-contradiction, then there does not seem to be any further arguments to offer.

Adopting van Fraassen's epistemic voluntarism therefore has a number of advantages. It rests upon a plausible conception of our epistemic lives that denies the need for a deeper level of philosophical justification for our day-to-day beliefs. In the context of the scientific realism debate, it also offers a fruitful way of articulating the opposition between scientific realism and its rivals, one that can accommodate their different methodological approaches and which helps to diagnose the sense of intractability that hangs over the debate as a whole. There are, however, difficulties with the approach. As Psillos (2007: 158–60) argues, even if we agree with the greater epistemological flexibility associated with epistemic voluntarism, it still seems to license *too much* insofar as it allows various epistemic policies that are clearly irrational. Indeed, any method of implicative inference can be made logically consistent provided one is willing to make the necessary adjustments elsewhere in one's web of beliefs, such as making inductive inferences upon scant evidence, refusing to make any inductive inferences at all or even making counter-inductive inferences upon one's evidence, where one concludes that the more times something has happened in the past, the less likely it is to happen again in the future. But that is a very strange conclusion to draw; indeed, it is precisely upon the basis of the blatant *irrationality* of counter-induction that so many casinos make their money.

According to Psillos, the basic problem is that a voluntarist conception of rationality is purely structural: it is concerned exclusively with the relationships that hold between an agent's beliefs, irrespective of the content of those beliefs. So, for example, a purely structural conception of rationality has nothing to say about when one should accept something as evidence, and thus has no capacity to condemn an epistemic policy that simply ignores any information inconsistent with what they already believe. Thus for the epistemic voluntarist, there is no substantial difference between the Creationist who tries to accommodate the fossil record into their own historical account, however plausible that account might be, and the Creationist who just refuses to accept that there is a fossil record to accommodate in the first place. But while we may be willing to accept some disagreement with the Creationist over the *importance* of certain phenomena such as the existence of the fossil record, we would not be willing to accept their *denial* that such evidence even exists – and indeed, most Creationists take it as part and parcel of their views that such phenomena must be explained one way or another. But on the voluntarist story, such denials would be perfectly rational, for if one does believe that the Earth was created in 4004 BC, then the easiest way to maintain consistency amongst one's beliefs in the face of a fossil record that appears to pre-date the act of creation is to simply reject the notion that there could be such a fossil record altogether. A concept of rationality that would legitimize the epistemological policy of never attending to any evidence cannot be *our* concept of rationality, and threatens to collapse the entire scientific realism debate into a debilitating form of epistemic relativism.

7.4. Chapter summary

- Constructive empiricism is the view that our scientific theories only aim at empirical adequacy. It is therefore a modern day successor to eliminative instrumentalism. In contrast to the latter position, however, constructive empiricism is based upon an epistemological distinction between observable and unobservable entities, rather than a semantic distinction between our observational and theoretical vocabulary.
- Specifically, constructive empiricism differs from eliminative instrumentalism in maintaining that our scientific theories should be understood as sets of models rather than sets of sentences, and in arguing that the unobservable content of our theories need not be reinterpreted or eliminated, but can be accepted – rather than believed – for practical purposes.
- The principal challenge for the constructive empiricist is to show that a principled distinction can be drawn between the observable and unobservable phenomena with which our theories are concerned. One problem is that since this is an empirical distinction, the constructive

empiricist must in fact rely upon his scientific theories in order to determine which parts of those very scientific theories he can legitimately believe.

- A more general problem is that the distinction between observable and unobservable phenomena seems arbitrary. In order to determine what we could observe in other circumstances, the constructive empiricist must rely upon certain counterfactuals. But it is difficult to distinguish between those counterfactuals that are plausible and those which are not. Moreover, it is not clear that the constructive empiricist can believe any counterfactuals at all, given his epistemological constraints.

- In recent work, however, van Fraassen has articulated constructive empiricism within a more permissive account of rationality. This has important consequences for how the constructive empiricist can respond to – or otherwise ignore – the foregoing criticisms. The problem, however, is that such a view risks descending the entire scientific realism debate into a debilitating form of relativism.

7.5. Further reading

The distinction between the syntactic and semantic account of theories is an important topic in the contemporary philosophy of science; a good starting point, however, is Suppe, F. (1989) *The Semantic Conception of Theories and Scientific Realism* (Chicago: University of Illinois Press). For a specific discussion of constructive empiricism in the context of a semantic account of theories – and a negative assessment of its important – see Turney, P. (1990) 'Embeddability, Syntax and Semantics in Accounts of Scientific Theories', *Journal of Philosophical Logic* 19: 429–51. I discuss the distinction between acceptance and belief in more detail in Dicken, P. (2010) *Constructive Empiricism: Epistemology and the Philosophy of Science* (Basingstoke: Palgrave Macmillan).

Another important issue relating to constructive empiricism concerns van Fraassen's account of explanation: see Kitcher, P. and Salmon, W. (1987) 'Van Fraassen on Explanation', *Journal of Philosophy* 84: 315–30 for some criticisms. Also of importance is how the constructive empiricist can accommodate the mathematical content of his scientific theories. See Rosen, G. (1994) 'What is Constructive Empiricism?', *Philosophical Studies* 74: 143–78 and Bueno, O. (1999) 'Empiricism, Conservativeness, and Quasi-Truth', *Philosophy of Science* 66: S474–S485 for further discussion. Churchland, P. M. and Hooker, C. A. (eds) (1985) *Images of Science: Essays on Realism and Empiricism with a Reply From Bas C. van Fraassen* (Chicago: University of Chicago Press) includes a number of useful articles on constructive empiricism. For recent discussion of van Fraassen's epistemic voluntarism, see Monton, B. (ed.) (2007) *Images of Empiricism: Essays on Science and Stances with a Reply From Bas C. van Fraassen* (Oxford: Oxford University Press).

Conclusion

If there has been one persistent theme present throughout the discussion of the scientific realism debate, it has been the suspicion that the entire topic is nothing more than a philosophical pseudo-problem. In a way, this point of view originated with Kant, who argued that it was impossible for us to ever know for sure that our scientific theories – or indeed, any of our ideas about the external world – accurately represented the world. The problem was that any attempt to answer such a question would involve comparing our representations with the objects they were supposed to represent, which would involve adopting a perspective outside of our own representational practices. The project is simply absurd, and if that is what is required in order to establish scientific realism, then the whole issue should be abandoned as futile.

Instead, Kant proposed what he called his Copernican Revolution in philosophy. Rather than asking whether or not our scientific theories accurately represent the external world, we should instead inquire into the necessary preconditions for such accurate representation. In simple terms, we should suppose that our scientific theories are approximately true and try to provide the best philosophical explanation for that fact. This does not automatically settle the question of scientific realism, since the best explanation for our scientific success may be extremely modest indeed – it might even prove impossible to provide any such explanation, leading us to revise our original supposition. What Kant did, however, was to replace a hopeless philosophical task with a more tractable query, and to establish a methodological approach that was to shape the rest of the scientific realism debate.

Kant's own response to the problem of scientific realism was to show how the basic principles of Newtonian Mechanics could be derived from the fundamental structure of our cognitive faculties. Our scientific theories were predictively successful because they were simply abstractions from the conditions for any possible experience. We can know that they accurately represent the world, because that world is partly constructed by our representational practices. It followed then that our scientific theories weren't just true, but that they were *necessarily* true. For all of its ingenuity, however, this result required some serious rethinking when the necessary truth of Newtonian Mechanics was shown to be empirically false by twentieth-century developments in geometry and physics. Kant's general approach was preserved, however, by philosophers like Reichenbach and Carnap, who simply transposed the Kantian framework from an investigation into the necessary structure of our cognitive faculties to the contingent structure of our scientific language. For Kant, Newtonian Mechanics was true because it followed from the conditions for any possible experience; for Reichenbach, Einstein's theory of relativity was true because it followed from our linguistic definitions of words like 'space' and 'time'.

This linguistic orientation in the scientific realism debate in turn motivated a closer examination of the structure of our scientific language, and in particular the relationship between the increasingly theoretical vocabulary of our scientific theories and the everyday observational terms to which they were related. The various attempts to reduce our theoretical vocabulary to our observational vocabulary, or to eliminate it altogether, eventually ran up against insuperable technical difficulties. But the main problem facing the logical empiricists was far more conceptual. If our scientific theories accurately represent the world because our scientific language partly *constitutes* that world, then it should follow that radically different linguistic frameworks will result in radically different worlds. But while plenty of postmodernist charlatans have built a career out of precisely this possibility, the fact remains that it is simply false, and refuted by the existence of even the most trivial instances of inter-translatability. Our linguistic frameworks are simply too flexible to perform anything like the role of Kant's faculties of sensibility and understanding – which is just to say that nothing can perform that role after all.

By the 1960s, therefore, the scientific realism debate had abandoned any notion that the world we attempt to describe is somehow constructed by our representational practices. The principal questions now concerned our epistemological access to an independently existing external world, and whether or not the beliefs we formed about the world could be justified. The debate, however, did not simply collapse back into the hopeless philosophical task of standing outside of our own representational practices, since it still preserved the general methodological approach of attempting to *explain* the predictive success of our scientific theories, rather than asking if success was really the case. The resulting situation was, however, a curious one. It was an epistemological investigation into the status of our scientific theories which simultaneously acknowledged that our scientific theories were the best guide to our epistemological investigations. Put so bluntly, it is hardly surprising that the two central considerations framing this way of articulating the scientific realism debate – the No-Miracles Argument and the Pessimistic Meta-Induction – were immediately rejected as simply presupposing what they were attempting to achieve.

While the problems with the contemporary scientific realism debate can be clearly seen to have arisen from a failure to think through all of the philosophical consequences of abandoning logical empiricism, it has proved considerably more difficult to provide a precise analysis of those problems and to suggest how they might be resolved. Perhaps the most perspicuous suggestion, however, is that all participants to the contemporary scientific realism are guilty of a widespread tendency to commit the Base Rate Fallacy. Both the No-Miracles Argument and the Pessimistic Meta-Induction are only compelling insofar as we can already assume something about the overall distribution of true and false scientific theories in our overall sample – yet it is precisely the purpose of these arguments to *establish* the overall distribution of truth and falsity amongst our scientific theories. This then would certainly explain why the various attempts of realists and anti-realists to convince one another of the relative likelihood of a predictively successful scientific theory being true have been so inconclusive. It also provides a formal framework for thinking about the general dilemma that faces the scientific realism debate: of either standing outside our own representational practices and offering an *a priori* assessment of the relevant base rates, or presenting a scientific argument that simply presupposes what it is attempting to establish.

The prospects for the scientific realism debate, however, are not exhausted by this particular episode. One option is to reformulate the scientific realism debate as a series of specific arguments targeting individual scientific theories. The emphasis is not upon the approximate truth of our scientific theories considered as a whole, or an assessment of the general reliability of our scientific methods, but with whether or not we have good reason to believe that *this* particular scientific theory is approximately true. This is a relatively new approach to an old question, and it remains an open question as to whether or not it will be successful. The worry with such an approach, however, is that by focusing too narrowly on the specifics of individual scientific theories at the expense of any philosophical generalization, it is no longer clear whether such case studies will have anything to add to the scientific practice with which they are concerned.

A more promising direction lies in those approaches to the scientific realism debate that have managed to avoid the No-Miracles Argument and the Pessimistic Meta-Induction altogether. Both the structural realist and the constructive empiricist offer accounts that seek to circumscribe how much of our scientific theories we need to believe. They are motivated by considerations relating to how our scientific theories manage to represent the world and the aim of our scientific theorizing – and not with the tiresome attempt to provide an epistemological evaluation of the very scientific theories that guide our epistemological evaluations. They are the direct descendants of the philosophical project originated by Kant, and all the better for it.

Bibliography

Achinstein, P. (2002) 'Is There a Valid Experimental Argument for Scientific Realism?', *Journal of Philosophy* 99: 470–95

Ainsworth, P. (2009) 'Newman's Objection', *British Journal for the Philosophy of Science* 60: 135–71

Bennett, J. (1990) 'Why is Belief Involuntary?', *Analysis* 50: 87–107

Blackburn, S. (2002) 'Realism: Deconstructing the Debate', *Ratio* 15: 111–33

Blackburn, S. and Simmons, K. (eds) (1999) *Truth* (Oxford: Oxford University Press)

Bonk, T. (2008) *Underdetermination: An Essay on Evidence and the Limits of Natural Knowledge* (Dordrecht: Springer)

Boyd, R. (1973) 'Realism, Underdetermination and a Causal Theory of Evidence', *Noûs* 7: 1–12

Boyd, R. (1984) 'The Current Status of the Scientific Realism', in J. Leplin (ed.) *Scientific Realism* (Berkeley: University of California Press), 41–82

Bueno, O. (1999) 'Empiricism, Conservativeness, and Quasi-Truth', *Philosophy of Science* 66: S474–S485

Burgess, J. and Rosen, G. (2000) *A Subject With No Object: Strategies for Nominalistic Interpretation of Mathematics* (New York: Oxford University Press)

Butterfield, J. (2012) 'Underdetermination in Cosmology: An Invitation', *Proceedings of the Aristotelian Society* (Supplementary Volume) 86: 1–18

Carnap, R. (1936) 'Testability and Meaning', *Philosophy of Science* 3: 419–71

Carnap, R. (1937) 'Testability and Meaning – Continued', *Philosophy of Science* 4: 1–40

Carnap, R. (1950) 'Empiricism, Semantics and Ontology,' *Revue Internationale de Philosophie* 4: 20–40; reprinted in his *Meaning and Necessity: A Study in Semantics and Modal Logic* (Chicago: University of Chicago Press, 1956), 205–21

Carnap, R. (1955) 'Meaning and Synonymy in Natural Languages', *Philosophical Studies* 6: 33–47; reprinted in his *Meaning and Necessity: A Study in Semantics and Modal Logic* (Chicago: University of Chicago Press, 1956), 233–47

Carnap, R. (1958) 'Beobachtungssprache und Theoretische Sprache', *Dialectica* 12: 236–48

Carnap, R. (1974) *An Introduction to the Philosophy of Science* (New York: Basic Books)

Chakravartty, A. (2003) 'The Structuralist Conception of Objects', *Philosophy of Science* 70: 867–78

Chakravartty, A. (2007) *A Metaphysics for Scientific Realism: Knowing the Unobservable* (Cambridge: Cambridge University Press)

Chakravartty, A. (2008) 'What You Don't Know Can't Hurt You: Realism and the Unconceived', *Philosophical Studies* 137: 149–58

Churchland, P. M. (1985) 'The Ontological Status of Observables: In Praise of the Superempirical Virtues', in P. M. Churchland and C. A. Hooker (eds) *Images of Science: Essays on Realism and Empiricism with a Reply From Bas C. van Fraassen* (Chicago: University of Chicago Press), 35–47

Churchland, P. M. and Hooker, C. A. (eds) (1985) *Images of Science: Essays on Realism and Empiricism with a Reply From Bas C. van Fraassen* (Chicago: University of Chicago Press)

Coffa, J. A. (1991) *The Semantic Tradition from Kant to Carnap* (Cambridge: Cambridge University Press)

Cohen, L. J. (1981) 'Can Human Irrationality Be Experimentally Demonstrated?', *Behavioral and Brain Sciences* 4: 317–70

Craig, W. (1953) 'On Axiomatisability Within a System', *Journal of Symbolic Logic* 18: 30–2

Craig, W. (1956) 'Replacement of Auxiliary Expressions', *Philosophical Review* 65: 38–55

Creath, R. (2007) 'Quine's Challenge to Carnap', in M. Friedman and R. Creath (eds) *The Cambridge Companion to Carnap* (Cambridge: Cambridge University Press), 316–35

Dainton, B. (2001) *Time and Space* (Durham: Acumen)

Davidson, D. (1974) 'On the Very Idea of a Conceptual Scheme', *Proceedings of the American Philosophical Association,* 47: 5–20; reprinted in his *Inquiries into Truth and Interpretation* (Oxford: Oxford University Press, 2001), 183–98

Demopoulos, W. (2013) *Logicism and its Philosophical Legacy* (Cambridge: Cambridge University Press)

Demopoulos, W. and Friedman, M. (1985) 'Critical Notice: Bertrand Russell's *The Analysis of Matter:* Its Historical Context and Contemporary Interest', *Philosophy of Science* 52, 621–39

Devitt, M. and Sterelny, K. (1987) *Language and Reality: An Introduction to the Philosophy of Language* (Oxford: Blackwell)

Dicken, P. (2010) *Constructive Empiricism: Epistemology and the Philosophy of Science* (Basingstoke: Palgrave Macmillan)

Donnellan, K. (1966) 'Reference and Definite Descriptions', *Philosophical Review* 75: 281–304

Duhem, P. (1914) *The Aim and Structure of Physical Theory*, translated P. W. Wiener (Princeton, NJ: Princeton University Press, 1954)

Earman, J. (1978) 'Fairy Tales versus an Ongoing Story: Ramsey's Neglected Argument for Scientific Realism', *Philosophical Studies* 33: 195–202

Evans, G. (1973) 'The Causal Theory of Names', *Proceedings of the Aristotelian Society* 47: 187–208

Field, H. (1973) 'Theory Change and the Indeterminacy of Reference', *Journal of Philosophy* 70: 462–81; reprinted in his *Truth and the Absence of Fact* (Oxford: Oxford University Press, 2001), 177–93

Field, H. (2001) *Truth and the Absence of Fact* (Oxford: Oxford University Press)

Fine, A. (1984a) 'The Natural Ontological Attitude', in J. Leplin (ed.) *Scientific Realism* (Berkeley: University of California Press), 83–107; reprinted in his

The Shaky Games: Einstein, Realism and the Quantum Theory (Chicago: University of Chicago Press, 1986), 112–135; reprinted in D. Papineau (ed.) *The Philosophy of Science* (Oxford: Oxford University Press, 1996), 21–44

Fine, A. (1984b) 'And Not Realism Either', *Noûs* 18: 51–65; reprinted in his *The Shaky Game: Einstein, Realism and the Quantum Theory* (Chicago: University of Chicago Press, 1986), 136–50

Foss, J. (1984) 'On Accepting van Fraassen's Image of Science', *Philosophy of Science* 51: 79–92

Fraassen, B. C. van (1980) *The Scientific Image* (Oxford: Clarendon Press)

Fraassen, B. C. van (1985) 'Empiricism in the Philosophy of Science', in P. M. Churchland and C. A. Hooker (eds) *Images of Science: Essays on Realism and Empiricism with a Reply From Bas C. van Fraassen* (Chicago: University of Chicago Press), 245–308

Fraassen, B. C. van (1989) *Laws and Symmetry* (Oxford: Clarendon Press)

Fraassen, B. C. van (1997) 'Structure and Perspective: Philosophical Perplexity and Paradox', in M. L. Dalla Chiara, K. Doets, D. Mundici and J. van Benthem (eds) *Logic and Scientific Methods* (Dordrecht: Kluwer), 511–30

Fraassen, B. C. van (2002) *The Empirical Stance* (New Haven, CT: Yale University Press)

Fraassen, B. C. van (2008) *Scientific Representation: Paradoxes of Perspective* (Oxford: Oxford University Press)

Fraassen, B. C. van (2009) 'The Perils of Perrin, in the Hands of the Philosophers', *Philosophical Studies* 143: 5–24

Frege, G. (1884) *The Foundations of Arithmetic: A Logico-Mathematical Enquiry into the Concept of Number*, translated J. L. Austin (Oxford: Blackwell, 1980)

French, S. and Redhead, M. (1988) 'Quantum Physics and the Identity of Indiscernibles', *British Journal for the Philosophy of Science* 39: 233–46

Friedman, M. (1982) 'Review of *The Scientific Image*', *Journal of Philosophy* 79: 274–83

Friedman, M. (1992) *Kant and the Exact Sciences* (Cambridge, MA: Harvard University Press)

Friedman, M. (1999) *Logical Positivism Reconsidered* (Cambridge: Cambridge University Press)

Friedman, M. (2013) *Kant's Construction of Nature* (Cambridge: Cambridge University Press)

Friedman, M. and Creath, R. (eds) (2007) *The Cambridge Companion to Carnap* (Cambridge: Cambridge University Press)

Frigg, R. and Votsis, I. (2011) 'Everything You Always Wanted to Know About Structural Realism But Were Afraid to Ask', *European Journal for the Philosophy of Science* 1: 227–76

Frost-Arnold, G. (2010) 'The No-Miracles Argument for Realism: Inference to an Unacceptable Explanation', *Philosophy of Science* 77: 35–58

Gardner, S. (1999) *Kant and the Critique of Pure Reason* (London: Routledge)

Godfrey-Smith, P. (2008) 'Recurrent, Transient Underdetermination and the Glass Half-Full', *Philosophical Studies* 137: 141–8

Gower, B. (2000) 'Cassirer, Schlick and "Structural" Realism: The Philosophy of the Exact Sciences in the Background to Early Logical Empiricism', *British Journal for the History of Philosophy* 8: 71–106

Guyer, P. (2006) *Kant* (London: Routledge)

Hacking, I. (1985) 'Do We See Through a Microscope?', in P. M. Churchland and C. A. Hooker (eds) *Images of Science: Essays on Realism and Empiricism with a Reply from Bas C. van Fraassen* (Chicago: University of Chicago Press), 132–52

Hanfling, O. (1981) *Logical Positivism* (New York: Columbia University Press)

Hardin, C. L. and Rosenberg, A. (1982) 'In Defence of Convergent Realism', *Philosophy of Science* 49: 604–15

Hempel, C. G. (1958) 'The Theoretician's Dilemma: A Study in the Logic of Theory Construction', in H. Feigl, M. Scriven and G. Maxwell (eds) *Concepts, Theories and the Mind-Body Problem* (Minneapolis: University of Minnesota Press), 37–98; reprinted in his *Aspects of Scientific Explanation, and Other Essays in the Philosophy of Science* (New York: Free Press, 1965), 173–226

Hempel, C. G. (1965) *Aspects of Scientific Explanation, and Other Essays in the Philosophy of Science* (New York: Free Press)

Horwich, P. (1991) 'On the Nature and Norms of Theoretical Commitment', *Philosophy of Science* 58: 1–14; reprinted in his *From a Deflationary Point of View* (Oxford: Oxford University Press, 2005), 86–104

Howson, C. (2000) *Hume's Problem* (New York: Oxford University Press)

Howson, C. (2013) 'Exhuming the No-Miracles Argument', *Analysis* 73: 205–11

Howson, C. and Urbach, P. (1989) *Scientific Reasoning: The Bayesian Approach* (La Salle, IL: Open Court)

Hylton, P. (1990) *Russell, Idealism, and the Emergence of Analytic Philosophy* (Oxford: Oxford University Press)

Hylton, P. (2007) *Quine* (New York: Routledge)

Jacobi, F. H. (1787) 'On Transcendental Idealism', supplement to his *David Hume on Faith; or Idealism and Realism, A Dialogue*; translated and reprinted in G. di Giovanni (ed.) *The Main Philosophical Writings and the Novel 'Allwill'* (Montreal: McGill-Queen's University Press, 1994)

James, W. (1948) 'The Will to Believe', in his *Essays in Pragmatism* (New York: Hafner Press), 88–109

Kahneman, D., Slovic, P. and Tversky, A. (1982) *Judgements Under Uncertainty: Heuristics and Biases* (New York: Cambridge University Press)

Kant, I. (1781) *Critique of Pure Reason*; translated N. Kemp Smith (London: Macmillan, 1929)

Kant, I. (1786) *Metaphysical Foundations of Natural Science*; translated M. Friedman, reprinted in H. Allison and P. Heath (eds) *The Cambridge Edition of the Works of Immanuel Kant Volume III: Theoretical Philosophy After 1781* (Cambridge: Cambridge University Press, 2002)

Ketland, J. (2004) 'Empirical Adequacy and Ramsification', *British Journal for the Philosophy of Science* 55: 409–24

Kirkham, R. (1992) *Theories of Truth* (Cambridge, MA: MIT Press)

Kitcher, P. (1978) 'Theories, Theorists and Theoretical Change', *Philosophical Review* 87: 519–47

Kitcher, P. (1993) *The Advancement of Science* (Oxford: Oxford University Press)

Koehler, J. (1996) 'The Base Rate Fallacy Reconsidered: Descriptive, Normative, and Methodological Challenges', *Behavioral and Brain Sciences* 19: 1–53

Kripke, S. (1980) *Naming and Necessity* (Cambridge, MA.: Harvard University Press)

Kukla, A. (1993) 'Laudan, Leplin, Empirical Equivalence and Underdetermination', *Analysis* 53: 1–7

Ladyman, J. (1998) 'What is Structural Realism?', *Studies in History and Philosophy of Science* 29: 409–24

Ladyman, J. (2000) 'What's Really Wrong with Constructive Empiricism? Van Fraassen and the Metaphysics of Modality', *British Journal for the Philosophy of Science* 51: 837–56

Ladyman, J. (2002) *Understanding Philosophy of Science* (London: Routledge)

Ladyman, J. (2004) 'Constructive Empiricism and Modal Metaphysics: A Reply to Monton and van Fraassen', *British Journal for the Philosophy of Science* 55: 755–65

Ladyman, J. and Ross, D. (2007) *Every Thing Must Go: Metaphysics Naturalised* (Oxford: Oxford University Press)

Ladyman, J., Douven, I., Horsten, L. and van Fraassen, B. C. (1997) 'A Defence of van Fraassen's Critique of Abductive Reasoning: Reply to Psillos', *Philosophical Quarterly* 47: 305–21

Lange, M. (2002) 'Baseball, Pessimistic Inductions and the Turnover Fallacy', *Analysis* 62: 281–5

Laudan, L. (1981) 'A Confutation of Convergent Realism', *Philosophy of Science* 48: 1–49; reprinted in D. Papineau (ed.) *The Philosophy of Science* (Oxford: Oxford University Press), 107–38

Laudan, L. (1984) 'Realism Without the Real', *Philosophy of Science* 51: 156–62

Laudan, L. (1990) 'Demystifying Underdetermination', in C. Wade Savage (ed.) *Scientific Theories*, Minnesota Studies in the Philosophy of Science, Vol. XIV (Minneapolis: University of Minnesota Press), 267–97; reprinted in his *Beyond Positivism and Relativism* (Boulder, CO: Westview Press, 1996), 29–54

Laudan, L. (1996) *Beyond Positivism and Relativism* (Boulder, CO: Westview Press)

Laudan, L. and Leplin, J. (1991) 'Empirical Equivalence and Underdetermination', *Journal of Philosophy* 88: 449–72; reprinted in L. Laudan, *Beyond Positivism and Relativism* (Boulder, CO: Westview Press, 1996), 55–74

Lewis, D. (1983) 'New Work for a Theory of Universals', *Australasian Journal of Philosophy* 61: 343–77

Lewis, D. (2009) 'Ramseyan Humility', in D. Braddon-Mitchell and R. Nola (eds) *The Canberra Programme* (Oxford: Oxford University Press), 203–22

Lewis, P. (2001) 'Why the Pessimistic Induction is a Fallacy', *Synthese* 129: 371–80

Lipton, P. (1993) 'Is the Best Good Enough?', *Proceedings of the Aristotelian Society* 93: 89–104; reprinted in D. Papineau (ed.) *The Philosophy of Science* (Oxford: Oxford University Press, 1996), 93–106

Lipton, P. (2000) 'Tracking Track Records', *Proceedings of the Aristotelian Society* (Supplementary Volume) 74: 179–205

Lipton, P. (2004) *Inference to the Best Explanation* (London: Routledge)

Mach, E. (1893) *The Science of Mechanics: A Critical and Historical Account of its Development*, trans. T. J. McCormack (La Salle, IL: Open Court, 1960)

Magnus, P. D. (2010) 'Inductions, Red Herrings, and the Best Explanation for the Mixed Record of Science', *British Journal for the Philosophy of Science* 61: 803–19

Magnus, P. D. and Callender, C. (2004) 'Realist Ennui and the Base Rate Fallacy', *Philosophy of Science* 71: 320–38

Maxwell, G. (1962) 'The Ontological Status of Theoretical Entities', in H. Feigl and G. Maxwell (eds) *Scientific Explanation, Space and Time* (Minneapolis: University of Minnesota Press), 3–27

Maxwell, G. (1971) 'Theories, Perception and Structural Realism', in R. Colodny (ed.) *Nature and Function of Scientific Theories* (Pittsburgh: University of Pittsburgh Press), 3–34

McAllister, J. W. (1993) 'Scientific Realism and the Criteria for Theory-Choice', *Erkenntnis* 38: 203–22

McCulloch, G. (1989) *The Game of the Name: Introducing Logic, Language, and Mind* (Oxford: Oxford University Press)

McMullin, E. (1984) 'A Case for Scientific Realism', in J. Leplin (ed.) *Scientific Realism* (Berkeley: University of California Press), 8–40

McMullin, E. (1987) 'Explanatory Success and the Truth of Theory', in N. Rescher (ed.) *Scientific Inquiry in Philosophical Perspective* (Lanham, MD: University Press of America), 51–73

Melia, J. and Saatsi, J. (2006) 'Ramseyfication and Theoretical Content', *British Journal for the Philosophy of Science* 57: 561–85

Menke, C. (2014) 'Does the Miracle Argument Embody a Base Rate Fallacy?', *Studies in History and Philosophy of Science* 45: 103–8

Mizrahi, M. (2013) 'The Pessimistic Induction: A Bad Argument Gone Too Far', *Synthese* 190: 3209–26

Monton, B. (ed.) (2007) *Images of Empiricism: Essays on Science and Stances with a Reply From Bas C. van Fraassen* (Oxford: Oxford University Press)

Monton, B. and van Fraassen, B. C. (2003) 'Constructive Empiricism and Modal Nominalism', *British Journal for the Philosophy of Science* 54: 405–22

Muller, F. A. (2004) 'Can a Constructive Empiricist Adopt the Concept of Observability?', *Philosophy of Science* 71: 637–54

Muller, F. A. and van Fraassen, B. C. (2008) 'How to Talk About Unobservables', *Analysis* 68: 197–205

Musgrave, A. (1985) 'Realism Versus Constructive Empiricism', in P. M. Churchland and C. A. Hooker (eds) *Images of Science: Essays on Realism and Empiricism with a Reply From Bas C. van Fraassen* (Chicago: University of Chicago Press), 197–221

Musgrave, A. (1988) 'The Ultimate Argument for Scientific Realism', in R. Nola (ed.) *Relativism and Realism in Science* (Dordrecht: Kluwer Academic Press), 229–52

Musgrave, A. (1989) 'NOA's Ark — Fine for Realism', *The Philosophical Quarterly* 39: 383–98; reprinted in D. Papineau (ed.) *The Philosophy of Science* (Oxford: Oxford University Press, 1996), 45–60

Musgrave, A. (1993) *Common Sense, Science and Scepticism* (Cambridge: Cambridge University Press)

Nagel, E. (1961) *The Structure of Science* (Indianapolis: Hackett)

Newman, M. (1928) 'Mr Russell's "Causal Theory of Perception"', *Mind* 37: 137–48

Norton, J. D. (2003) 'A Material Theory of Induction', *Philosophy of Science* 70: 647–70

Papineau, D. (ed.) (1996) *The Philosophy of Science* (Oxford: Oxford University Press)

Poincaré, H. (1902) *Science and Hypothesis*, translated W. J. Greenstreet (London: Walter Scott Publishing Company, 1905)

Potter, M. (2000) *Reason's Nearest Kin* (Oxford: Oxford University Press)

Psillos, S. (1995) 'Is Structural Realism the Best of Both Worlds?', *Dialectica* 49: 15–46

Psillos, S. (1996) 'On van Fraassen's Critique of Abductive Reasoning', *The Philosophical Quarterly* 46: 31–47

Psillos, S. (1997) 'Kitcher on Reference', *International Studies in the Philosophy of Science* 11: 259–72

Psillos, S. (1999) *Scientific Realism: How Science Tracks Truth* (London: Routledge)

Psillos, S. (2001) 'Is Structural Realism Possible?', *Philosophy of Science* 68: S13–S24

Psillos, S. (2007) 'Putting a Bridle on Irrationality: An Appraisal of van Fraassen's New Epistemology', in B. Monton (ed.) *Images of Empiricism: Essays on Science and Stances with a Reply From Bas C. van Fraassen* (Oxford: Oxford University Press), 134–64

Psillos, S. (2009) *Knowing the Structure of Nature: Essays on Realism and Empiricism* (Basingstoke: Palgrave Macmillan)

Psillos, S. (2011a) 'Moving Molecules Above the Scientific Horizon: On Perrin's Case for Realism', *Journal for General Philosophy of Science* 42: 339–63

Psillos, S. (2011b) 'On Reichenbach's Argument for Scientific Realism', *Synthese* 181: 23–40

Putnam, H. (1965) 'Craig's Theorem', *Journal of Philosophy* 62: 251–60; reprinted in his *Philosophical Papers Vol. I: Mathematics, Matter and Method* (Cambridge: Cambridge University Press, 1975), 228–36

Putnam, H. (1975a) 'What is Mathematical Truth?', in his *Philosophical Papers Vol. I: Mathematics, Matter and Method* (Cambridge: Cambridge University Press, 1975), 60–78

Putnam, H. (1975b) 'The Meaning of Meaning', in K. Gunderson (ed.) *Language, Mind and Knowledge*, Minnesota Studies in the Philosophy of Science, Vol. VII (Minneapolis: University of Minnesota Press), 131–93; reprinted in his *Philosophical Papers Vol. II: Mind, Language and Reality* (Cambridge: Cambridge University Press, 1975), 215–71

Quine, W. V. O. (1951a) 'Two Dogmas of Empiricism', *The Philosophical Review* 60: 20–43; reprinted in his *From a Logical Point of View* (Cambridge, MA: Harvard University Press, 1953), 20–46

Quine, W. V. O. (1951b) 'Carnap's Views on Ontology', *Philosophical Studies* 2: 65–72; reprinted in his *The Ways of Paradox, and Other Essays* (Cambridge, MA: Harvard University Press, 1966), 203–11

Quine, W. V. O. (1975) 'On Empirically Equivalent Systems of the World', *Erkenntnis* 9: 313–28

Quine, W. V. O. (1986) 'Reply to Hellman', in L. E. Hahn and P. A. Schlipp (eds) *The Philosophy of W. V. O. Quine* (La Salle, IL: Open Court), 206–8

Ramsey, F. P. (1929) 'Theories', reprinted in R. B. Braithwaite (ed.) *The Foundations of Mathematics and Other Logical Essays* (London: Routledge & Kegan Paul, 1931)

Redhead, M. (2001) 'The Intelligibility of the Universe', in A. O'Hear (ed.) *Philosophy at the New Millennium* (Cambridge: Cambridge University Press), 73–90

Reichenbach, H. (1920) *The Theory of Relativity and A Priori Knowledge*,
translated M. Reichenbach (Los Angeles: University of California Press, 1965)
Rosen, G. (1994) 'What is Constructive Empiricism?', *Philosophical Studies* 74:
143–78
Russell, B. (1912) *The Problems of Philosophy* (Oxford: Oxford University Press)
Russell, B. (1927) *The Analysis of Matter* (London: George Allen & Unwin)
Saatsi, J. (2005) 'On the Pessimistic Induction and Two Fallacies', *Philosophy of
Science* 72: 1088–98
Saatsi, J. (2010) 'Form vs. Content-Driven Arguments for Realism', in
P. D. Magnus and J. Busch (eds) *New Waves in Philosophy of Science*
(Basingstoke: Palgrave Macmillan), 8–28
Salmon, W. (1984) *Scientific Explanation and the Causal Structure of the World*
(Princeton, NJ: Princeton University Press)
Sklar, L. (1981) 'Do Unborn Hypotheses Have Rights?', *Pacific Philosophical
Quarterly* 62: 17–29
Smart, J. J. C. (1963) *Philosophy and Scientific Realism* (London: Routledge
Kegan Paul)
Stanford, P. K. (2001) 'Refusing the Devil's Bargain: What Kind of
Underdetermination Should We Take Seriously?', *Philosophy of Science* 68:
S1–S12
Stanford, P. K. (2003) 'Pyrrhic Victories for Scientific Realism', *Journal of
Philosophy* 100: 553–72
Stanford, P. K. (2006) *Exceeding Our Grasp: Science, History, and the Problem of
Unconceived Alternatives* (Oxford: Oxford University Press)
Suppe, F. (1989) *The Semantic Conception of Theories and Scientific Realism*
(Chicago: University of Illinois Press)
Tarski, A. (1944) 'The Semantic Conception of Truth and the Foundations of
Semantics', *Philosophy and Phenomenological Research* 4: 341–76; reprinted
in S. Blackburn and K. Simmons (eds) *Truth* (Oxford: Oxford University Press,
1999), 115–43
Turney, P. (1990) 'Embeddability, Syntax and Semantics in Accounts of Scientific
Theories', *Journal of Philosophical Logic* 19: 429–51
Votsis, I. (2007) 'Uninterpreted Equations and the Structure–Nature Distinction',
Philosophical Inquiry 29: 57–71
Williams, B. (1973) 'Deciding to Believe', in his *Problems of the Self* (Cambridge:
Cambridge University Press), 136–51
Worrall, J. (1989) 'Structural Realism: The Best of Both Worlds?', *Dialectica* 43:
99–124; reprinted in D. Papineau (ed.) *The Philosophy of Science* (Oxford:
Oxford University Press), 139–65
Worrall, J. (2007) 'Miracles and Models: Why Reports of the Death of Structural
Realism May Be Exaggerated', *Royal Institute of Philosophy* (Supplementary
Volume) 82: 125–54
Worrall, J. (2009) 'Underdetermination, Realism and Empirical Equivalence',
Synthese 180: 157–72
Worrall, J. and Zahar, E. (2001) 'Ramseyfication and Structural Realism', in
E. Zahar, *Poincaré's Philosophy: From Conventionalism to Phenomenology* (La
Salle, IL: Open Court), 236–51
Wray, K. Brad (2010) 'Selection and Predictive Success', *Erkenntnis* 72: 365–77

Wylie, A. (1986) 'Arguments for Scientific Realism: The Ascending Spiral',
    American Philosophical Quarterly 23: 287–98
Yudell, Z. (2010) 'Melia and Saatsi on Structural Realism', *Synthese* 175: 241–53
Zahar, E. (2001) *Poincaré's Philosophy: From Conventionalism to Phenomenology*
    (La Salle, IL: Open Court)

Index